Let This Be Known

Let This Be Known

Finding the Shin Buddhist Path

JAMES POLLARD

Buddhist Education Center

Let This Be Known
Copyright© 2020, James Pollard
Second edition, 2021

Published by Buddhist Education Center
Anaheim, California

All rights reserved. No part of this book
may be reproduced without written
permission and consent of the publisher.

Printed in the USA
ISBN 978-0-9966581-7-1 (paperback)
ISBN 978-0-9966581-6-4 (eBook)

For Sachi and Masako,
our sangha's most dedicated Dharma listeners

Contents

Synopsis x
Preface xi
Abbreviations xv
Acknowledgements xvi
Image Credits xvii

Part I. Seeking the Way

The Turning Point 2
Beginner's Mind 5
Beyond Hope 7
Beyond Faith 11
Beyond Charity 15

Part II. Buddhahood

Putting Away Samsara 24
Dying and Living 27
The Most Important Day 31
Do I Want to Become a Buddha? 35
Learning and Non-Learning 37
Leaving the World, Leaving the Mountain 40
Authenticity 45

Part III. Skillful Means

Meaning and Metaphor 52
We Receive the Dharma in Three Ways 57
Hearing and Reflecting 60
'It's Only a Story' 66
True Teachings and Provisional Teachings 71
Pure Land Birth 76
'He Returned to the Pure Land' 83

Part IV. Self-Awareness

The Karmic Seed 88
My First Dharma Teacher 91
Birth and Death...96
Divine Messengers...100
Underground Man 104
Alone and Unknown 109
'I Might Do Anything' 112

Interlude. Shinran's Uniqueness

Disciple of Śākyamuni 116

Part V. Our Rituals

What Is the Purpose? 122
The Chanting Experience 124
Why Meditate? 126
Reenactments...128
Devotion and Morality 132
'Meditation Is Not Part of Our Tradition' 135
'I Am Incapable of Any Other Practice' 139

Part VI. Our Community

Becoming a Truth-Seeker..146
Creating a Favorable Environment 149
Remembering Our Predecessors 152
Institutional Buddhism 157
Merit-Making 161
Your Island...167

Part VII. What Nature Teaches

Bugs, Germs, and People 174
Where Do We Come From? 177
Evolution Is Buddha-dharma 181
What Doesn't Go Away 186
Looking for the Self 189
The Mind of a Beginner 194
Cause and Effect 199

Part VIII. What Shinran Teaches

The Teaching for Our Era 206
His Path to Realization 212
Teacher and Poet 214
To Liberate All Sentient Beings 219
A Narrow Road to the Interior 223
Is Life Refuted? 227
True Settlement 231
Postscript 238
Conclusion 240
About the Author 241
Notes 243

Synopsis

It is said:
Attaining Buddhahood through the nembutsu is
the true teaching.

Further, it is said:
The true teaching is difficult to encounter.

Let this be known.[1]

—Gutoku Shinran

"Let this be known" (or "Reflect on this") appears frequently in Shinran's writings, indicating that his teaching is concerned with *self-knowing*. He challenges our customary reliance on *self-acting*, namely, ethical conduct and religious practices.

Preface

When my wife and I first came to Orange County Buddhist Church, we had no awareness of Buddhism, and we were not looking for a spiritual path. Janis's brother, Kent Hirohama, had been a Taiko instructor at the temple. Sadly, Kent died of cancer at the age of forty, and we went there for his funeral, which we thought would be our one-and-only visit. However, the minister encouraged us to return for a class called "Buddhist Views of Life and Death." This was our introduction to Buddhism, and it proved to be a turning point. Having experienced the loss of a family member, our minds had somehow opened to the Dharma. Soon we began to learn about Jōdo Shinshū (or Shin Buddhism), the teachings and life experience of Shinran (1173-1263). For us to have encountered this path was quite unexpected. Dharma gateways are said to be innumerable, but Shin Buddhism is the only gateway that we were temperamentally suited to enter. We made no conscious effort to discover it, but that is where causes and conditions led us.

Then as now, my primary reason for being at the temple is to hear and reflect on the teachings. The essays in this book are an attempt to share what I have received from my teachers, but the views expressed (and any errors therein) are mine. In the Buddhist Churches of America (BCA) we benefit from a diversity of views. If you listen to enough talks at BCA gatherings, you will hear speakers contradicting each other's statements. Rather than being a weakness, this diversity is a source of strength. Words and concepts cannot capture the depth of the Dharma. Thus, Shinran was relentless in seeking new meanings in ancient texts—should we not do the same? Each person must reflect on the teachings in light of his or her life experience. Each of us must encounter an *upāya*, or point of entry. Perhaps my way of expressing the teachings is helpful to you. If not, please consider what others have to say.

Simply stated, to follow the Buddhist path is to seek liberation from meaninglessness. In traditional terms, meaninglessness is samsara (the world of delusion), and liberation is nirvana (the world of awakening). Meaninglessness would appear to be a clear and present danger that must be avoided. However, at one time or another we may adopt views that lead us *not* to seek liberation. Here are three examples:

First, the satisfied view. Suppose that I feel my life is already meaningful. I have my work, my family, and my recreation: these are sufficient to fulfill my life. To talk of liberation is unnecessary. All I ask of my church or temple is that I be given a nice funeral. The satisfied view resembles the state of Siddhattha Gotama's mind while he was living in his palace, prior to meeting with impermanence. His encounter with aging, illness, and death negated the things he considered to be meaningful—his wealth, family, and pleasures. His sense of satisfaction evaporated. We cannot know when impermanence might disrupt our satisfied view. At some point, Gotama's experience might become our own.

Second, the practical view. Suppose that I want my religion to yield spiritual benefits. I am looking for an ethical teaching that will make me a better person, a more likeable person, a happier person. In the time remaining to me, I expect to make progress toward my goal. By taking the practical view, what I am seeking is self-improvement rather than liberation. In that case I don't really need Buddhism. Some other approach to life-enhancement might be more suitable. Many people find meaning on the path of spiritual self-improvement, but Shinran describes this approach as provisional or incomplete. For Shinran, liberation arises through self-awareness, not through self-improvement.

A third possibility is to experience the human condition, but to disengage from it. I work, eat, sleep, and I don't ask questions— "stuff happens." There is no meaning to be found through either secular or spiritual pursuits. I'm off the hook as far as asking Why is there suffering? or What am I? If that is my view, then Buddhism has nothing to offer me. Still, to have been born into human life and to choose disengagement is a sad outcome. By not searching for meaning, I have chosen to waste this rare and wondrous life that I was given. Socrates believed that the unexamined life is not worth living. Thus, when the

Athenians convicted him of impiety, he chose to be executed rather than to curtail his unsettling questions.

In trying to make sense of the world, human beings have looked to religion, one form of which is a system of beliefs about the forces of nature. These powerful forces were once thought to have a quasi-personal character, such that they could be pacified by devout observances. Eventually, through reasoning and experimenting, it was shown that nature has its own workings, which are not influenced in any way by religious beliefs and practices. As faith in the effectiveness of devout observances declined, religion came to focus on ethical conduct and on hopes and fears about the afterworld; these remain key issues for many religious followers today. Whether I embrace such religious views or reject them, I must still pay heed to my inner life. The wish for liberation from meaninglessness never disappears.

Buddhism, as I regard it, is not a system of beliefs about forces outside of me. It is a teaching about my sickness (samsara) and its cure (nirvana). It is not concerned with people in general, but rather with my own subjective situation. If I objectify the teachings and use them to judge others, the essential meaning is destroyed. A distinguishing feature of Shinran's teaching is that recognizing my sickness and realizing its cure are simultaneous. This sets Jōdo Shinshū apart from some other forms of Buddhism in which liberation is deferred to a future existence. For Shinran, the cure is here and now; it is to receive self-awareness (known as *shinjin*) by looking into the mirror of the teachings.

This book explores aspects of Shin Buddhism that are, in my estimation, of key importance. These writings are a subjective response to what I have received—they are not the product of objective scholarship. Admittedly, I am partial to Jōdo Shinshū, and I lack scholarly qualifications. Nor is this book a sectarian tract, since my way of reading Shinran diverges from institutional doctrines.

A word on nomenclature. The historical Buddha was a spiritual teacher who lived in northern India during the 5th century BCE. The Pāli suttas refer to him as the renunciant Gotama or the Blessed One, while the Pure Land literature calls him Śākyamuni or the World-Honored One. Because these are two quite distinct portrayals of the Buddha, I will identify him as *Gotama* or as *Śākyamuni*, depending on the specific teaching being considered.

I am deeply indebted to many teachers. Some, like Shinran, are historical figures whom I know through the works they left behind. Of the teachers I've known personally, I owe a special debt to three: Rev. Marvin Harada, Dr. Nobuo Haneda, and Rev. Tetsuo Unno. Without their kind instruction given over many years, I could never have encountered the teachings or become part of a sangha—the Buddhist community. I am grateful to Rev. Dr. Mutsumi Wondra for guiding me on questions of translation and interpretation. My wife and I are fortunate to have formed lasting ties with sanghas at Orange County Buddhist Church, Vista Buddhist Temple, Senshin Buddhist Temple, and the Maida Center of Buddhism. Our dear friends, Mrs. Sachi Ochiai and Mrs. Masako Hamada, have been a source of continual inspiration and amazement. Finally, the present-day person to whom I owe the most is Janis Hirohama, my fellow traveler on the path of the Dharma.

About the Second Edition

Along with editing and formatting changes, the second edition of this book contains two new essays: "Leaving the World, Leaving the Mountain" in Part II, and "Devotion and Morality" in Part V. I am grateful to the many Dharma friends who read the first edition and who kindly responded with encouragement and helpful suggestions.

Abbreviations

In this book, citations of Shinran's writings, the Pure Land sutras, and related commentaries are abbreviated as follows:

CWS: *The Collected Works of Shinran* (Jōdo Shinshū Hongwanji-ha, 1997), 2 vols.

DTS: *Shinran's Kyōgyōshinshō*, trans. Daisetz Teitarō Suzuki (Oxford Univ., 2012).

RTS: *Ryūkoku Translation Series* (Ryūkoku Univ., 1966-1983), 7 vols.

TPLS: *The Three Pure Land Sutras* (Jōdo Shinshū Hongwanji-ha, 2003, 2009), 2 vols.

PLW: *The Pure Land Writings* (Jōdo Shinshū Hongwanji-ha, 2012, 2018), 2 vols.

SIT: Yoshifumi Ueda and Dennis Hirota, *Shinran, An Introduction to His Thought* (Hongwanji International Center, 1989).

The Pāli suttas cited in this book are all available online at https://suttacentral.net/, a resource for convenient access to the entire Canon. I also cite the following guides to the suttas:

IBW: Bhikkhu Bodhi, *In the Buddha's Words: An Anthology of Discourses from the Pāli Canon* (Wisdom Publications, 2005).

WBT: Walpola Sri Rahula, *What the Buddha Taught* (Grove Press, 1974).

Acknowledgements

Excerpts from *The Collected Works of Shinran*, vols. I and II, *The Three Pure Land Sutras*, vols. I and II, and *The Pure Land Writings*, vol. 1, copyright © 1997, 2003, 2009, 2012 Jōdo Shinshū Hongwanji-ha, are used with permission.

Excerpts from *Shinran, An Introduction to His Thought* by Yoshifumi Ueda and Dennis Hirota, copyright © 1989 Hongwanji International Center, are used with permission.

Excerpts from *The Myth of Sisyphus* by Albert Camus, translated by Justin O'Brien, translation copyright © 1955, copyright renewed 1983 by Penguin Random House LLC. Used by permission of Alfred A. Knopf, an imprint of Knopf Doubleday Publishing Group, a division of Penguin Random House LLC. All rights reserved

Excerpts from Joseph Campbell's *The Hero with a Thousand Faces*, copyright © Joseph Campbell Foundation (jcf.org) 2008, are used with permission.

Excerpt from Joseph Campbell's *Historical Atlas of World Mythology*, vol. II: *The Way of the Seeded Earth*, copyright © Joseph Campbell Foundation (jcf.org) 1988, is used with permission.

Excerpts from *Myths to Live By* by Joseph Campbell, copyright © 1972 by Joseph Campbell. Used by permission of Viking Books, an imprint of Penguin Publishing Group, a division of Penguin Random House LLC. All rights reserved.

Excerpts from *An Open Life: Joseph Campbell in Conversation with Michael Toms*, copyright © 1989 by the New Dimensions Foundation, are used by permission of HarperCollins Publishers.

Image Credits

Cover / James Pollard photos

The Turning Point / Attasit saentep / Shutterstock.com

Beyond Charity / Enrico Della Pietra / Shutterstock.com

Hearing and Reflecting / James Pollard photo

My First Dharma Teacher / The Picture Art Collection / Alamy Stock Photo

Alone and Unknown / James Pollard photo

Reenactments / James Pollard photo

Creating a Favorable Environment / James Pollard photo

Merit-Making / James Pollard photo

Where Do We Come From? / Peter Barritt / Alamy Stock Photo

The Mind of a Beginner / ijARTup / Shutterstock.com

The Teaching for Our Era / Mirko Kuzmanovic / Shutterstock.com

True Settlement / chai chaiyo / Shutterstock.com

Part I

Seeking the Way

Midway upon the journey of our life
　I found myself within a forest dark,
　For the straightforward pathway had been lost.

Alas! How hard a thing it is to say
　What was this forest savage, rough, and stern,
　Which in the very thought renews the fear.

I cannot well repeat how there I entered,
　So full was I of slumber at the moment
　In which I had abandoned the true way.[2]

　　—Dante Alighieri (1265-1321)

The Turning Point

I once attended a funeral at our temple for a man I had never met. Three hundred of his friends and relatives came to the service. From what was said about him, this man was an exemplary human being. He had a successful career and a rich family life. According to his friends, he considered himself to be the luckiest person in the world. He passed away at the age of seventy-seven, a few years after learning he had a terminal illness. He lived out his days with dignity. By any measure, he realized the fulfillment of his life. Could any of us ask for more than this?

Family and friends had a lot to say about the man, all of it inspiring. But I noticed there was no mention of religion. Apparently, that was not among his interests, although he pursued many other activities. As far as I could tell, he wasn't a temple member, and he did not follow the Buddhist path. This man realized the fulfillment of his life on the path of secular transcendence, where value is to be found in personal accomplishments. Such a path is well suited to people in the modern era, when time-honored religious traditions have lost their vitality. It is the path followed by many members of my family, and from all I can tell, it is very suitable for them. Even for people who have a specific religious affiliation, fulfillment may still be found on the secular path. They participate in social and cultural activities at the church or temple, but they have yet to encounter the teachings of their tradition in a meaningful way. For the time being, they are focused on work, recreation, and family.

However, there are those who are unable to find ultimate value in personal accomplishments or to fulfill their lives on the secular path. That is the case for me, and perhaps it is true for you also. Most importantly, it was true for Siddhattha Gotama, who became the historical Buddha. Like the poet Dante, Gotama awoke to find himself in a dark forest of anxiety: *How hard a thing it is to say, / What was this forest savage, rough, and stern, / Which in the very thought renews the fear*. Meeting with impermanence, he experienced grave doubts—he saw his worldly aspirations negated:

> "I too, being liable to be reborn, sought what is also liable to be reborn. Being myself liable to grow old, fall sick, die, sorrow, and become corrupted, I sought what is also liable to these things."[3]

Gotama concluded that his life up to that point was meaningless, and that he would never find fulfillment on the secular path. He persisted in his questioning, and presently his thoughts took a new direction:

> "Then it occurred to me: 'Why do I, being liable to be reborn, grow old, fall sick, sorrow, die, and become corrupted, seek things that have the same nature? Why don't I seek the unborn, unaging, unailing, undying, sorrowless, uncorrupted supreme sanctuary, *nibbāna*?'"
>
> "Sometime later, while still black-haired, blessed with youth, in the prime of life—though my mother and father wished otherwise, weeping with tearful faces—I shaved off my hair and beard, dressed in ocher robes, and went forth from the lay life to homelessness."[4]

Having renounced his possessions and family ties, Gotama took to the road, seeking a way toward liberation from meaninglessness.

In ancient India, unless you were an aristocrat, you could not avoid seeing aging, illness, and death. They were everyday realities. Not so, here in 21st century America, where we have technology to keep impermanence hidden through most of our lives. We are like Gotama living in his palace, dreaming up distractions to keep the truth under wraps: *So full was I of slumber at the moment / In which I had abandoned the true way.*

But there may come a time when something causes us to ask, Why is my life bound up with sorrow? Perhaps the trigger is not accompanied by drama—it's just a gnawing sense of dissatisfaction. Is *this* all there is to life? Why do my joys seem to evaporate so quickly? Have I encountered anything that can be called *true*? To ask these questions is the turning point, when we become seekers like Gotama, when the Buddhist teachings cease to be abstractions, when the scriptures become personal. To have an experience that causes us to question our secular values is evidence that the Buddhist path has opened for us.

For the admirable man whose funeral I attended, a fulfilled life on the secular path was possible. During most of my adult life, I was confident that it was the right path for me. However, I was misinformed.[5]

Beginner's Mind

In starting out on the Buddhist path, we participate in bowing, meditating, chanting, and offering incense, but our understanding of these activities is likely to be incomplete or even wrong. Misunderstanding might seem to be an obstacle that we should avoid, but in fact it's an essential aspect. Why is this so?

I was brought up in a Christian denomination in which a good understanding was required before one could perform practices. It was considered necessary for the mind of a beginner to be replaced by the mind of an expert. Starting at age twelve, I received two years of doctrinal instruction before participating in the sacrament of Holy Communion. Being a competitive student, I probably earned an *A* in the class. To understand before participating is sound logic if, like Martin Luther, you aim to reject the mysticism of the Catholic Church. Luther conjectured that salvation is brought about by faith on the part of the believer. Faith rests on a firm understanding of doctrines. Once it is attained by this route, then the believer can perform religious practices. So I was taught.

Eastern religion reverses that logic by saying that participation comes *before* true appreciation. I engage in actions without grasping the meaning of what I'm doing. The key is to enter the path with a beginner's mind. When I try to figure out everything in advance, when I work to develop my expertise, then my ego turns this effort to its own advantage. Therefore, I must participate with an outlook in which

> ... there is no thought, "I have attained something." All self-centered thoughts limit our vast mind. When we have no thought of achievement, no thought of self, we are true beginners. Then we can really learn something.[6]

The nature of the path is such that I will have mistaken ideas about it. Gotama and Shinran each went through a stage of misunderstanding before they experienced awakening. It would be vain to imagine outdoing them by avoiding this stage. Awakening means to recognize the limitations of my ideas about Buddhism. Although I am unable to do away with my wrong ideas, gradually *I am made aware of them* through listening with the mind of a beginner. As the Dharma acts on me, a genuine sense of appreciation may develop. My misconceptions and my ego-centered view may be transcended. On the other hand, if I think, "I have attained faith," or "I have corrected my wrong ideas," then the true meaning is lost. I have become an expert.

A question arises concerning the beginner's mind. Do I remain just as I was the first time I came to the temple? Is the beginner's mind an untransformed mind? I don't think so. There's a traditional way of explaining Jōdo Shinshū, which says, "You are saved just as you are." A person who is unfamiliar with Shinran's teaching would be led astray by such advice. From it you might conclude that there is no need to engage with the teachings, because you will be fine without doing anything. It suggests that the path offers no possibilities, a view that epitomizes the mind of an expert: "There's nothing more I can learn from Buddhism. I choose not to read or to listen." That is the opposite of a beginner's mind.

No, I don't stay just as I was at the time of my first visit to the temple. I don't remain a "beginner" in the sense of the Dharma not yet having a presence in my life. Through continual listening to the teachings, the beginner's mind deepens. Possibilities multiply—a transformation is taking place. I start to appreciate the Dharma in every aspect of life, to perceive it as something that is always fresh and new, to never feel that I have become an expert and have "attained something." In this way the Buddhist path can be seen as a dynamic way of living, as a teaching that challenges me every time that I approach it. The path is nothing other than perfecting the mind of a beginner.[7]

Beyond Hope

Are you beyond hope? Am I beyond hope? It's a phrase we sometimes hear in connection with a negative situation, such as a terminal illness. Or it might be used to describe a person who, in our estimation, is clearly lacking in common sense. I want to suggest that to seek the way in Shin Buddhism is to be "beyond hope." First, consider how hope is expressed in everyday situations, as in the following examples:

I hope to visit Japan again. I would enjoy spending more time in Japan. My wife and I have had wonderful experiences there, and we would certainly like to go back. Hope, in this context, is an expression of my desire for future enjoyment.

I hope to get over this cold soon. I want my current illness to end. I remember what it was like to be healthy, and I wish that I could feel that way again. I yearn for a future in which I will be free of suffering.

In a political context the single word—*Hope*—next to the image of a candidate, can express the aspiration for social change. Another example from politics: *We have hope for the future.* Or, on the contrary: *The national situation is hopeless.* We hold opinions about the direction the country is taking, and whether we see that direction as favorable or unfavorable.

In these examples, hope is based on a distinction between good and bad outcomes. It arises from dualistic values. If my hopes are realized, then I will feel satisfaction. If my hopes are not realized, then I will feel regret. Hope is future-oriented, and regret is past-oriented. Thinking in that way, it's difficult to focus on what is happening here and now. These attributes show that hope, in the examples given, is non-Buddhistic.

In contrast, consider this statement. *Every day is a good day!* These are the words of Zen master Baso, spoken when he was on his death bed.[8] He was able to say this even while suffering and dying. "A good day" refers to absolute values, not relative ones. Every day is good in an absolute sense, regardless of one's circumstances. The master was beyond hope, medically speaking. He was also beyond hope in the sense of transcending our usual system of relative values and our judgments about good and bad.

Next, consider hope in a religious context. The idea is central to the teachings of Christianity, and it appears frequently in Christian signage, perhaps as a command—*Hope!*—or as a promise of what you will find when you come to the church.[9] For some people, the problem of life and death can be resolved only through teachings about an afterworld. Hence, the thought arises, *I hope I will go to heaven; I hope I will not go to hell.* This is the religion of hope for many people.

How about an idea that is more Buddhistic? *I hope to have a favorable rebirth.* The cycle of death and rebirth is a fundamental principle in Indian religion, going back centuries before the time of Gotama Buddha. Undoubtedly, the Buddha saw death and rebirth in samsara as the basic condition of the unawakened life. But did he teach that we should hope for a favorable rebirth? That has been the view of many Buddhists throughout history. They hope to acquire enough good karma to be reborn as heavenly beings or humans, rather than as hungry ghosts, animals, or hell-dwellers. To hope for a favorable rebirth is to think that the problem of life and death will be resolved not in the present life but in the distant future.

Religions that teach hope are generally aimed at a future existence, but the path taught by Gotama should not be counted among them. Future rebirth in samsara is not the aim of his teaching.[10] Rather, one aspires to become an awakened person—a buddha—and thereby to be liberated from the cycle of death and rebirth, just as Gotama was liberated:

> "A vision of true knowledge arose in me thus: My heart's deliverance is unassailable. This is the last birth. Now there is no more rebirth."[11]

The Buddha has put an end to the mentality of death and rebirth. He is no longer bound by that way of thinking. Shinran, in his understanding of Jōdo Shinshū, was faithful to the spirit of Gotama's teaching. Accordingly, Shin Buddhist awakening means to resolve this problem here and now, without relying on a hoped-for future existence. For awakened persons,

> ... there is no further state of existence into which we must be born, no further realm into which we must pass. Already the causes leading to the six courses and the four modes of birth have died away and their results become null. Therefore, we immediately and swiftly cut off birth-and-death in the three realms of existence.[12]

In Buddhist cosmology, samsara's "three realms of existence" are the worlds of Desire, Form, and Formlessness. The world of Desire contains the "six courses" of rebirth—gods, humans, fighting demons, hungry ghosts, animals, and hell-dwellers. On the path identified by Shinran, repetitive existence in samsara is "immediately and swiftly cut off (*soku ton danzetsu*)."

Consider this statement. *I hope to become enlightened.* This kind of hope is a little closer to the mark. The basis of Jōdo Shinshū is the *Larger Sutra of Immeasurable Life*. Using symbolic language, the sutra evokes the innermost desire to become a buddha and to liberate all beings. Even so, the phrase, "I hope to become enlightened," appears to lack conviction; it implies that I am not quite sure about the path: "Maybe I will be enlightened or maybe not; it depends." By contrast, consider these lines from *Sanbutsuge*, often chanted by Shin Buddhists:

> *I will make offerings*
> *To all these Buddhas;*
> *Nothing surpasses my determination*
> *To seek the Way steadfastly and untiringly.*
>
> *Even if I should be subjected to*
> *All kinds of suffering and torment,*
> *Continuing my practice undeterred,*
> *I would endure it and never have any regrets.*[13]

These are the words of Bodhisattva Dharmākara, the hero of the story in the *Larger Sutra*. The bodhisattva's Vow is different from saying, "I hope to become enlightened." The focus is removed from the goal (a future outcome) and placed entirely on seeking the way (fulfillment here and now). The bodhisattva performs practices for countless eons, which, in itself, is to realize the aspiration for limitless seeking. Endlessly, Dharmākara is becoming a buddha called Immeasurable Light (*Amitābha*), and his Land of Perfect Bliss (*Sukhāvati*) is being established.

An important question arises. Are Amida and the Pure Land the distant objects of our religious hope, or are they close at hand? A passage in the *Amida Sutra* says that the Pure Land is "beyond a zillion Buddha-lands westwards from here," which means that it's far removed from our world of delusion. However, in the *Contemplation Sutra*, Śākyamuni says, "Do you know that Amida Buddha is not very far from here?" He is speaking to Vaidehī, a woman who has awakened the aspiration to seek the way. Whether nirvana is nearby or far away is a matter of one's perspective. For Shinran, the awakened person "lives the truth and reality of the Pure Land," despite being "always impure and creating karmic evil." The heart of this person "already and always resides in the Pure Land."[14]

As I see it, hope, as it's often understood by religious followers, is not an aspect of the Shin Buddhist path, which is none other than seeking the way untiringly here and now. To seek steadfastly is to live with confidence, to feel truly settled as a follower of Jōdo Shinshū, to live the truth and reality of the Pure Land. Resolving the problem of life and death does not mean hoping to become enlightened in a future existence. In seeking the way untiringly, one can go beyond that kind of hope.

Beyond Faith

Can you justify your beliefs? In some cases, it's unnecessary to do so. When it comes to personal preferences, such as, "That was a great-tasting sandwich," or "I don't like plaid slacks," we are entitled to be arbitrary. Choices made on the basis of views about food and fashion are largely inconsequential. However, when we speak of "beliefs" we usually are referring to important matters, such as how the world works, how we should behave, and how society is organized. Ideally, I would carefully weigh the evidence rather than rely on emotional reactions, but, in fact, my consequential beliefs can be just as arbitrary as my preferences regarding sandwiches or slacks. I will use the word *belief* to designate an arbitrary opinion about the world. Under this definition, a *belief system* is a collection of opinions that are not based on evidence. Buddhism teaches us to go beyond this kind of belief system.[15]

In ancient India, it was customary for spiritual teachers to give their opinions on questions such as Is the world eternal? or Is the world infinite? or Does a buddha exist after death? It was impossible to determine whether the answers were true or false, and therefore these opinions were called *speculative views*. By contrast, on the path taught by Gotama Buddha, one does not engage in speculative discussions. He declined to respond when questioned about such matters, because his teachings arose from experience and not from speculation. "These speculative views have been left undeclared by the Blessed One, set aside and rejected by him," because they do not lead "to peace, to direct knowledge, to enlightenment, to *nibbāna*."[16]

Gotama did not teach a collection of arbitrary opinions, that is, a belief system, as I have defined the term. He awakened to direct knowledge of the path leading to liberation, as revealed in his own life experience. The Buddha offered a teaching that was open to all, and he invited each person to test it against his or her own experience. We must not hold an unquestioning belief in the teacher's words. However, we face a difficulty when first encountering the Dharma, because our ability to understand what the Buddha is teaching is feeble. We cannot grasp the depth of the Dharma based on perceptions that are shallow and unfocused. How are we to get through this difficulty? It's at this crucial stage that faith can be said to play a role in Buddhism.

As a teenager I listened to many sermons on the topic of faith, but eventually I turned away from my ancestral religion. So, decades later, I am surprised to be thinking about faith again in a Buddhist context. The word "faith" has many non-Buddhist interpretations. It can mean a collection of beliefs that contradict the evidence from the natural world, as in relying on a "faith-healer" to cure an illness. In the familiar phrase, "faith in God," it means a relationship with an all-powerful deity. Formerly in the Buddhist Churches of America, faith was used as a translation for the term shinjin or Shin Buddhist awakening. It was also used in translating the text of the Three Treasures: "I put my faith in Buddha. I put my faith in Dharma. I put my faith in Sangha." These usages are not wrong, but I want to suggest a different meaning for the word.

There is no difficulty in recognizing that we live in a world of delusion. Samsara is manifested in all aspects of our culture. It's easy to see delusion in other people, and, once in a while I am made to see my own deludedness, as well. However, it's very difficult to sense that the Buddhist world of awakening exists in the midst of samsara. "World of awakening" means Buddhahood, nirvana, liberation. Can we accept the idea that liberation exists, that it can be realized at the personal level? This is an opinion for which we lack supporting evidence at the outset. With so many distractions in our lives, it seems impossible for the world of awakening to register with us. No matter how many Buddhist services we attend or how many talks we listen to, direct experience may still be absent. We accept the idea that the Buddha realized nirvana, but accepting the idea of our own liberation is difficult.

The teachings identify two types of doubt or distorted views: first, that there is *no path to liberation*, and second, that even if a path were to exist, there is *no one to walk it*.[17] By reflecting seriously on religious questions we may experience such doubts, which cannot be overcome merely by thinking things over. Without direct experience, no amount of cogitation can convince us that there is a path to awakening, and that we are able to walk it. There has to be another way around the distorted views. To hold the belief that a path exists, before we have actually found it, is what I call *Buddhist faith*. It is to affirm the existence of a path to liberation when the evidence is lacking. To affirm this, in spite of doubts, is what motivates us to keep listening.

The archetype of one who seeks the way is Siddhattha Gotama. Unable to find meaning in his secular life, he resolves to abandon his home and family and to become a renunciant. Persisting in his search for six years, he endures rigorous training and hardships, but during that time the direct experience of liberation eludes him. Why doesn't Gotama abandon his search? It is because he has faith that a path exists and that he will find it. This faith does not come about through his powers of reasoning. In Buddhist terms, faith is a product of his karma—the flow of causes and effects from the distant past. The scriptures speak about past lives in which he performed countless meritorious deeds, leading up to his final birth as a "great man" destined to attain Buddhahood.[18] We might not explain our own background in such a colorful way, but the same principle applies. All the things we have experienced and all the choices we have made, whether foolish or wise, determine whether we are able to believe that the path exists prior to our actually finding it.

Once Gotama has attained awakening, his faith is transcended. He has direct experience of the way. Faith, as I have defined it, ceases to be an attribute of the Buddha. Remarkably, the same pattern applies in Shin Buddhism. Under the influence of our karma, we hold the unsupported belief that a path exists before we have actually encountered it. The stage of unsupported belief is transcended when shinjin or true settlement is realized; it means that a foolish being is headed irreversibly toward liberation.[19] Rather than the belief that a path exists, there is now direct experience of the path. The moment is beautifully depicted in Shan-tao's parable of the two rivers, when the traveler exclaims, "As I cannot escape death in any way, I would rather follow this path. Since there is a path, it must be possible to cross."[20]

How is our initial faith transformed into direct experience? What is the evidence that enables us to go beyond faith? First, we must meet a *buddha*, in the sense of hearing and appreciating the powerful life stories of Gotama and of Shinran, our teachers who lived long ago. They taught others how to experience the world of awakening. The experience was carried in turn from teacher to student down to the present day, and we are now able to receive it.

Second, we must meet a *sangha*, a community of people who seek the way. Today there are many heirs of Gotama and of Shinran, and our initial belief that a path exists will enable us to encounter them. Previously, I said that Gotama is our archetype. But in one sense we are not like him, the exceptional person who found the path to liberation on his own. The Shin Buddhist path is experienced as part of a community. The world of awakening is revealed to us in the lives of others. When this happens, we become receptive to the teachings. We gain a desire to understand what has transformed our fellow sangha members.

Third, we must engage with the *dharma* by listening deeply and reflecting on the teachings. In particular, we must commit to being students of Shinran. His writings speak powerfully to our condition here and now, if we make the effort to become familiar with his language. Through listening and learning in the favorable environment of a sangha, the Shin Buddhist life of awakening emerges as a reality. We become able to accept the idea of liberation at the personal level. The stage of unsupported belief that a path exists is transformed into direct experience of the path. Encountering this path, we are able to go beyond faith.

Beyond Charity

Man is neither angel nor brute, and the unfortunate thing is that he who would act the angel acts the brute.[21]

—Blaise Pascal

Faith, hope, and charity are three Christian virtues lauded in a famous passage from the New Testament.[22] So far, I have suggested that faith and hope are transcended in the context of Shin Buddhism. Now I would like to consider the third virtue, charity, depicted on the following page as an allegorical figure by the artist, Giotto (1266-1337). Every detail of this wonderful painting is meant to teach a lesson. The figure of Charity appears as an intermediary between the divine realm and the human realm. Beneath her feet are moneybags representing greed, which she is treading down on. With her left hand, rather alarmingly, Charity holds out her anatomically accurate heart to the Lord Jesus, while in her right hand she carries a bowl of flowers and fruit to give to the needy.

The word charity comes from *caritas* in Latin, corresponding to *agape* in Greek. These words mean divine love, which is said to be the supreme virtue. When we love God above all things, we are able to extend this divine love to other people, just as, in the painting Charity gives her heart to God, and in doing so she can benefit others. To love God is what leads to a moral and ethical way of living. By "moral and ethical" I mean the standards for conducting our lives and for dealing with our fellow humans.

Buddhism is pointing beyond faith and beyond hope, as they are generally understood in Christianity. Similarly, Shinran's teaching can be seen as pointing beyond charity, namely, beyond the love of God and of our fellow human beings. It is difficult to accept this idea, because it challenges our favorable self-image—we consider ourselves to be ethical people. What would it mean to go beyond charity?

Spiritual paths generally contain an affirming aspect and a negating aspect. In Buddhism, impermanence negates my ego self and affirms my interdependent self. The affirming aspect of Christian charity was just mentioned, i.e., one's love of God, which inspires moral and ethical behavior. But there is also the negative aspect of Christian charity, namely divine punishment for disobedience. Theistic religion is concerned with how we respond to God's commands. Moral and ethical standards are central to the teachings: obey and be rewarded, or disobey and be punished. Failing to love God, i.e., being without *caritas*, is the worst kind of disobedience. Historically, the Church was not content to await God's Last Judgment, and it made zealous efforts to punish the ungodly in the present life. The Bible celebrates the annihilation of the Canaanite tribes and the unbelievers,[23] which led Christians to see themselves as privileged executioners whose actions were virtuous. Their catalog of barbarities included crusades against Muslims, inquisition against heretics, *pogroms* against Jews, torture and execution of "witches," and forced conversion and enslavement of indigenous peoples. However, in the words of Albert Camus, there are *no* privileged executioners. Rather, *all executioners are of the same family*.[24]

Destructive aspects arise when one's religious view is centered on standards of conduct; as Pascal warns: *he who would act the angel acts the brute*. And, it's not unique to Christianity. Despite Gotama's example of strict non-violence, Buddhist followers have persecuted those whose religion or ethnicity differs from theirs.[25] The Buddhist-led campaign of ethnic cleansing directed at Muslims in Myanmar is the latest such atrocity.

We face a serious difficulty in following a path where the primary emphasis is on morality and ethics. There is a temptation to shift the focus away from where it should be, namely, the recognition of my own deluded ideas. Instead, standards of conduct give me a pretext for judging the apparent moral and ethical failings of others. Misdirecting my focus in this way prevents me from becoming a spiritually mature person. So, for me it is not a skillful means to make charity (i.e., right conduct) the basis of a spiritual path. The aim in Jōdo Shinshū is to gain self-awareness, rather than to uphold ethical standards. When this was first explained to me, I realized that Jōdo Shinshū would be my path and that Shinran would be my teacher.

Do our temple customs accord with Shinran's views? In the Buddhist Churches of America, a text called the Golden Chain is often recited. It exists in various versions, one of which says, in part,

> I will try to be kind and gentle to every living thing and protect all who are weaker than myself. I will try to think pure and beautiful thoughts, to say pure and beautiful words, and to do pure and beautiful deeds, knowing that on what I do now depends not only my happiness or unhappiness, but also those of others.

That is a fine religious sentiment, entirely in accord with Christian charity. However, Shinran's view can be paraphrased this way: "Because I cannot tell right from wrong, or false from true, I am incapable of thinking, saying, or doing anything pure and beautiful."[26] He is brutally honest in a way that few of us can match. Do we know what a pure and beautiful thought is? Can we be confident that our calculated actions will lead to a pure and beautiful outcome? Even in simple cases (e.g., Should I give money to a beggar?) our attempts to be ethical can go awry. The outcome is often beyond our control, and we may fail to uphold the most basic standard of conduct: "First, do no harm."

Because the authorship of the Golden Chain is not generally given, temple members might assume that it comes from Shinran or that it was promoted by Hongwanji in Japan. In fact, this text originated one hundred years ago with European Buddhists living in Hawaii.[27] They drew on the Theravāda tradition, which emphasizes ethical behavior for monks and for lay people. The key idea is that one's good actions bring good consequences, and one's bad actions bring bad consequences, as an automatic aspect of existence. The text we recite aligns very well with that teaching, and it is therefore misleading with respect to Shinran's experience of the Buddhist path—actions that we think are "good" may, in fact, lead to "bad" consequences:

> There is virtue that is produced from a defiled mind and that does not accord with dharma-nature. Whether with regard to their cause or to their fruition, the good acts of foolish human beings and devas and the recompense of human beings and devas are all inverted (*tendō*) and empty/false (*kogi*). Hence, they are called [unreal] virtue.[28]

For Shinran, believing in the recompense of good and evil is the cause of "provisional" birth in the Pure Land and prevents the realization of "transformative" or true birth.[29] Ironically, it's fitting that the text we recite is called the Golden Chain. In the *Larger Sutra*, those "who believe in the recompense of good and evil [and] doubt the inconceivable Buddha-wisdom" are symbolized as young princes fettered with gold chains![30]

To be a disciple of the Buddha, one generally must adopt training rules or precepts. These are ethical guidelines that one aspires to live by. Gotama recommended five precepts for lay people: not to kill, not to steal, not to lie, not to commit adultery, and not to become intoxicated.[31] Monks and nuns have many additional precepts to observe. Aspiring to follow the guidelines was fundamental to the Buddhist path in ancient India, and it remains so in many Buddhist traditions today.

However, Shin Buddhism has no ceremony in which one takes the five precepts.[32] Did Shinran think lightly of killing, stealing, lying, and so forth? No, he did not view the precepts as being wrong in that sense. Rather, he identified them as a provisional understanding that may eventually lead us to the true teaching. Shinran undoubtedly revered the precepts (and so should we), but they were not the means for his liberation:

> Know that it is impossible to be born in the true, fulfilled Pure Land by simply observing precepts, or by self-willed conviction, or by self-cultivated good.[33]
>
> *Thus it is that those fundamentally evil who break precepts ardently enter the path of birth in the Pure Land.* Know that *thus it is* means "being made to become so"; that

is, according to the way the Pure Land is, those who break precepts or have no precepts as well as those of deep evil karma will all attain birth.[34]

Shinran was liberated when shinjin or self-awareness arose in him through his listening to the words of teachers. At that point, he abandoned the notion that he was a charitable person.

Shinran was not primarily concerned with ethical standards, and in that sense his teaching is beyond charity. As noted in a modern commentary,

> ... given the fundamental rejection of the secular world's systems of logic and value in Shinran's thought, it is quite natural that conventional systems of ethical norms or principles are not present therein.[35]

However, this aspect of Jōdo Shinshū became a stumbling block for followers who were caught up in the "licensed evil" controversy during the 13th century. There were those who advocated "offensive or even malicious conduct stemming from the presumption that one is guaranteed birth in the Pure Land."[36] Advocacy of licensed evil rests on the belief that the Pure Land is strictly an after-death realm. However, Shinran's writings do not support this belief.[37] He admonished such persons:

> It is deplorable that you have told people to abandon themselves to their hearts' desires and to do anything they want. One must seek to cast off the evil of this world and to cease doing wretched deeds; *this* is what it means to reject the world and to live the nembutsu.[38]

It is indeed sorrowful to give way to impulses with the excuse that one is by nature possessed of blind passions—excusing acts that should not be committed, words that should not be said, and thoughts that should not be harbored—and to say that one may follow one's desires in any way whatever.[39]

As rumors of misdeeds gradually spread, Shinran wrote in a letter, "Do not take a liking to poison just because there is an antidote." This was in order to put an end to that wrong understanding. It by no means implies that evil can obstruct one's attainment of birth.[40]

In his writings during the controversy, Shinran did not put forward a code of conduct. Rather, he sought to correct the distorted views that had arisen concerning Shin Buddhist liberation. Nevertheless, his descendants drew on Confucian ethics and imperial law to promote rules of conduct in an effort to gain social acceptance.[41]

In Jōdo Shinshū the first order of business is self-knowing—an awakening to the ego self and to the interdependent self. Even so, do we ever get back to the idea of moral and ethical behavior? As a Shin Buddhist, should I aspire to be a compassionate person? The question does not arise in religions that teach the duality of good and evil, of God and the devil. There you find standards of charitable conduct that a faithful person must observe.

Can there be any basis for charitable actions within Shin Buddhism? As I see it, ethical behavior is a derived property of an awakened life. To live in a truly charitable manner is not possible without self-knowing. Lacking this, our calculated attempts to be charitable or compassionate only serve to amplify the ego. By way of illustration, has this thought ever crossed your mind? *The nerve of those people. I was so generous, and they didn't even thank me!* I suspect that most of us have felt resentment when our good deed was thwarted or not appreciated. If that is so, then were we motivated by true generosity or by a desire for recognition? On rare occasions we might perform a spontaneous or unreflective act of compassion, but it seems that most of our actions are based on calculated self-interest.

Is there a bodhisattva in your life? I hope that is the case. Indeed, there are many beings among us who are bodhisattvas, but we should not think of ourselves as playing that role. A wonderful trait of a bodhisattva is to perform charitable actions unconsciously. Only the beneficiary regards the actions as compassionate. True charity is possible when the bodhisattva awakens to wisdom. This awakening is to attain humility, and therein lies the dilemma—my own striving cannot make me humble. My conscious, calculated efforts cannot transform me into a bodhisattva. On the Shin Buddhist path, we can be liberated when self-knowing arises through listening to the Dharma. Most directly, it is to hear and reflect on the meaning of the *myōgō* or Buddha's Name, *Namo Amida Butsu*, which can be translated as the command, "Know thyself!" When Shinran understood this, he abandoned the idea of observing precepts. It was the death of his efforts to become a charitable person and his birth as a humble person. Only at this stage could his actions unconsciously manifest true compassion. A bodhisattva is one who *listens*, who is made to *awaken*, and who becomes *humble*. For me, this is what it means to go beyond charity.

Part II

Buddhahood

The wanderer Vacchagotta asked the Blessed One, "Then does Master Gotama hold any speculative view at all?"

"Vaccha, 'speculative view' is something that the Tathāgata has put away." [42]

—Aggivacchagotta Sutta

Putting Away Samsara

Since ancient times, people have speculated about how old the world is, but today there are accurate measurements that bear on this question. The age of the known universe (13.80 ± 0.02 billion years) comes from observations of the cosmic microwave background radiation.[43] The age of the earth (4.54 ± 0.05 billion years) comes from radiometric dating of terrestrial, lunar, and meteoritic samples. This means that the earth has been revolving around the sun for fifty million times longer than a human life span!

Challenged by what nature is teaching us, we might react with denial. How could the world have existed without us for billions of years? This egocentric view gives rise to the popular misconception that the earth and its inhabitants came into existence only a few thousand years ago. By contrast, people in ancient India had an intuitive grasp that the world was far older than the span of a human life. They proposed a cosmology with a time-scale vastly longer than 13.8 billion years.

In our Buddhist services we recite a text called the Three Treasures, which states, "How rare and wondrous it is to be born into human life! Now I am living it." The recognition that it is *rare* to be born into human life follows from the Indian idea that the world is inconceivably old, and that a human life lasts for only a brief instant. The teaching is meant to challenge my egocentric perspective.

The text of the Three Treasures continues: "How rare and wondrous it is to encounter the teachings of the Buddha! Now I can hear them." It was only through the rarest of circumstances that I received life in human form. Just as extraordinary were the events that led me to encounter the Dharma. It is said that a buddha appears in the world just once within a very long span of time. To be alive at such a moment and to meet with a buddha is an exceedingly unlikely event. The way of life taught by Gotama Buddha persisted in India for 1500 years before dying out there. His teachings would have perished too, had they not been brought to other parts of Asia by Buddhist propagators who risked their lives to do so. Centuries later the teachings took root in America, having been carried here initially by Buddhist followers from China and Japan. Through these improbable and heroic efforts, I am able to receive the Dharma today.

And here is the punch line from the Three Treasures: "If I do not find a path to liberation in the present life, no hope is there that I will be freed from sorrow in the ocean of birth and death." Liberation means ending the pattern of repetitive existence called samsara. Traditional Indian religion conceived of a literal cycle of transmigration within the six realms of rebirth, as the *ātman* or unchanging identity experiences death and rebirth repeatedly. Gotama found a path for putting away the idea of *ātman* and with it the mentality of samsara. For noble disciples, awakening meant the removal of illusions:

> "Being disillusioned, desire fades away. When desire fades away, they're freed. When they're freed, they know they're freed. They understand: 'Rebirth is ended, the spiritual journey has been completed, what had to be done has been done, there is no return to any state of existence.'"[44]

From a Pure Land perspective, desires and illusions are an inherent aspect of human life, and there is no prospect that they will fade away. Yet, the text of the Three Treasures is given a new meaning:

> The beings of the ten quarters in the same way transmigrate within the six courses endlessly; revolving in circles, they flounder in the waves of desire and sink in the sea of pain. It is rare to meet with the Buddhist path or receive birth into human existence; now, already, we have met with them. It is rare to hear the Pure Land teaching; now, already, we have heard it. It is rare to awaken shinjin; now, already, we have awakened it.[45]

Gotama's final words were a summary of everything he had taught: "All conditioned things are impermanent. Seek your liberation with diligence."[46] Given the exceptionally favorable circumstances of (a) being born into human life and (b) being able to listen to the teachings of the Buddha, I must put away the "ocean of birth and death" here and now, and not dream of doing so in a future existence—a lesson evoked by the metaphor of the house-builder:

> *Houses are impermanent—*
> *on and on, life after life.*
> *I've been searching for the house-builder—*
> *painful is birth again and again.*
>
> *I've seen you, house-builder!*
> *You won't build a house again.*
> *All your rafters are broken,*
> *your ridgepole is shattered.*
> *My mind is released from limits:*
> *in this very life it will dissipate.*[47]

Dying and Living

Dying is inevitable—certainly, that is our biggest problem. But, to go on living is *not* inevitable—that is our next biggest problem. Can we know whether life is or is not worth living? In Buddhist terms, the human condition is *duhkha*—it is unsatisfactory and sorrowful. But rather than reflecting on life's tragic aspect and on our precarious existence, we crave excitement that takes our mind off it. By filling our waking hours with distractions, we avoid thinking about dying and living. However, the great writers have given voice to thoughts that we try to repress:

> *To be, or not to be, that is the question:*
> *Whether 'tis nobler in the mind to suffer*
> *The slings and arrows of outrageous fortune,*
> *Or to take arms against a sea of troubles,*
> *And by opposing, end them. To die, to sleep—*
> *No more, and by a sleep to say we end*
> *The heart-ache and the thousand natural shocks*
> *That flesh is heir to; 'tis a consummation*
> *Devoutly to be wish'd. To die, to sleep—*
> *To sleep, perchance to dream—ay, there's the rub,*
> *For in that sleep of death what dreams may come,*
> *When we have shuffled off this mortal coil,*
> *Must give us pause.*[48]

Are death and its unknown consequences preferable to a life of troubles? Hamlet is famously unable to make up his mind. Choosing to end the heartache would be logical, he says, if not for "the dread of something after death, the undiscover'd country from whose bourn no traveller returns." Another of Shakespeare's tragic heroes comes down on the side of dying, regardless of what may follow:

> *To-morrow, and to-morrow, and to-morrow,*
> *Creeps in this petty pace from day to day,*
> *To the last syllable of recorded time;*

And all our yesterdays have lighted fools
The way to dusty death. Out, out, brief candle!
Life's but a walking shadow, a poor player
That struts and frets his hour upon the stage
And then is heard no more. It is a tale
Told by an idiot, full of sound and fury,
Signifying nothing.[49]

Macbeth, who is soon to be slain in battle, concludes that life is without meaning and ought not to continue. The poor player's sound and fury deserve to be heard no more. And as King Lear came to understand, it would be better never to have received life in human form:

> *When we are born, we cry that we are come to this great stage of fools.*[50]

In difficult circumstances, one might become despondent and therefore wish to die, but that is a personal problem rather than a universal one. Here, we are considering the universal aspect of *duhkha* that is bound up with impermanent existence and so applies to everyone, regardless of circumstances. Life appears to be meaningless if it is impermanent, as Shinran recognized:

> But with a foolish being full of blind passions, in this fleeting world—this burning house—all matters without exception are empty and false, totally without truth and sincerity.[51]

Albert Camus (1913-1960), one of the great literary voices of the 20th century, restated Hamlet's dilemma:

> There is but one truly serious philosophical problem, and that is suicide. Judging whether life is or is not worth living amounts to answering the fundamental question of philosophy.[52]

We may have the good fortune to live in comfortable circumstances, but still the world is full of suffering and cruelty that are without any apparent meaning. The unreasonableness of the world is opposed by "the wild longing for clarity whose call echoes in the human heart." The consequence of this opposition, according to Camus, is the feeling of the *absurd*.

> At this point of his effort man stands face to face with the irrational. He feels within him his longing for happiness and for reason. The absurd is born of this confrontation between the human need and the unreasonable silence of the world.[53]

Why pursue happiness in the midst of meaningless suffering? Is suicide a solution to the absurd, a means of deliverance from it, as Hamlet wonders? Shakespeare declines to answer, but Camus proposes a way forward. If one affirms the logic arising from the confrontation with the irrational, then choosing to end one's life is not admissible. *Absurd man*, defined as one who questions the silence of the world, rejects suicide because it would put an end to his questioning. He does not turn away from the human condition. He is liberated from meaninglessness through his conscious dissatisfaction. In effect, Camus affirms the Buddha's injunction: you must comprehend fully that *your life is duhkha*. Seeing the human condition clearly, absurd man refuses to be tempted by heaven or terrified by hell:

> Hence, what he demands of himself is to live *solely* with what he knows, to accommodate himself to what is, and to bring in nothing that is not certain. He is told that nothing is. But this at least is a certainty. And it is with this that he is concerned: he wants to find out if it is possible to live *without appeal*.[54]

Absurd man acknowledges no court of appeal before which he might argue his case.

Camus's reasoning finds a parallel in the story of Siddhattha Gotama. The question of whether life is or is not worth living inspires Gotama to leave his home and family and to seek the way. He experiences great difficulties in his search, and the austerities he practices are a form of gradual self-destruction.[55] Yet, Gotama stops short of death, which would end his questioning. His awakening comes with the clear realization that the human condition is *duhkha*. Examining the self to its ultimate depth, he discovers that everything in him is constantly moving, turning, and evolving. The self to which he has been clinging is impermanent and without intrinsic substance. He realizes that the self is interdependent with the whole of existence. He awakens to the Dharma—limitless, formless reality—and becomes one with it.

To go on living is not a matter of inevitability. Rather, it is a conscious choice for the person who confronts *duhkha*, the tragic dimension of life. Gotama's urgent questioning of the human condition—his wild longing for clarity—led him to seek the way. An authentic human existence is realized through a commitment to search for meaning. It is to accept the confrontation with the unreasonable silence of the universe.

The Most Important Day

What is the most important event of the year for members of the Buddhist Churches of America? Undoubtedly, it is the Obon festival, which draws the big crowds and is the principal fundraiser. It derives from the Hungry Ghost festival in Chinese folk religion, a non-Buddhist holiday marking the temporary return of ancestors from the spirit world. In adapting this observance for Buddhist temples, the *Ullambana Sutra* is often cited. Here, the Buddha teaches his disciple to make offerings that will free the disciple's deceased mother from the hungry ghost realm. However, neither the Obon festival nor the *Ullambana Sutra* figure at all in the teachings of Shinran. He held that there is no practice we can perform that will give merit to our ancestors.[56] Instead, the meaning we might attach to Obon has to do only with gratitude: our lives are sustained by what we have received from those who came before us.

What is the most important event of the year for Hongwanji, the BCA's parent organization in Japan? It is *Hō-onkō* in January, which commemorates the death of Shinran. Its prominence dates to the time of Shinran's great-grandson, Kakunyo (1270-1351), who asserted that Shinran was the incarnation of Amida Buddha.[57] The architecture at Hongwanji in Kyoto reflects the primary institutional purpose of memorializing the founder.[58] The two main temple buildings are the *Amida-dō*, dedicated to Amida Buddha, and a more imposing structure, the *Goei-dō*, in which the central image on the altar is a portrait statue of Shinran that serves as "the spiritual and functional 'double' of the deceased master."[59] However, Shinran's writings do not suggest that he wanted to be enshrined in this way or to have elaborate services performed in his memory.

What about Shinran's own perspective? What might he say is the most important day of the year? Rather than claiming to be a founder, he saw himself as a disciple of Śākyamuni and a student of Jōdo Shinshū, the teaching that he received by way of the Pure Land masters. He honored the historical Buddha above all other teachers, because

> ... in his compassion, Śākyamuni, the great hero sought indeed to bless those committing the five grave offenses, those slandering the dharma, and those lacking the seed of Buddhahood.... [He] appeared in this world and expounded the teachings of the way to enlightenment, seeking to save the multitudes of living beings by blessing them with this benefit that is true and real.[60]

This suggests that Shinran, to acknowledge his indebtedness, might regard Bodhi Day, commemorating the Buddha's awakening, as the most important event of the year.

Twenty-five hundred years ago, Indian society was organizing into urban centers where people made a living through commerce rather than agriculture.[61] The traditional Vedic religion, with its ritual sacrifices and rigid caste system, was unsuited to a society of enterprising city dwellers. In response to changing spiritual needs, new religious paths were being formulated by mendicant teachers who considered religious awakening to be an individual matter. A core issue for them was the problem of karma and rebirth.

Indian spirituality posits that the world is inconceivably old, having neither beginning nor ending. All beings possess an inherent self that undergoes cyclic existence, in which death is followed by rebirth in an endless round of transmigration. Not only humans, but heavenly beings, hell-dwellers, and the rest, are all subject to death and rebirth. The law of karma says that thoughts, words, and deeds have inevitable consequences, as an automatic aspect of existence, and the karma that we generate will bear fruit in subsequent lives. With this understanding, the spiritual imperative was finding a path to a favorable rebirth of the self.

Like many of his contemporaries, Gotama renounced the householder's life to seek the way as a mendicant. By studying with teachers of yoga, he became a master of meditation. Through such techniques, it was said that one could transcend the ego and realize the eternal, absolute self. Gotama attained the highest states of yogic meditation, but rather than encountering the absolute self, he came to doubt that human beings have any such intrinsic or permanent essence.

Next, he tried to achieve liberation through ascetic practices that punish the body and mind, but this method also proved to be ineffective.

At one point, Gotama recalled an incident from his boyhood, when, seeing bugs being eaten by birds, he felt spontaneous compassion for suffering creatures. He decided to replicate this experience of non-ego through a set of wholesome activities known as the Eightfold Path. The path culminated when he attained liberation under the Bodhi Tree. He became Gotama Buddha, a human being who had transcended samsara and realized nirvana. He was freed from the thirst for renewed existence that drives the cycle of death and rebirth.

Buddhahood meant that Gotama no longer identified with the constituents of the self as we generally understand it. How might one then describe him? A brahmin named Doṇa, amazed by the Buddha's confidence and serenity, sought to know what manner of being he was. Gotama framed his answers with reference to rebirth:

"Sir, might you be a god?"
"I will not be a god, brahmin."
"Might you be a heavenly spirit?"
"I will not be a heavenly spirit."
"Might you be an earthly spirit?"
"I will not be an earthly spirit."
"Might you be a human?"
"I will not be a human."
"What then might you be?"
"Remember me, brahmin, as one who woke up."

I could have been reborn as a god,
or as a heavenly spirit flying through the sky.
I could have become an earthly spirit,
or returned as a human.
But the defilements that could bring about these rebirths
I've ended, smashed, and gutted.
Like a graceful lotus,
to which water does not cling,
the world doesn't cling to me,
and so, brahmin, I am a buddha.[62]

Gotama's life example and teachings were so powerful that Buddhism eventually grew into a world religion. In light of all the above, I think Shinran might say that the Buddha's awakening was the most important event in human history.

Do I Want to Become a Buddha?

A minister related the following incident to me. Once, when a group of Jōdo Shinshū priests in Japan was asked, Do you want to become a buddha? they all answered No. At first, I found their response baffling, even shocking. What did they have in mind when they recited the Three Treasures, or when they received ordination? Later, it occurred to me that the question has a variety of interpretations. What is meant by "become a buddha?" What is meant by "want to?" For that matter, what am I, a being that wants or doesn't want to become a buddha?

For the early disciples, Buddhahood or nirvana was "the destruction of lust, the destruction of hatred, the destruction of illusion."[63] The disciples practiced the Eightfold Path to become *arahants* or "worthy ones." *Nibbāna* was realized in the present life, and physical death meant the end of cyclic rebirth in samsara. However, today we are very unlikely to meet an *arahant*, and we have scarcely any chance of becoming one. For most of us, that route is closed. A few centuries after the Buddha's passing, Mahāyāna teachers shifted the focus to the way of the bodhisattva. It is the idealized path of one who is oriented toward nirvana while working for universal liberation. The bodhisattva awakens the aspiration to become a buddha, cultivates the *pāramitā* practices over many lives, and forgoes final enlightenment until all sentient beings have been liberated.

In the present day, how can one attain Buddhahood? Do I expect to become an *arahant* like the early disciples? Do I see myself as following the bodhisattva path? Have I vowed to liberate all sentient beings? Will I engage in *pāramitā* practices over long eons and through countless rebirths? Perhaps when the ministers in Japan answered No, it was because they were aware of their own weaknesses. They might have been acknowledging their inability to let go of attachments in this life. The calculating mind cannot genuinely aspire to liberate *all* beings, with no exceptions. To think of oneself as a bodhisattva is presumptuous.

Shinran teaches that foolish beings cannot awaken the mind aspiring for enlightenment (*bodhicitta*) through the effort of the ego self:

> *The aspiration for enlightenment through self-power taught*
>   *in the Path of Sages*
> *Is beyond our minds and words;*
> *We foolish beings ever sinking in transmigration—*
> *How could we awaken it?*[64]

Rather, *bodhicitta* is "the inconceivable working of the power of the Vow," which is shinjin.[65] Entering the path, we find that the poisons of greed, anger, and ignorance are standing in the way of liberation, so we want to eliminate them. In fact, we face a greater obstacle than the three poisons. It is the religious ego, which turns our spiritual aspirations toward the task of self-aggrandizement. Shin Buddhism recognizes this more difficult obstacle. The poisons of greed, anger, and ignorance remain intact, but they no longer prevent our liberation. The reality of the passions is what teaches us to be humble. On this path, eventual Buddhahood becomes certain despite our wavering aspiration. It is attaining nirvana without "wanting to."

Learning and Non-Learning

As young children we continually ask What? How? and Why? We come equipped with natural curiosity—the desire to understand the world and our place in it. Sustaining this curiosity leads to life-long learning. However, as adults we may be overwhelmed by difficulties and lose our natural curiosity—we may cease to be learners. Another trap is to become cynical or ideological: we prefer the comfort of our ego-centered version of reality. To lose our natural curiosity is to cease being truly human; it is to abandon the search for meaning. Rather than arriving at this dead end, we ought to make life-long learning a goal. Nevertheless, there is a form of Buddhism in which the aim is to put an end to learning. How can that be?

By listening to Gotama Buddha and following his teachings, a direct disciple could become an *arahant*—one whose attainment of *nibbāna* was the same as that of the Buddha. This Way of the Hearers (*śrāvakayāna*) could be a slow process extending over many lifetimes of practicing, but if a disciple had enough good karma to live as a monk, he could progress through a series of stages in which the passions were eradicated one by one. The stages of noble discipleship are the stream-enterer, the once-returner, the non-returner, and the *arahant*, each having the two phases of path and fruition.[66]

By cultivating wisdom through years (or lifetimes) of practicing, one could realize the highest stage attainable by a disciple of the Buddha—to see *nibbāna* and to dwell in it. Such an *arahant* was called an "adept" or "one beyond training" (*asekha*).[67] The Japanese term is *mugaku*, the stage in which all religious practice has been completed and nothing remains to be accomplished. That is contrasted with the stage of the *gakunin* or trainee, one whose learning and practice are incomplete.[68] The trainee can see the supreme goal of *nibbāna* but is unable to dwell in it, because ignorance has not been eliminated. There is still learning to be accomplished.

Gotama Buddha described his liberation this way: "Knowledge and vision arose in me: my freedom is unshakable; this is my last rebirth; now there are no more future lives."[69] Unshakable freedom means that nothing can undo the realization of *nibbāna*—Buddhahood is irreversible. For Gotama, the samsaric mentality of rebirth has been destroyed. Clearly, this describes a person with no further questions to ask and nothing more to learn. That was the meaning of Buddhahood for the early disciples. The path of personal liberation culminated in *mugaku* or non-learning when all questions had been answered.

Fast forward to Shinran in 13th century Japan. For him, the way of the early disciples ("Hīnayāna sages") was not accessible; practice and realization on that path died out long before. He could not become an *arahant* by eradicating the passions: "Being filled with blind passions, we are unable to liberate ourselves from birth-and-death, whatever practices we may carry out."[70] Shinran found a life of awakening in Jōdo Shinshū, the path that was "now vital and flourishing." People who hear and reflect on the meaning of Namo Amida Butsu can be liberated, despite their living in a time and place far removed from ancient India. Rather than the ideal of non-learning, the *Larger Sutra* teaches the aspiration for limitless learning. Rather than eradicating the passions and becoming an *arahant*, it teaches a life of awakening "without severing blind passions."

Through practicing under Gotama's guidance, a disciple advanced in stages from an "uninstructed worldling" to an *arahant*. By contrast, the Shin Buddhist life of awakening does not involve upward advancement. We remain foolish beings, but we are given a new awareness of our situation. In one sense, nothing changes. In another sense, there is a complete transformation of our perspective. The transformation requires ceaseless effort, but it is effort that we cannot take credit for.

In Shin Buddhism we never stop learning. The ideal is not *mugaku* but rather *gakunin*, the stage of a trainee who still has much to learn.[71] As one of my teachers stated, "If you attain enlightenment, you may have no further need for Buddhism. However, foolish people like us must study endlessly."[72] Awakening in Shin Buddhism is to understand that I am a foolish person who trusts in his abilities and who swims against the flow of limitless reality. Asking questions is the essence of this path, the most important question being What am I? Or, put in a different way, What is Namo Amida Butsu? On this path we spend our whole lives asking these questions; the stage of learning is itself the goal.

In Shin Buddhism the only transformative practice is listening to the Dharma with self-reflection. This approach resembles superficially the manner in which the early disciples listened to the Buddha, but there are crucial differences. Our teachers are ministers and sangha members, all of whom are foolish beings, not *arahants*. We also receive the Dharma through everyday difficulties that reveal our human frailty. There is no end to the difficulties that teach me what I am—I must be open to learning from them. Otherwise, I am not genuinely listening and reflecting. Shin Buddhist followers never arrive at the non-learning stage. As trainees with a lot to learn, I hope that we will retain our curiosity and will keep asking questions.

Leaving the World, Leaving the Mountain

If the starting point is pure, then the fulfillment is also pure. This we should know.[73]

—T'an-luan

To realize the potential of any spiritual path, we must begin in the right way. Let's consider what is the fulfillment of the Dharma path and what might be the necessary point of departure for realizing it. Inevitably, we bring with us mistaken ideas about Buddhism, but even so, it can be said that there is a "pure" or right starting point.

Gotama and Shinran, while living sixteen centuries apart and in very different cultures, realized the fulfillment of the Dharma path, which is *Buddhahood*. This fulfillment is universal—it applies also to us in 21st century America. Recall what is recited in the Three Treasures text: "May I discover the highest aspiration, which is to become a Buddha." Here is a concise statement of what this aspiration means:

> Buddhism focuses on our attainment of true human growth as we search for a higher way of life by awakening supramundane [i.e., world-transcending] wisdom. One who realizes the fulfillment of such wisdom is called a "buddha," and Buddhism reveals the path leading to the attainment of buddhahood.[74]

Becoming a Buddh*ist* means to embrace this perspective. One sets out on the path of "true human growth" by awakening to wisdom that transcends the secular world's value systems.

Taken broadly, Buddhism has attributes that partake of secular values—for example, a religious organization, a social and cultural affiliation, a framework for political engagement, a catalog of self-help prescriptions, a marketing cachet for stylish products, and so forth. Here, I consider only the primary attributes of Buddhism, as expressed in the above quotation.

In Japanese the phrase "to become Buddha (*jōbutsu*)" is sometimes equated simply with physical death. That usage can be misleading; it suggests that one becomes Buddha eventually without following any spiritual path, or (even worse) that Buddhism refutes human life. Shinran, however, gives a concrete explanation of what it means to attain Buddhahood. In his understanding, those who follow the Dharma path and receive shinjin are made to see a *little bit* of world-transcending wisdom.[75] It means that one's mind is turned around entirely, and that the present life necessarily reaches fulfillment. Such a life of awakening ends in perfect completion at physical death, with nothing left unresolved as far as one's spiritual path. The path culminates in Buddhahood.[76] This is why in Shin Buddhism it is crucial to discover the right starting point. As the epigraph states, "If the starting point is pure, then the fulfillment is also pure."

There was once a minister in the BCA named Gyodo Haguri (1881-1965), who had a keen appreciation for Shinran's teaching. He said this:

> The first step in *becoming* a Buddhist—no one is born a Buddhist!—is to awaken to the true nature of the self.[77]

Seeing the true nature of the self, which Rev. Haguri identified as "blind ignorance," entails doubting the conventional self and its value system. Starting on the path in this way is a matter of *becoming*—of nurturing the mind. There must be a process of discovery to encounter one's true spiritual vocation. Because questioning the conventional self is not an instinctive desire, one cannot be born into this world as a Buddhist.

Gotama and Shinran each realized the universal goal of Buddhahood by finding the right starting point and by following the path leading from it. The starting point, too, contains aspects that are universal. One such aspect is to doubt our system of values, as indicated here:

> Buddhism encourages us to engage in profound reflection on the reality that we human beings lead lives of ignorance,

emptiness, and falsity in our everyday, secular lives. Through a penetrating insight into ourselves, we are subjectively made to negate the present state of our being, which remains buried in the secular world.[78]

Without coming to doubt secular values, it would not be feasible to start on the Dharma path, or on any spiritual path, for that matter. The values in question are of course wealth and fame, but also social status, career, family, and recreation. Gotama chose "the going forth from home life into homelessness," because he saw that wealth, fame, and all the rest were hollow values. Knowing that the things he cherished were fated to pass away, he concluded that his life up to that point was without any substance that he could rely on.[79]

Consider for a moment an opposing point of view—that of the person who never comes to doubt secular values. Such a person has no need to look for a spiritual vocation. By affirming one's present state of being, human life can be fulfilled through secular accomplishments, without recourse to Buddhism. Gotama and Shinran, however, were driven to spiritual seeking because they could not escape the consciousness of doubt. In this regard, they can be seen as role models. Absent a sense of identification with them, it would be very difficult to find the Shin Buddhist path.

How to describe the secular world? Among other things, it is full of suffering, cruelty, and unrestrained egotism. Anyone not blind to this fact stands to be overtaken by doubt. One is driven to look for a spiritual path that leads beyond the negative aspects of the secular world, that offers a way of life—or even a world separate from this one—where suffering, cruelty, and egotism are eliminated. Could *that* be the aim of the Buddhist path?

In fact, that is not the aim. I have stated that rejecting secular values is the right starting point, but something different must be said concerning the fulfillment. When Gotama awakened to world-transcending wisdom, he did not remain in the condition of negating the secular world, but rather returned to that world to manifest wisdom and compassion.[80] He began a forty-five-year mission to share the Dharma, the content of his awakening experience. Likewise, on the

Shin Buddhist path, seeing a little bit of world-transcending wisdom will certainly change our perspective. In a life of awakening, the secular world, including both negative and positive aspects, becomes a learning place, a place for the attainment of true human growth, a place where unavoidable suffering is no longer meaningless, where human life is affirmed and not refuted.[81] Indeed, the life-examples of Gotama and Shinran attest to this.

Shinran left the secular world at the age of eight to follow the path of monastic discipline on Mt. Hiei. However, taking up such a life did not constitute the right starting point for him. Twenty years later, in departing from the mountain, what he renounced was not *secular* values, but rather, his *religious* values. That decision became the right starting point for Shinran.

It may be hard for us to understand what led him to abandon monastic life. A special focus of Mt. Hiei Buddhism was extreme practices that would bring a monk to the point of physical and mental collapse, such as uninterrupted circumambulation about a Buddha statue for ninety days at a stretch.[82] It was held that these daunting tests would purify the mind, a view that was accepted by the young Hannen (as Shinran was then known). His departure from the mountain seems not to have been motivated by failure at physical practices. On the contrary, one can imagine him performing these to the letter. The reason for discarding physical practices was his conclusion that they were hollow and lacked any substance he could rely on. They could not transform Shinran's mind. The same conclusion had been reached by his predecessor Gotama when he abandoned ascetic practices. Thus, Shinran was on firm ground in renouncing his religious values. Even so, he did not discard everything when he left the mountain. His activities there included the intense study of Buddhist scriptures, and for the remainder of his life he continued to deepen his reading and reflecting.[83]

A universal aspect of the right starting point in Buddhism is to doubt our *secular* value system. Hence, Gotama abandoned his home and his social status to seek the way. Another universal aspect of the right starting point is to doubt our *religious* value system. This aspect is the central focus of Jōdo Shinshū, as understood by Shinran. One must "leave the mountain," at least figuratively, in order to take up the path of Shin Buddhism.[84]

What is implied here is a process of self-discovery, of understanding the self more clearly, and it might go like this: Something about Buddhism catches our interest. We explore the teachings and find them to be applicable in our life. We feel a certain level of commitment to the path and seek fulfillment there. We create a religious value system, modeling it after the secular way of thinking, because this is the only type of logic available to us. Based on the secular goal of self-improvement, we arrive at a value system of ethical conduct and religious practices. We become followers of what Shinran calls "provisional" Buddhism.[85] In Jōdo Shinshū, the Buddhism based on self-improvement is the figurative "mountain" that we need to abandon.

Can we do so? Alas, as foolish beings, we never abandon provisional Buddhism entirely. Not even Shinran could do that. But what we can do is learn to question our values by hearing and reflecting on Shinran's teaching and life experience. Doubting our values is to see the religious ego at work in the way we approach the spiritual path. Motivated by the religious ego, we gravitate to the idea of self-improvement. To be more clearly aware of our selfish spiritual motivations is to see *a little bit of world-transcending wisdom*, which is to receive shinjin. In the Shin Buddhist life of awakening—a life of true human growth—this way of seeing our motivations more clearly is ever-deepening.

Authenticity

Anyone searching for a spiritual path wants to find authenticity—the quality of being genuinely felt or compellingly experienced. Such a path cannot be purely our own invention. It must have a history of teachers and students who have gone before us, and there must be present-day followers for us to encounter. Buddhism seems to fit the bill, but it takes many different forms. Is each of them authentic? We might claim that authentic Buddhism is what was taught in ancient India by Gotama Buddha. That would be *historical authenticity*, which is accorded great importance in some religions. But is it attainable?

Buddhism lacks physical artifacts dating to the time and place of origin, namely the 5th century BCE in India. The earliest tangible records of Gotama's existence are stone inscriptions made in the 3rd century BCE by King Aśoka. As far as the historical status of Buddhist texts, it's likely that the teachings were transmitted orally for hundreds of years before being written down. During these centuries, Indian Buddhism was splitting into dozens of schools and regional variants. Eventually, Gotama's words were transcribed and recopied in various dialects. The Pāli Canon is the version that happens to have survived in the most complete form, and it includes thousands of suttas or sermons. The suttas offer a wealth of detail that makes them sound more like history than like a fable. There is a degree of self-consistency, suggesting that the teachings flowed originally from a single intelligence, namely the mind of Gotama Buddha.[86] However, authenticity in a strict historical sense remains an elusive goal.

For Shin Buddhists, the history of the teachings is even murkier. In fact, historical authenticity *might not be a virtue*. Shin Buddhism is based on the Pure Land sutras, which are a subset of the very extensive writings of Mahāyāna Buddhism. These texts are quite unlike the Pāli suttas. In Mahāyāna writings, the Buddha transcends his original identity as a flesh-and-blood teacher. Now called Śākyamuni rather than Gotama, he becomes a character in a drama in which the events are mostly imagined rather than historical.

Authoritatively calling itself the Great Vehicle, Mahāyāna emerged in the 1st century BCE as a movement within the fragmented Indian Buddhist community.[87] Certainly, Mahāyāna flows from the Buddha's awakening experience, but its authenticity relies less on what the historical Buddha said and more on the perception of his dynamic way of being. Mahāyāna sutras are richly creative literary works composed by teachers who lived in India certainly, but possibly also in central Asia and in China. The identity of the writers is unknown, but we can be confident that they experienced the same awakening as Śākyamuni. They were Mahāyāna bodhisattvas—teachers who expressed the Dharma in a way that could liberate all sentient beings.[88]

Perhaps in the centuries after the Buddha's passing there were some who saw the existing forms of practice and realization as narrow and stagnant. They sought to regain authenticity by giving voice to the Buddha's innermost aspiration or *Hongan*. Here, liberation does not result from following a renunciant lifestyle or from learning fixed doctrines. Liberation is the deepening spiritual awareness that emerges when we meet with teachers and teachings. Mahāyāna is authentic in a way that transcends both history and social circumstance. One might say that it pre-dates the historical Buddha.[89] It calls forth an aspiration from our unconscious mind, a desire that has been shared by human beings in all times and places—the desire to live the most meaningful life possible, to become an awakened person. Assuming that such a universal path exists, would we not be justified in calling it authentic?

The term *general Buddhism* refers to a subset of the teachings endorsed by many Buddhist schools, including basic principles like the Four Noble Truths and Eightfold Path, and ethical ideals such as pacifism and vegetarianism. No doubt there are people today who think of themselves as general Buddhists, and there may be organized groups that identify in this way, but to establish a community a specific identification is usually needed. To embrace a particular tradition and its history helps to build a case for authenticity.

In the Buddhist Churches of America, the form that we focus on is Jōdo Shinshū, the teachings and life experience of Shinran. Surprisingly, Shinran's writings say nothing concerning the Four Noble Truths and the Eightfold Path.[90] Nor does he teach ethical behavior in the usual sense: he does not put forward a code of conduct. Therefore, Jōdo Shinshū is *not* general Buddhism. For Shinran, a different path to liberation had to be found. After studying many sutras and commentaries, he concluded that *Hongan*, the Buddha's deepest wish, is most clearly expressed in the *Larger Sutra of Immeasurable Life*. He came to regard the teaching, practice, and realization set forth in the *Larger Sutra* as the culmination of Buddhist history. For Shinran, the Buddha came into the world solely to teach *Hongan*.[91]

Jōdo Shinshū is a sharp change of direction from the religious views that prevailed in Shinran's day. Even now, his words are a challenge to our preconceptions about Buddhism:

> "To abandon the mind of self-power" admonishes the various and diverse kinds of people—masters of Hīnayāna or Mahāyāna, ignorant beings good or evil—to abandon the conviction that one is good, to cease relying on the self, to stop reflecting knowingly on one's evil heart, and further to abandon the judging of people as good and bad.[92]

Being made to abandon the mind of self-power is Shinran's description of liberation. He speaks confidently about what he has received:

> The radiant light, unhindered and inconceivable, eradicates suffering and brings realization of joy; the excellent Name, perfectly embodying all practices, eliminates obstacles and dispels doubt. This is the teaching and practice for our latter age; devote yourself solely to it.[93]

Remarkably, he does not portray himself as having attained a true understanding, or as acting from good motives:

> *I am such that I do not know right and wrong*
> *And cannot distinguish false and true;*
> *I lack even small love and small compassion,*
> *And yet, for fame and profit, enjoy teaching others.*[94]

> I know nothing at all of good or evil. For if I could know thoroughly, as Amida Tathāgata knows, that an act was good, then I would know good. If I could know thoroughly, as the Tathāgata knows, that an act was evil, then I would know evil.[95]

Shinran's ever-deepening self-awareness is what gives Jōdo Shinshū its claim to authenticity.

Are we in touch with Shinran? The experience of American Shin Buddhists during World War II had consequences that are still with us today. Under the difficult conditions of incarceration and resettlement, the wish of Japanese Americans to assimilate was quite understandable. There was a desire not to be seen as closely tied to Japan. Shinran's words, just quoted, are at odds with ideas that most Americans believe in—ideas like personal autonomy and the willingness to make moral judgments. The authentic flavor of Jōdo Shinshū had to be de-emphasized to give Buddhism a form that would be more palatable in America.[96] I've been told by long-time BCA members that they grew up hearing nothing at all in English concerning Shinran's teaching. Consequently, they were quite surprised when they encountered it later in life.

Seventy-five years after the incarceration, what should be the path forward for the BCA? My wish is that we would reconnect with what is authentic in Jōdo Shinshū by making Shinran our teacher and experiencing what he did as a person of the nembutsu. Not so long ago, there were very few published translations that would help us to do this. It wasn't until the 1990s that the Pure Land sutras and Shinran's writings became readily available to English speakers. I feel that we must do more to share the content of these foundational texts. We should not remain within the confines of general Buddhism.

Here are the key points. First, historical authenticity in Buddhism is difficult to attain, because direct evidence from the time of Gotama Buddha is lacking. Second, Mahāyāna Buddhism aims for an authenticity that transcends the historical Buddha. It seeks to awaken us to *Hongan*, the universal aspiration. Finally, Shinran, as a teacher of Mahāyāna, found the definitive expression of *Hongan* in the *Larger*

Sutra. For me, learning to appreciate his teachings is the most direct route to authenticity in Buddhism.

Part III

Skillful Means

When Śākyamuni was about to enter nirvana, he said to the monks, "From this day on, rely on dharma, not on people who teach it. Rely on the meaning, not on the words....Words are the finger pointing to the meaning; they are not the meaning itself. Hence, do not rely upon words." [97]

—Bodhisattva Nāgārjuna (2nd century CE)

Meaning and Metaphor

We are drawn to the Dharma in order to give meaning to our lives and to discover something of lasting value that brings a sense of fulfillment. Where is meaning to be found as we walk the Dharma path? I want to suggest that metaphor plays a crucial role.

During the lifetime of Gotama Buddha, many disciples were inspired to emulate their teacher by renouncing secular life. For renunciants, the Buddha's guidelines for mental training and personal conduct were to be understood literally. The words and actions of Gotama defined once and for all the kind of life they should lead. It was a sober, pragmatic approach for seeing the danger of attachments and for letting go of them. Even so, emulating the teacher's lifestyle was not the only way. There were many non-renunciant lay people among Gotama's direct disciples, but after his passing their path came to be seen as inferior to that of the monks.[98]

Buddhism eventually found a new direction in Mahāyāna, a path to Buddhahood that embraces all beings. Mahāyāna sutras express a deep truth that the historical Buddha was pointing toward, even though the conditions for transmitting it arose centuries later. Among these scriptures, Shin Buddhists consider three Pure Land sutras to be primary: the *Amida Sutra*, the *Contemplation Sutra*, and the *Larger Sutra of Immeasurable Life*. These texts reflect a stage of development that seems far beyond what could have been realized during the lifetime of the historical Buddha. Nevertheless, his life and teachings provided the source material.

In the Pure Land sutras, we meet Śākyamuni Buddha not as the historical teacher, but as a character in a drama that extends the possibility of liberation to all of humanity. According to Shinran, to teach this universal awakening is the purpose for which the Buddha appeared in the world.[99] Although emulating the Buddha's lifestyle is not required, how are we to follow a path that offers no such guidelines for behavior? What is needed are teachings that transcend the literal reading, that go beyond words and concepts. Consider this passage:

> The Buddha then said to Śāriputra, the Elder, "Beyond a [zillion] Buddha-lands westwards from here, there is a land called 'Perfect Bliss.' In that land there is a Buddha called Amida who is expounding the Dharma at this moment."
>
> "Śāriputra, why is that land called Perfect Bliss? It is because the people of that land experience no suffering. Rather, they only know every kind of pleasure. That is why it is called Perfect Bliss."[100]

Here the *Amida Sutra* is guiding us toward the world of awakening using poetic or figurative language. The style is entirely metaphorical, using words that point beyond our pre-fabricated concepts.

Shinran adopts a literary style that makes frequent use of metaphor, as when he states (quoting Vasubandhu) that to encounter Amida's Vow is to "enter the great treasure ocean of virtues (*kinyū kudoku dai hōkai*)."[101] We have ready-made ideas to go with treasure and to go with ocean, but entering the great treasure ocean suggests something quite different, an immersion that surpasses our concepts. At times Shinran is unable to contain his poetic impulse and bursts forth with a string of rapid-fire metaphors:

> As I humbly contemplate matters, I see that the inconceivable Universal Vow is the *great ship* which conveys us across the *sea that is difficult to cross*; the *unhindered Light* is the *sun of wisdom* which dissipates the *darkness of ignorance*.[102]
>
> Thus, when one has boarded the *ship of the Vow* of great compassion and sailed out on the vast *ocean of light*, the *winds of perfect virtue* blow softly, and the *waves of evil* are transformed. The *darkness of ignorance* is immediately broken through, and quickly reaching the *land of immeasurable light*, one realizes great nirvana and acts in accord with the *virtue of Samantabhadra*. Let this be known.[103]

For a further illustration of metaphor, consider the language of classical music. I see a parallel between the way we find meaning in the sutras and the way we perceive the meaning of a musical theme like this one:[104]

This simple-looking theme carries tremendous meaning, but I cannot explain it in words. Ignore for a moment any specific moods or pictorial impressions (e.g., moonlight) that it might call to mind. The message goes deeper than that. Just as spoken words allow us to communicate, music is a language that conveys meaning. It has a grammar that one learns by studying harmony and counterpoint, and a great composer has complete mastery of the grammar. Beethoven's theme is the door to a world whose existence we had not suspected. To enter that door resembles the way we encounter the Buddhist world of awakening.

Focus for a moment on a single tone—analogous to a single word taken in isolation. Does a tone have meaning, say the C-sharp in the first measure of the theme? Or does an interval have meaning, say G-sharp/C-sharp? There may be no inherent meaning in tones themselves, but when structured in a musical phrase using the rules of grammar, they point metaphorically to something beyond mere acoustic vibrations. A great American musician, Leonard Bernstein (1918-1990), said this:

> Metaphor accomplishes the supremely difficult task of providing a name for everything. And by everything, [I

mean] our interior lives, the things that can't be named otherwise, our psychic landscapes and actions. And it is thus that [music] can and does name the unnamable and communicate the unknowable.[105]

In the same way, we are brought into contact with limitless, formless reality by literary devices that "name the unnamable." Accordingly, the language of the Pure Land sutras speaks to us through metaphor.

The sutras tell of the music of the Pure Land, which surely includes Beethoven's theme, just mentioned:

> "Śāriputra, in that Buddha-land, when a gentle breeze begins to blow, causing the arrayed jeweled trees and decorative jeweled nets to stir, they produce subtle, harmonious sounds. It is as if a hundred thousand musical instruments were being played simultaneously. Everyone who hears those sounds becomes spontaneously mindful of the Buddha, the Dharma, and the Sangha."[106]
>
> "Again, music spontaneously arises there in all its myriad forms, the sounds of which are without exception those of the Dharma. Being clear and serene, they are exquisite and harmonious. They are the most excellent in all the worlds of the ten quarters."[107]

When reading such passages, I'm reminded of Dorothy's famous line: "Toto, I've got a feeling we're not in Kansas anymore."

It's impossible to describe the world of awakening with engineer's blueprints, and so the sutras use poetic language that is intended to open our perceptions. In the manner of a musical phrase, the words convey a transcendent message. Of course, the Buddha did not teach exclusively through words. It is said that he once gave a sermon simply by holding up a flower, but only one of the disciples was able to grasp the meaning of that wordless sermon. Most of us are not like that disciple. We have to rely on words, however inadequate they may be, to show us the world of awakening.[108] Limitless reality fills and surrounds us, here and now, but without the language of metaphor we would be incapable of perceiving it. With our perceptions opened, we can listen to the teachings in a way that grows deeper and deeper. On the Shin Buddhist path, I think this is how we find meaning in our lives.

We Receive the Dharma in Three Ways

Myth is a directing of the mind and heart, by means of profoundly informed figurations, to that ultimate mystery which fills and surrounds all existences.[109]

—Joseph Campbell

Since ancient times, the teachings of Buddhism have been preserved in a large and diverse collection of written records. Most of the Pāli suttas are plain-spoken accounts of the career of the historical teacher, Gotama Buddha, but some suttas retain the context of earlier Indian religion, wherein Gotama interacts with deities such as Śakra and Brahmā. Mahāyāna sutras are populated with numerous buddhas and bodhisattvas—non-historical characters who attend when the teachings are given and who carry on dialogs with Śākyamuni, the present Buddha. There are also legends of supernatural deeds and tales of the Buddha's previous lives leading to his final incarnation as a prince of the Śākya clan. To elucidate this diverse material, Mahāyāna has a special framework called the *trikāya*, without which we would have great difficulty making sense of Buddhist teachings and rituals. A buddha is said to be manifested as "three bodies"—the truth body, the enjoyment body, and the emanation body. This nomenclature imparts a theological coloring; we can do better by viewing the *trikāya* as three ways or modes—voiceless, symbolic, and human—by which the Dharma is transmitted.[110]

Dharma-kāya, the voiceless way, points to limitless reality, beyond all words and concepts. It is said to be the essence of all buddhas. Attempting to name it, we use terms like nirvana, impermanence, suchness, and emptiness. It is formless, impersonal, and, like a display of fireworks that lights up the sky and vanishes, it is not a "thing" that can be grasped.[111] If, once in a while, *dharma-kāya* breaks through the shell of our ego, that is not because of any effort on our part. We might perceive it momentarily by seeing a flower, by hearing a musical phrase, by taking a breath, or in an instant between two thoughts. Zen Buddhism emphasizes the voiceless way—direct apprehension of *dharma-kāya* by practitioners who have special ability.

Sambhoga-kāya, the symbolic way, conveys the world of awakening through myths and stories about transcendent buddhas, buddha-lands, and bodhisattvas, as in Mahāyāna texts like the Pure Land Sutras. These teachings are intended for ordinary people who lack special ability, and they offer a skillful means that we can name or visualize or participate in. The *Larger Sutra* tells of a spiritual seeker who aspires to attain supreme, perfect enlightenment and to liberate all living beings. To fulfill the aspiration, the seeker spends eons learning from innumerable buddhas and is thereby becoming Amida, the Buddha of Limitless Light and Life. The story is reenacted each time that we say Namo Amida Butsu, or offer incense before the altar, or chant the verses of *Sanbutsuge* and *Jūseige* from the *Larger Sutra*.

Nirmāna-kāya, the human way, refers to historical teachers who actualize the timeless principle of spiritual seeking that Amida represents. Symbols must finally reach us in human form if they are to carry any force, and thus we encounter the historical figures Gotama and Shinran, along with their current-day successors whom we meet in person. The activity of the teacher is regarded as "emanating" from limitless reality into our present world to manifest boundless compassion. Through the power of skillful means, the teacher gives voice to the *myōgō*, Namo Amida Butsu, and exhorts us to wake up.

The *trikāya* is a framework of great beauty and cogency that appeals to both mind and heart. It explains how historical teachers are encouraging us through metaphors and symbols so that we may turn our gaze toward limitless reality. Thus considered, Mahāyāna Buddhism becomes a properly functioning whole, one element of which is a well-nurtured mythology. Without this insight, our constrained imagination is tempted to read Mahāyāna texts as though they were history or geography, as Joseph Campbell observes:

> And herein resides the irony of mythology—namely, that its poetic metaphors, through which transcendent revelations are delivered, become translated by what Nietzsche called the "Socratic" mind into prose, so that not

only is the revelation lost, but an additional leaden weight of delusion is laid upon the mind.[112]

And, since Nietzsche has been invoked, let's hear from him directly. He says that spiritual seeking, severed from its mythic roots and contained within the narrow field of history, is finally undermined:

> It is the fate of every myth to insinuate itself into the narrow limits of some alleged historical reality, and to be treated by some later generation as a solitary fact with historical claims… For this is the manner in which religions are wont to die out: when under the stern, intelligent eyes of an orthodox dogmatism, the mythical presuppositions of a religion are systematized as a completed sum of historical events, and when one begins apprehensively to defend the credibility of the myth, while at the same time opposing all continuation of its natural vitality and luxuriance; when, accordingly, the feeling for myth dies out, and its place is taken by the claim of religion to historical foundations.[113]

Hearing and Reflecting

The Name of this Buddha surpasses the names of all other Tathāgatas, for it is based on the Vow to save all beings.[114]

—Gutoku Shinran

In Shin Buddhism we are encouraged to recite the Name of Amida Buddha throughout our lives. In so doing, the Name takes on a meaning that reflects our personal experience. It could be viewed as an expression of gratitude, for example. However, the significance cannot be purely subjective—reciting the Name must carry meaning that is universal. This is why Shinran emphasizes "hearing and reflecting" in contrast to mere recitation.[115]

The Name or *myōgō* is a combination of six *kanji* characters that do not form a grammatical sentence in Chinese or Japanese. It is a transcription, or sounding-out, of a Sanskrit phrase, the syllables of which are *na-mo-a-mi-da-butsu*. The basic English rendering is, "Take refuge in limitless wisdom!" These words have universal significance.

A hallmark of Zen Buddhism is that practitioners of superior ability can directly apprehend the Dharma, or limitless reality, without words. Through silent meditation they realize voiceless and formless truth. By contrast, in Pure Land Buddhism the Dharma is conveyed through words and images, which are the Buddha's *upāya* or skillful means. A modern commentary describes two modes of expression presented in the Pure Land sutras:

> When Amida, as a symbolic expression [of ultimate truth], is revealed as form, it is discussed in terms of buddha-body or buddha image. When it is expressed as language or word, it is explicated as the Buddha's Name (*myōgō*).[116]

Limitless wisdom and compassion are made visible in the human-like figure of Amida and are verbalized in the syllables of the Name. However, the Dharma cannot be fully expressed by any of our words and images.

SKILLFUL MEANS

Shinran was apparently the first Pure Land teacher to place on the altar a scroll with the *myōgō* in Chinese characters hovering over a lotus pedestal, as seen here.[117] The pedestal serves as an exclamation point, reminding us what a curious arrangement this is. Rather than calling for a traditional image of Amida on the pedestal, Shinran preferred the written Name in its imperative aspect. For him, the *myōgō* itself (and not the human-like figure) is the *gohonzon* or focus of reverence.

Because an Amida image is effective for many people, Shin Buddhist temples typically have a painting or statue as the focus of reverence, even though it was not Shinran's preference. Note that the characters of the *myōgō* displayed on a scroll have the appeal of a calligraphic image to be visualized. Hence, even for ritual purposes the *myōgō* can be just as suitable as the human-like figure.

Some forms of Eastern religion include the recitation of mystical sounds or *mantras* that are believed to carry special powers, but Shinran did not conceive of the *myōgō* in that manner. He teaches that liberation is through the condition of hearing the Name (*monmyō*) and grasping its meaning, rather than through vocalizing it to bring about a result.[118] Hearing is taken broadly to mean one's own study, recitation, and reflection, as well as listening to the words of Dharma teachers.

Shinran emphasizes passages in the *Larger Sutra* that proclaim the fulfillment of the Buddha's *Hongan* through hearing the Name,[119] with the main attention focused on Vows 17 and 18:[120]

> *When I have fulfilled the Buddha-way,*
> *My Name shall pervade the ten quarters;*
> *Should there be any place it is not heard,*
> *May I not attain perfect enlightenment.*[121]
>
> *The power of the Buddha's [Hongan] is such that*
> *Those who, hearing the Name, aspire for birth,*
> *All reach that land,*
> *And their attainment of non-retrogression comes about of itself.*[122]

When the Name is recited, it's commonly given the meaning of "I take refuge in Amida." However, for Shinran the *myōgō* is the commanding voice of the Dharma:

> The word *namo* means *kimyō* [Come take refuge!]... *Kimyō* is to be summoned by the *Hongan*; it is like the sovereign's command.[123]
>
> *Namo* means "to take refuge." [It] is to respond to the command and follow the call of the two honored ones, Śākyamuni and Amida.[124]

To hear the Name as a command was a sharp break from the views that were prevalent in medieval Japan, which held that the effort of recitation and refuge-taking would cause Amida Buddha to welcome the practitioner to the Pure Land at the hour of death (*rinjū no raikō*). By contrast, Shinran recognized that he was incapable of any religious practice that would be the cause of his liberation. The *Larger Sutra* showed him the path of hearing the Name and reflecting on its meaning, a path that does not rely on self-conceived efforts to become worthy of Amida's welcoming.[125]

According to Shinran, if one hears the Name but does not understand its universal significance, then there is "imperfect realization of hearing."[126] Hearing must be accompanied by "searching" or self-examination, i.e., one must "hear and reflect (*monshi*)."[127]

> Beings throughout the ten directions are grasped and guided by the Light and the Name, provided that their shinjin arises from searching and reflection.[128]

> "Good sons! There are two kinds of shinjin: one is trust and the other is searching. Such people, although they have trust, are incapable of searching. Therefore, theirs is termed 'imperfect realization of shinjin.' Again, there are two kinds of shinjin: one arises from hearing and the other from reflection. These people's shinjin has arisen from hearing but not from reflection. Therefore, it is called 'imperfect realization of shinjin.'"[129]

So that self-examination will take place, Shinran made a point of expressing the Name in language that was more immediately understandable than the Sanskrit phrase. He favored the ten-character *myōgō* consisting of a Chinese sentence, *Kimyō jin jippō mugekō nyorai*, which translates as "Take refuge in the Tathāgata of unhindered light filling the ten directions!"[130] Unhindered light (*mugekō*) is a metaphor for the wisdom that makes us see our own greed, hatred, and ignorance:

> *Mugekō nyorai* is light; it is wisdom. This wisdom is itself Amida Buddha. Since people do not know the form of Amida Buddha, Bodhisattva Vasubandhu, exhausting all his resources, created [the ten-character sentence] in order that we might know Amida's form with perfect certainty.... Although the words are different, whether we say "Amida" or "unhindered light," the meaning is one.[131]

> In order to make it known that supreme Buddha is formless, the name "Amida Buddha" is expressly used; so I have been taught. [The name] "Amida Buddha" fulfills the purpose of making us know the significance of *jinen* [i.e., suchness].[132]

These passages are evidence that Shinran did not regard Amida Buddha (i.e., *mugekō nyorai*) as an anthropomorphic divinity,[133] consistent with his preference for a scroll displaying the *kanji* rather than a human-like figure.

Shinran's teacher Hōnen considered recitation of the Name to be the direct path to an intuitive faith in Amida:

> In China and Japan, many Buddhist masters and scholars understand that the nembutsu is to meditate deeply on Amida Buddha and the Pure Land. However, I [Hōnen] do not understand the nembutsu in this way. Reciting the nembutsu does not come from studying and understanding its meaning. There is no other reason or cause by which we can utterly believe in attaining birth in the Pure Land than the nembutsu itself.[134]

I think that Shinran would affirm Hōnen's statement, while clarifying and expanding on it. Sincere recitation of the Name and intuitive faith do not "come from" scholarly study. Rather, understanding arises from hearing and reflecting upon the Name when it is recited.

The path to liberation in Shin Buddhism requires that the meaning of the command be clearly understood; therefore, Shinran expressed the Name in Chinese and Japanese sentences that his contemporaries could comprehend. In fact, all of his writings amount to the translation and unfolding of Namo Amida Butsu. Here are a few examples of what the *myōgō* meant to Shinran, rendered into imperative English:

> *In the Tathāgata of Immeasurable Life, take refuge!*
> *In the Light that surpasses all thoughts or ideas, take refuge!*[135]

The Right Dharma is indeed something wonderful, transcending things of this world! Let us, therefore, feel no hesitancy in listening to it and reflecting on it![136]

Those whose minds are dark and whose understanding is deficient, endeavor in this way with reverence! Those whose evils are heavy and whose karmic obstructions are manifold, deeply revere this shinjin![137]

As we become familiar with Shinran's writings, we are able to reflect on the deep layers of meaning in the command, "Take refuge in limitless wisdom!"

'It's Only a Story'

Near the end of his life, Gotama Buddha spoke to his disciples: "It may be that you will think: 'The Buddha's instruction has ceased; now we have no teacher!' It should not be seen like this, Ānanda, for what I have taught and explained to you as dharma and discipline will, at my passing, be your teacher."[138]

Thus, the teachings live on when the teacher exits history. Through deep listening, we learn to appreciate the awakening experience and to become participants in it. From a Mahāyāna perspective, the historical Buddha is not the only person to have woken up; many others preceded and followed him. The central teaching in Mahāyāna is the awakening experience, rather than the historical career of Gotama Buddha. This emphasis differs from what one finds in other world religions, where great significance is attached to having a historically accurate account of the founder's life.

Does historical accuracy have any value in Buddhism? The question cannot be answered in general terms; we must reflect on the content of particular scriptures. As far as valuing historical accuracy, a broad distinction can be made, corresponding to two portrayals by which the Buddha is remembered. Joseph Campbell describes two ways of viewing a cultural or mythic hero:

> The first view would lead one to imitate the master literally, in order to break through, in the same way he has, to the transcendent, redemptive experience. But the second states that the hero is rather a symbol to be contemplated than an example to be literally followed.[139]

Thus, we have *Gotama* and *Śākyamuni*.

Gotama Buddha, as portrayed in the Pāli suttas, is a teacher of ordinary human beings. He offers wise and compassionate answers to those who seek him out. He meets with the full range of humanity—people who have quirky, individual traits. Some arrive with pleas for help; some bring arguments to use against him. He converses with political figures, and he himself is a kind of politician involved in worldly affairs. Gotama resembles a flesh-and-blood individual, albeit a very special one. And the Pāli suttas, for the most part, read *as though they were historical records*.[140] That is the literary form of the texts, although there is no corroborating evidence dating to the Buddha's lifetime that would satisfy a historian. The intent is for the reader to imagine himself or herself learning from and emulating the example of Gotama, a specific real-life teacher. We cognize the experience in that way, as a teaching directed to our rational, conscious mind—namely, the mind that aims for self-improvement.

Now consider the portrayal that is the basis of Shin Buddhism. In the Pure Land sutras, the historical Buddha is called Śākyamuni rather than Gotama. Instead of a flesh-and-blood teacher or politician, Śākyamuni is the "world-hero" in a drama or screenplay. Rather than giving answers to ordinary human beings, he carries on dialogs with characters who, like himself, are larger-than-life. Rather than quirky, individual personalities, they are archetypes of universal human experiences. The literary form is not history or geography—it is *mythology*. And here is the key distinction: the teaching is not directed to our rational, conscious mind; it is meant to engage us at a deeper level, the level of the unconscious—by which I mean the repository of subliminal memories, motivations, and automatic reactions not governed by conscious awareness. Śākyamuni's teaching is aimed at the "unsavable" person whose conscious mind is incapable of self-improvement, but whose unconscious mind may contain the seeds of liberation. The meaning of the teaching is not to be found in a literal reading of the story (even if such were possible). Campbell urges us to recognize the deeper meaning:

> And so, to grasp the full value of the mythological figures that have come down to us, we must understand that they are not only symptoms of the unconscious (as indeed are all human thoughts and acts) but also controlled and intended statements of certain spiritual principles, which have remained as constant throughout the course of human history

as the form and nervous structure of the human physique itself.[141]

[Myths] are telling us in picture language of powers of the psyche to be recognized and integrated in our lives, powers that have been common to the human spirit forever, and which represent that wisdom of the species by which man has weathered the millenniums.[142]

Coming from the distant past, the picture language transmits timeless spiritual principles to our unconscious mind. It's impossible for this deeper experience to take place if we assign value to historical accuracy.

Finding myths to live by was perfectly natural for premodern people. There was no contradiction between the stories they told and their way of life. Myths were a template for growing from childhood into responsible adulthood and on into old age.[143] The stories were a model for an integrated way of life along the human arc from birth to death. Today, by contrast, we appreciate myths mainly as entertainment. A preeminent example is the immensely popular *Star Wars* franchise, whose fans go so far as to dress up in costumes, attend conventions, and perform rituals with other costumed enthusiasts. However, I doubt that this kind of fan appreciation yields much insight for the participants. The myths prevalent in popular culture are secular, in that they do not connect with any deeply-rooted spiritual path. I see them as stories to enjoy, but not myths to live by.

It's difficult for modern people to access the power of myth when it comes to religion. Hence the great popularity of secularized Buddhist meditation and mindfulness training, in which the mythological basis of the teaching is ignored. We neglect the "wisdom of the species by which man has weathered the millenniums." Instead, we moderns tend to regard historical accuracy as a spiritual virtue. Some insist on a literal reading of the scriptures. Others find a literal interpretation to be implausible and think, "It's only a story"—but still perhaps useful as a moral lesson for children. A duality is thereby established. A scripture that is historically accurate is suitable for rational adults; if it's not accurate, then it's a fairy tale for children. Sadly, when we hold such views, the teaching cannot bear fruit; its spiritual power cannot be felt.

> The imagery of mythology is symbolic of spiritual powers within us: when these are interpreted as referring to historical or natural events which science in turn shows could not have occurred, then you [have to] throw the whole thing out. You see, myths do not come from a *concept* system; they come from a *life* system; they come out of a deeper center.[144]

Imagery that is symbolic of spiritual powers within us—that is an apt description of *Hongan*, the Buddha's deepest wish, as taught in the *Larger Sutra*. The story tells of a hero who meets a teacher and is so moved that he resolves to become a buddha and to liberate all of humanity. The hero performs practices for countless eons to fulfill his Vows, and in so doing he is becoming Amida, the Buddha of Immeasurable Light and Life. As we allow the symbols to speak to our deeper center, this quality of the Buddha's *Hongan* is unexpectedly awakened in us, and the Vows are thereby fulfilled. Assuredly, it's *not* only a story. The message is actualized in our lives, here and now. For this reason, Shinran called the teaching of the *Larger Sutra* "true and real."

The *Larger Sutra* spoke so forcefully to Shinran that he came to regard it as the most important text in Buddhism. He saw that it expresses a fundamental psychic reality and opens a path to human liberation, corresponding to the universal pattern noted by Campbell:

> So there are two stages to this: one is going inward, and finding the relationship of your own deepest self to the ground of being so that you become transparent to transcendence; the other is bringing this realization back into operation in the field, which is the work of the artist—to interpret the *contemporary* world as experienced in terms of relevance to our inner life.[145]

Using Pure Land terminology, Shinran describes the Buddhist path in precisely this way—the going inward, being made to see our limitations in the light of limitless reality, and then manifesting this insight in everyday life.

Gotama is the portrayal of the Buddha in the Pāli suttas, in which the teachings are cast in the framework of historical accounts. Gotama's teaching is directed to the conscious mind that aims at self-improvement. Contrast that with the portrayal of Śākyamuni in the Pure Land sutras. It is picture language, coming to us out of the remote past and speaking to our unconscious mind, the deeper center. It deals with spiritual qualities that are to be recognized and integrated in our lives. The meaning transcends a literal reading of the story. For the person who receives the teaching, historical accuracy ceases to be of any concern.

> Myths come from where the heart is, and where the experience is, even as the mind may wonder why people believe these things. The myth does not point to a fact; the myth points beyond facts to something that informs the fact.... Essentially, mythologies are enormous poems that are renditions of insights, giving some sense of the marvel, the miracle, and wonder of life.[146]

True Teachings and Provisional Teachings

Impermanence or continual change is the basis of Buddhism, but we, as foolish beings, have difficulty coping with it. One type of change that may provoke discomfort is to revise the words used to express the teachings. Yet, to keep the words fixed is impossible. From ancient India to medieval Japan to 21st century America—the differences in language and culture are serious obstacles to our understanding. Every person who attempts to translate and interpret will offer a limited perspective. How can we find words to express the spirit of Śākyamuni and of Shinran?

In Mahāyāna Buddhism the Buddha's words are not pointing toward physical objects or historical events; they are pointing toward that which is beyond words and concepts. Thus, a basic teaching is that words cannot fully capture the meaning:

> "Consider, for example, a person instructing us by pointing to the moon with his finger. [To take words to be the meaning] is like looking at the finger and not at the moon. The person would say, 'I am pointing to the moon with my finger in order to show it to you. Why do you look at my finger and not at the moon?' Similarly, words are the finger pointing to the meaning; they are not the meaning itself. Hence, do not rely upon words."[147]

For anyone who grew up learning Biblical doctrines, as I did, this imperative, "do not rely upon words," is astonishing in a religious context. At the church I attended, the Word of God, as recorded in the Bible, was inherently the truth. It was true at all times and in all places—varying translations notwithstanding. The Bible describes the life of Jesus this way: "In the beginning was the Word: the Word was with God, and the Word was God.... The Word became human, he lived among us."[148] Inspiring, to be sure, but my foolish brain cannot grasp it.

Mahāyāna is compelling precisely because it has nothing analogous to the Word of God. Words are an expedient that can point us toward limitless reality, but their effectiveness is temporary. Eventually, as circumstances change, a prior choice of words will cease to be appropriate. The most important scriptures in Shin Buddhism are the Pure Land sutras. These are very durable teachings, having shown people the path to awakening for at least two thousand years. However, they too must be seen as a temporary expression.

At the outset, our ability to grasp a meaning that is beyond words is feeble. To help us through this difficulty the Buddha devises *skillful* or *provisional means* that are suited to our circumstances. His words are appropriate for the situation, but they are a transformed or disguised version of what he truly aims to teach:

> "Knowing that living beings have various desires and things to which they are deeply attached, I have taught the Dharma according to their basic nature, using a variety of causal explanations, parables, other kinds of expression, and the power of skillful means."[149]

This is illustrated by a parable in the *Lotus Sutra* that tells of children playing inside a burning house. Being fixated on their games, they refuse to flee the inferno until their father entices them outside with the promise of precious carriages. The carriages might not be real, but the children would perish if not for this deception. Likewise, we would fail to seek liberation without the power of the Buddha's skillful means.

It would appear that the Buddha intends for us eventually to recognize and transcend our reliance on disguised teachings. Shinran's contribution was to identify a framework for doing so within the Pure Land sutras.[150] He calls the teachings of the undisguised Dharma *true*, and he calls the disguised teachings *provisional*. The distinction is of crucial significance. We might say that clarifying the distinction between true and provisional is itself Jōdo Shinshū:

> Now, based on the true purport of the Buddha's teachings and the expositions by masters in the past, I shall

clarify that the teachings of the Path of Sages are provisional and those of the Pure Land are true...¹⁵¹

> Monks of Śākyamuni's tradition in the various temples, however, lack clear insight into the teaching and are ignorant of the distinction between true and provisional; and scholars of the Chinese classics in the capital are confused about practices and wholly unable to differentiate right and wrong paths.¹⁵²

"Path of Sages" refers to Buddhism that teaches spiritual self-improvement, encompassing all forms found "in the various temples," namely, forms that are not Pure Land Buddhism. Moreover, Pure Land followers themselves take up provisional teachings on the path of self-improvement:

> Since there are thousands of differences in the causes of birth in the provisional Buddha-lands, there are thousands of differences in the lands.... Being ignorant of the distinction between true and provisional, people misunderstand and lose sight of the Tathāgata's vast benevolence.¹⁵³

Hence, for Pure Land followers, there are two types of practice and shinjin:

> Generally stated, with regard to the Vows, there is true-and-real practice and shinjin (*shinjitsu gyō shin*), and there is practice and shinjin that are provisional means (*hōben gyō shin*).¹⁵⁴

"Practice" is what brings about a psychological transformation on the Buddhist path, and "shinjin" means self-awareness or a life of awakening.

The *Larger Sutra* teaches that all beings can be liberated by *Hongan*, the Buddha's universal Vow. As well, *Hongan* is our own deeply hidden desire to become Buddha—to live the most meaningful life possible. Shinran identifies six of the Vows in the *Larger Sutra* as the true-and-real expression of *Hongan*.[155] He designates two other Vows as provisional expressions of *Hongan*.[156] Shinran's writings are, by and large, the elucidation of these eight Vows; they are the central structuring elements of his teaching, analogous to the pillars and beams supporting a building. The *Larger Sutra* does not reveal this structure explicitly; it arises from Shinran's unique interpretation.

In setting forth these categories, he does not make metaphysical claims about what may be true ultimately or theoretically. He emphasizes the term *shinjitsu* or true-and-real: the Buddha's Vows are pointing toward a timeless *truth* which, according to the *Larger Sutra*, is necessarily fulfilled or made *real* in history.[157] It is with respect to the present human condition that a particular teaching is either true or provisional—the basis is *psychological* and *historically contingent*. Hence, the Path of Sages teachings were formerly true-and-real, but they are no longer so:

> Indeed, we know that the various teachings of the Path of Sages are practicable for the Buddha's time and for the Age of Right Dharma and not for [subsequent Ages]. The time for those teachings has already passed, and they do not agree with the capacities of sentient beings.[158]

According to Shinran, "monks of Śākyamuni's tradition in the various temples" were attached to teachings and practices that had ceased to be appropriate when circumstances changed.

Shinran carefully applies the term *shinjitsu* (true-and-real) to indicate that the *Larger Sutra*'s teaching, practice, shinjin, and realization exist as historical facts.[159] On the other hand, he applies the term *shin* (true) to Amida Buddha and the Pure Land to indicate that they are symbols representing *dharma-kāya*—they are not historical, and hence he does not use *shinjitsu*.[160] The published translations of Shinran's writings often neglect this distinction and employ the English word "true" for *shinjitsu*.

Throughout his long life, Shinran was never content with fixed interpretations. In many cases, his understanding of a sutra text was quite different from the standard reading of the Chinese characters.[161]

By continually discarding his preconceptions about Buddhism and by looking beyond the words for the deeper meaning, he came to appreciate the distinction between true and provisional. Shinran did not simply reject the provisional teachings; after all, they are the words of the Buddha, which are fulfilled and made real in history.[162] What he discovered in them was a skillful means residing on the surface, pointing to the deeper meaning within: "How noble is [the Buddha's] intent to guide [us] with the provisional Vows!"[163]

Shinran interpreted the disguised teachings as representing stages of spiritual growth that a person goes through to realize awakening.[164] At times, I have heard the view that we can access true-and-real Buddhism directly without following provisional Buddhism. To me, this view seems mistaken. Of necessity, we embrace disguised teachings that fit our preconceptions. Thus, when we speak about Buddhism at all, we are generally considering provisional teachings and practices, rather than those which Shinran calls true-and-real. Our calculating mind is drawn in that direction, and we never completely turn away from it. But, through the painful encounter with our limitations, the weakness of our Path of Sages mentality is exposed, allowing a glimpse of the true-and-real teaching of *Hongan*. Shinran discovered in the Pure Land sutras a template that has universal resonance. To make his experience our own is to have found the Shin Buddhist path.

Pure Land Birth

Buddhist scriptures use the literary devices of metaphor, symbol, and myth as basic forms of expression. A *metaphor* is a figure of speech that carries meaning beyond a literal reading of the words, as for example, "All the world's a stage" or "The amber waves of grain." A metaphor defines a *symbol* when applied to a specific object that stands for something else, often a visible form representing an abstract idea. A familiar example is the Statue of Liberty, a human-like figure expressing the aspiration for political freedom. A *myth* is a symbol-laden narrative describing archetypes of the human experience. It portrays our inner landscapes—psychic realities that we all share. Examples of mythic heroes are Odysseus journeying homeward to Ithaca, and Dante being led through Hell, Purgatory, and Paradise. A mythic hero is the original pattern of our own growing and maturing. A myth may flow out of historical events, but it's not to be understood in a narrow sense as history. Rather, it carries a message that transcends a literal reading.

Certainly, the teachings of Buddhism can be expressed without resorting to literary devices. To emulate the ethical example of Gotama Buddha, one may rely on plain-spoken accounts of his life and on monastic rules of conduct, as exemplified by Theravāda Buddhism. Another example of a plain-spoken approach is the contemporary practice of secularized meditation favored by Western converts. These paths are suited to practitioners who possess the necessary abilities, but from a Mahāyāna perspective they are too narrow. To broaden the reach of the Buddha's teachings, Mahāyāna scriptures describe the world of awakening with metaphorical language. Timeless aspects of the human condition are revealed not through rules for ethical conduct and self-improvement, but through the power of myth. This power is given full expression in the Pure Land sutras, which teach liberation by *Hongan*, the aspiration to attain Buddhahood and to awaken all sentient beings.

The *Larger Sutra* tells a story that carries universal implications. Astounded by the radiance of Śākyamuni's face, the disciple Ānanda asks, "Are you, the present Buddha, now thinking of all other Buddhas (*nen sho butsu*)?" In response, Śākyamuni shares the story of the bodhisattva who is becoming the Buddha of Limitless Light and Life residing in the western Pure Land. The questioner Ānanda is an archetype, the original pattern of our own experience of meeting with the Dharma by way of a teacher. The *Larger Sutra* reveals a path for people like Ānanda who have no aptitude for religious or therapeutic practices. Those who are unable to eradicate the passions or to follow self-improvement prescriptions can still be liberated, because nirvana (limitless reality) has a dynamic aspect that penetrates our self-created world of striving and delusion. Given the limited nature of words and concepts, this "inconceivable" teaching can be conveyed only through metaphors and symbols. Hence, Amida Buddha and the Pure Land are ideas that express the dynamic aspect of nirvana—they are not "substantial entities."[165] When considered as a human-like figure and a material realm, Amida and the Pure Land have an entirely symbolic existence. They point toward *limitless reality*, which, however, is certainly not "mythical" or "symbolic," in the sense of being limited by human contrivances.

From a Shin Buddhist perspective, Mahāyāna teachings as a whole comprise two categories—the Path of Sages (*shōdō*) and the Pure Land (*jōdo*). Bodhisattvas on the Path of Sages perform practices and advance through a series of levels, the crucial level being the *stage of non-retrogression*, which assures the eventual attainment of Buddhahood. Prior to Shinran, it was generally held that foolish, ordinary people are incapable of reaching this stage in the present world of delusion. Birth in the Pure Land after physical death was seen as necessary for idealized practicing, by means of which non-retrogression could be attained. Shinran overturns that view when he states that non-retrogression is realized in everyday life; after-death practicing to reach this stage is not part of Jōdo Shinshū. According to Shinran, the attainment of birth and the stage of non-retrogression are realized immediately with shinjin:

> *They then attain birth* [*soku toku ōjō*] means that when a person realizes shinjin, he or she is born immediately. "To

be born immediately" is to dwell in the stage of non-retrogression. To dwell in the stage of non-retrogression is to become established in the stage of the truly settled. This is also called the attainment of the equal of perfect enlightenment. Such is the meaning of *they then attain birth.*

Then means immediately; "immediately" means without any passage of time and without any passage of days.[166]

When we are grasped by Amida, immediately—without a moment or a day elapsing—we ascend to and become established in the stage of the truly settled; this is the meaning of *attain birth.*[167]

Know that the ocean of the One Vehicle of the [*Hongan*] is the ultimate sudden teaching, the teaching of sudden and instantaneous attainment, the perfectly fulfilled teaching, the consummate teaching.[168]

Shinran's view of the completion of human life faithfully reflects the path of Gotama Buddha: parinirvana (*daihatsu nehan*) is realized at death by a person of shinjin.[169] This refers not to the aspect of nirvana that penetrates the world of delusion, but rather to its ultimate aspect (*shinnyo jissō*, limitless formless reality). Parinirvana means that our self-created world of delusion, along with all of its metaphors and symbols, is brought to an end. The mythological description of the Pure Land given in the sutras is transcended—at physical death our words and concepts cease to have efficacy. Accordingly, Shinran attaches no value to the popular "deathbed rites that prepare one for Amida's coming."[170]

Shinran uses the term *ōjō jōdo* (going-birth pure-land) less frequently than one might anticipate—for example, *ōjō* does not appear in the great doctrinal summary *Shōshinge*. I translate *ōjō jōdo* as "Pure Land birth" to suggest that it's a transformation. On the other hand, the usual rendering as "birth in the Pure Land" suggests reappearance in another world. This aligns with a widely held view that "birth" occurs in the future—at physical death—and not during everyday life, which is to say that the Pure Land is actualized when the present life ends. In this view, one chooses *not* to take Shinran's statements on the immediate attainment of birth (cited above) at face value; instead, one chooses to associate *ōjō jōdo* solely with *daihatsu nehan*. However, Shinran's writings do not suggest to me that parinirvana is to be equated with "birth in the Pure Land," an afterworldly idea that calls to mind the fulfillment of human desires. That kind of "birth" cannot be parinirvana.

Shinran is specific in his language. He states that "great shinjin… is the true cause for realization of *dai nehan*"[171]—it is "the cause of Buddhahood"—he does not say that shinjin is the future cause of *ōjō*. He states (1) that the Vow of shinjin is the cause of "attaining equal-enlightenment and realizing *dai nehan*," (2) that "the fulfilled land's true cause" is Amida's Vow, Vow-mind, One-mind, or Vow-power, and (3) that "true settlement's cause is shinjin alone."[172] These ideas are clear enough in the original texts, but the published translations suggest *different* meanings by inserting the English word "birth" into passages where Shinran does not write *ōjō*.

In letters to personal friends Shinran makes statements such as, "It is certain that I will go to birth in the Pure Land before you, so without fail I will await you there."[173] However, I choose not to take *those* remarks at face value, the like of which never appears in his many commentaries and verses! A case can be made that to a certain degree Shinran was medieval in his outlook and that he viewed the Pure Land, in one of its facets, as a dualistic afterworld.[174] Limited by the medieval reference frame, he could never be a universal teacher like Gotama; his Buddhism would have remained provisional, rather than becoming true-and-real. Yet, in many respects Shinran's doctrinal writings are sharply at odds with the prevailing secular and religious views of his era and instead seem tailored for a modern audience.[175] I contend that once he had embraced the radical message contained in the *Larger Sutra*, Shinran ceased to *live* in the reference frame of his contemporaries, even if occasionally he chose to *visit* them there. However, to sojourn in the medieval world is not a requirement of the Shin Buddhist path in the 21st century.

Shinran is famous for interpreting the sutras and commentaries in ways that go beyond the basic meaning of the *kanji* characters. Consider a statement by Shan-tao concerning the 18th Vow in the *Larger Sutra*: "Practicers who aspire to be born are brought by the power of the Vow to the attainment of birth [*shōtoku ōjō*] when their lives end."[176] Shan-tao's basic meaning is consistent with the after-death view of Pure Land birth. However, Shinran's interpretation takes a surprising direction:

> [Shan-tao's statement] refers specifically to practicers who aspire for birth during the final moments of their lives. To be grasped by the great Vow's karmic power is what it means to attain birth, as with people who have already realized shinjin in ordinary times. Still, there are some who, for the first time at the hour of death, become definitely settled in shinjin and benefit by being grasped. However, those who receive the diamond-like mind and dwell in true settlement are protected and embraced by the heart and light [of Amida] in ordinary times, not only at their dying hour. To have been constantly protected and never abandoned in ordinary times is called "the attainment of birth," and therefore is designated as "the powerful condition of birth" [by Shan-tao].[177]

The phrase "attainment of birth when their lives end" has to do with deathbed conversions only. Shinran could not have stated this more plainly.

What is this thing that he says is realized here and now, namely, attainment of birth and the stage of non-retrogression? Obviously, it is not parinirvana (life's completion), nor is it "becoming Buddha with this very body" (sudden realization on the Path of Sages).[178] One might choose to view "the attainment of birth" as a *transitional* state in which a person is headed irreversibly toward Buddhahood. Yet, by a hair-splitting distinction, the transitional state is viewed as something other than "Pure Land birth." I am not attuned to that way of reasoning. The following thoughts from a modern commentary are more persuasive:

Life in this defiled world does not intrinsically divide us from the Buddha; hence, it is not physical death itself that signifies entrance into the sphere of enlightenment.[179]

Instead of maintaining temporal and spatial conceptions of the practicer's movement to enlightenment, Shinran breaks through such frameworks and brings Pure Land thought into correspondence with basic Mahāyāna insight, in which samsara and nirvana are non-dual.[180]

Concerning what is realized here and now, Shinran says this:

> Shinjin is wisdom. This wisdom is the wisdom attained because we are grasped by the light of [*tariki*]. The Buddha's light is also wisdom. Thus, we can say that the person of shinjin and the Tathāgata are the same. "Same" means that, in shinjin, they are equals.[181]

And he has this to say concerning the Pure Land:

> Shan-tao, the Master of the Kuang-ming temple, explains that the heart of the person of shinjin already and always resides in the Pure Land. "Resides" means that the heart of the person of shinjin constantly dwells there.[182]

Pure Land birth, as an idea, is actualized "already and always" for a person of shinjin in ordinary times. There is no need to await Amida's welcoming at the hour of death:

> *It is regrettable indeed that sentient beings doubt what*
>   *should not be doubted;*
> *The Pure Land is right before us and never out of harmony*
>   *with us.*
> *Do not ponder whether Amida will take you in or not;*
> *The question is whether or not you wholeheartedly turnabout*
>   *at heart.*[183]

Through a wholehearted turnabout (*senshin e*), one is brought face-to-face with the Pure Land (*jōdo taimen*) here and now.

The difficulty with the afterworldly interpretation of Pure Land birth is not religious in nature—it arises as a literary problem, namely, a lack of appreciation for literary devices. Concerning Amida and the Pure Land, the present life is the time and place for human beings to actualize the ideas in the intended manner. To find meaning in the symbols here and now as a foolish being is what defines Pure Land birth. For a person of shinjin, life's ending defines parinirvana. At the hour of death, the symbols are transcended and abandoned. This is what I learn from Shinran.

'He Returned to the Pure Land'

> *Know that because of doubt one remains in the house of birth-and-death.... We are to realize that up to now we have been wandering for eons in such a realm of illusion.*[184]
>
> —Gutoku Shinran

It is sometimes said of a person who has died that he or she has "returned to the Pure Land." This might be simply a poetic expression intended to comfort the bereaved, but could it have a more concrete meaning? The words "return to" indicate that the person resided in the Pure Land in some form prior to physical birth and is doing so again after physical death. The idea of a deceased person "returning to" the Pure Land occurs only rarely in Shinran's writings. In the *Kōsō wasan* verses, Shinran speaks of his teacher Hōnen as having previously appeared as the historical masters Tao-ch'o and Shan-tao, as Bodhisattva Mahāsthāmaprāpta, and as Amida Buddha.[185] The verses say that Hōnen's death was marked by auspicious signs and that "he returned to the Pure Land (*jōdo ni kaeri*)." These words express Shinran's feeling of deep gratitude toward his teacher.

Shinran never speaks in this way regarding his own past or future. On the contrary, he states that as a foolish being he has transmigrated vainly in samsara "through countless kalpas and innumerable lives," and, if it were not for Hōnen, "this present life also would pass in vain."[186] Concerning himself, Shinran does not say that a prior existence in the Pure Land interrupted his transmigration.[187] He was not a bodhisattva in a past life, nor is he one in the present life, and hence he will not "return to" the Pure Land. It seems to me that if we accept Shinran as our teacher, we should not imagine ourselves as having resided in the Pure Land previously and as "returning" there at physical death.

The Buddhist concept of *ekō* ("directing of virtue") is a pervasive theme in Shinran's teaching. To say that a deceased person has "returned to the Pure Land" might reflect a certain mechanistic view of *ekō*. In this view, *ekō* is conceived of as a two-way system of supernatural transport carrying beings between the pre-birth/after-death Pure Land and the present world of delusion. However, this notion misrepresents Shinran's reinterpretation of *ekō*. "Directing of virtue" is not a mechanism utilized by foolish beings. Rather, it is a metaphor for Amida Buddha's activity toward us:

> In general, the term *directing virtue* may be interpreted as meaning that the bodhisattva [Dharmākara] gives all the virtues he has gathered to sentient beings and brings them to enter the Buddha-way together [with him].[188]
>
> However, sentient beings of the countless worlds, floundering in the sea of blind passions and drifting and sinking in the ocean of birth and death, lack the true and real mind of directing virtues; they lack the pure mind of directing virtues.[189]
>
> ...the great practice is not a foolish being's practice of directing his or her own merit toward attainment of birth. It is the fulfilled practice that Amida directs to beings out of great compassion, and therefore is called "not-directing virtue [on the part of beings]."[190]

Amida Buddha's *ekō* is highlighted in the opening paragraphs of Chapters 1 through 4 of the *Kyōgyōshinshō*. Here is how Shinran begins Chapter 1:

> Thinking with reverence about Jōdo Shinshū, it seems to me that there are two aspects of *ekō*: first, the going aspect and second, the returning aspect. In the going aspect there are the true-and-real teaching, practice, shinjin, and realization.[191]

The *Collected Works* translation of this passage inserts the phrases, "our going forth to the Pure Land" and "our return to this world," which are not in Shinran's original text. These phrases applying to *ekō* were inserted by the translator throughout the *Collected Works* in passages where the phrases are not present in the original.[192] To represent

Shinran as speaking of "our going forth" and "our return" is misleading. Directing of virtue is the practice of Amida Buddha (a symbol for the dynamic aspect of nirvana); it is not the practice of foolish beings who have no such virtue to direct.

Amida's *ekō* has a nirvanic "going aspect" and a samsaric "returning aspect", as Shinran explains in three of his *Kōsō wasan*.[193] In the first *wasan*, "mind" (single-mindedness or shinjin) and "practice" (bodhisattva activity) are the fulfillment of *ekō* in its two respective phases:

> *Amida's ekō is fulfilled*
> *In the two aspects of going and returning.*
> *It is indeed through this ekō*
> *That both mind and practice are received.*

In the second *wasan*, culmination of the going aspect is when "shin" (shinjin) and "practice" (hearing the Name) are realized simultaneously, which takes place here and now, without waiting for an after-death Pure Land:

> *The going aspect of ekō is such that*
> *When Amida's skillful means culminate,*
> *The compassionate Vow's shin and practice are realized;*
> *Immediately, samsara is nirvana.*

To awaken shinjin is to transcend the duality of samsara and nirvana—the terms no longer refer to worlds that are separated from each other. In the third *wasan*, fulfillment of the returning aspect equates to "immediately turning toward all beings" and engaging in the compassionate activity of a bodhisattva in the present life:[194]

> *The returning aspect of ekō is such that*
> *By teaching and guiding we benefit others;*
> *Immediately turning toward all beings,*
> *We cultivate the bodhisattva practices [of the 22nd Vow].*

Considering these verses, it is not justified to say that "going" and "returning" are centered around physical death. On the contrary, receiving the "mind" of shinjin is *concurrent* with receiving the "practice" of benefiting others. Hence, Shinran states that "the person who realizes true and real shinjin through the Tathāgata's two aspects of *ekō* necessarily dwells in the stage of the truly settled"[195]—meaning that shinjin is brought about by the simultaneous operation of the nirvanic and samsaric aspects. It is to realize nirvana, even in the midst of samsara, an outcome that is "inconceivable."

> Know, then, that although they neither seek nor know the indescribable, inexplicable, and inconceivable virtues of the Pure Land of happiness, those who entrust themselves to the [*Hongan*] are made to acquire them.... How can this be conceivable? [It is] beyond thought and measure, beyond understanding and words; this should be known.[196]

Careful consideration ought to be given to Shinran's choice of words. He does not imagine himself residing in the Pure Land prior to his birth in samsara, and consequently he will not "return to" the Pure Land at physical death. His metaphoric labels for the two aspects of Amida's *ekō* do not require a mechanistic interpretation as "our going forth to the Pure Land" and "our return to this world." In regard to the going and returning aspects, he does not propose that foolish beings gain access to a two-way transport system between a pre-birth/after-death Pure Land and the present world of delusion.

The mechanistic view is further reflected in the translator's phrase, "Pure Land Way," which appears prominently throughout the *Collected Works* translation. However, Shinran does not use this phrase (浄土道). For him, the Pure Land (a symbol) is not a "way" to accomplish something. Rather, he says that Jōdo Shinshū (a teaching) is the "way to realization" (証道).[197]

Part IV

Self-Awareness

"But an educated noble disciple has seen the noble ones, and is skilled and trained in the teaching of the noble ones.... They regard form like this: 'This is not mine, I am not this, this is not my self.' They also regard feeling ... perception ... choices ... whatever is seen, heard, thought, known, sought, and explored by the mind like this: 'This is not mine, I am not this, this is not my self.'" [198]

—Alagaddūpama Sutta

The Karmic Seed

One of my teachers has said that when the Buddhist path opens, the direction of our life is turned around, like making a 180° turn. My case can be better described as two 90° turns that occurred thirty years apart. As a teenager I had considerable enthusiasm for the religion in which I was brought up. However, at age twenty I concluded that this belief system was without any factual basis (at least for me), and I abandoned it. It was my first 90° turn, when I left my initial path and chose not to walk in that direction any more.

That's how things stood for the next thirty years. I had no religious affiliation, but I encountered many important teachers. Among these was the writer Albert Camus, who sought to know if one could live a meaningful life without recourse to religion. Where to find meaning was an urgent question in the first half of the 20th century, when Europe was suffering through an age of barbarism. Murder, justified by a perverted logic, was carried out on a vast scale by the Nazi and Bolshevik state terrorist regimes. Camus witnessed the Nazi occupation of France, and he joined the Resistance as editor of the underground newspaper *Combat*. His novels, plays, and essays earned him the Nobel Prize for literature in 1957. Camus was called "the conscience of his generation" for his eloquent opposition to tyranny. Tragically, he died as the passenger in a car accident at the age of forty-six.

Camus saw that the world is full of suffering and cruelty, as amplified to an unprecedented level in the 20th century. If one is not persuaded by the claims of religion, then human suffering would appear to be meaningless. We are led to ask if life is or is not worth living in the presence of universal suffering. For Camus, deciding whether to go on living is the one philosophical question that is truly serious, assuming we are prepared to follow through on our answer.[199]

For Buddhists, Camus's question has a familiar ring to it. Twenty-five centuries ago, Siddhattha Gotama asked if there can be meaning in a life that contains suffering. Gotama's life had been a pleasurable cocoon, which he came to regard as a prison. Breaking free of it to seek the way, he asked whether there could be liberation from suffering. Surely, he knew that he might have to end his life if no answer could be found.

Camus reasoned that even in a world full of meaningless suffering, suicide is not logical. We are compelled to accept "the desperate encounter between human inquiry and the silence of the universe."[200] There must be a questioner to accept this encounter, and even though the situation is absurd and hopeless, it is still illogical to negate oneself through suicide. Meaning is found precisely in the questioner's rebellion. Camus chose as his hero the character Sisyphus from Greek mythology, a man who is punished for defying the gods. Sisyphus is condemned to push a boulder up the side of a mountain, only to have it roll back down, again and again. Yet, in Camus's interpretation the hero attains awakening, and his burden is transformed:

> But Sisyphus teaches the higher fidelity that negates the gods and raises rocks. He too concludes that all is well. The universe henceforth without a master seems to him neither sterile nor futile. Each atom of that stone, each mineral flake of that night-filled mountain, in itself forms a world. The struggle itself toward the heights is enough to fill a man's heart. One must imagine Sisyphus happy.[201]

The first stage of Gotama's awakening was to experience absurdity and hopelessness, upon learning that there was nothing permanent in him or in the things that he had valued. Impermanence negated everything that he was clinging to. It was his desperate encounter with the silence of the universe. The second stage of awakening was when, instead of swimming against the universal flow, the Buddha became one with it. He accepted and affirmed the encounter. Then, a new way of life opened for him.

The events that allow the Dharma to break in on us cannot be predicted. For many people, it is like discovering something previously unrecognized yet strangely familiar. Prior to the encounter, the cause is within us, but we remain unaware of it. Mahāyāna Buddhism teaches that all of our thoughts and experiences produce karmic seeds that reside in our unconscious mind. For me the hidden seed was having learned from teachers like Albert Camus. The seed was present for many years, but it failed to sprout because favorable conditions were lacking.

The situation changed because of my late brother-in-law, Kent Hirohama. I met Kent in 1994 when I married his sister Janis. Due to the family dynamic that existed at that time, there was not much genuine communication between family members. I knew very little about Kent's life, although I was aware that he was involved with a Buddhist temple and that he performed in a Taiko group, both of which were remote from my concerns. Regrettably, I never spoke to Kent about it or attended any of the performances he gave as a Taiko musician and instructor.

Prior to 2006, when Kent died of cancer, there was no reason to think that Janis and I would follow the Buddhist path. Many friends came to visit Kent during the final weeks of his life. From them we began to learn things about him that we had not suspected. Janis and I met members of the Taiko group, and we met Rev. Harada who came frequently to the hospital where Kent was being treated.[202] Attending the funeral service at the temple really struck a chord with us, although we did not figure on going back. However, Rev. Harada encouraged us to join a study class he was giving called "Buddhist Views of Life and Death." Since then, we have been able to learn from many wonderful Dharma teachers. This was the second 90° turn in my life.

The intent of the teachings is to overturn our preconceptions—an exceedingly difficult task. We should not expect that our *upāya* (or skillful means) will be pleasant or agreeable. For Janis and me, the seed for finding the Dharma path sprouted because of the sad and painful experience of a death in the family. Although Kent died unaware of it, he is the reason that our lives took a new and surprising direction.

My First Dharma Teacher

We are made to awaken to the Dharma, or limitless reality, through the influence of teachers, typically in the form of spoken words or books that we read. We also may be influenced by images, such as the statue of Amida Buddha on the altar. The Dharma might be made known to us through a difficult experience like the loss of a family member. Or, it could be through a wonderful experience that causes us to stop and say, "Wow!" It was not until age fifty that I met with a Buddhist sangha, but the Dharma was reaching me in other ways at earlier times in my life.

To find Dharma teachers we most often look to Asia, but such teachers have arisen in Europe, too. Strangely enough, in the West it is rare to meet them in the sphere of religion. There, rather than in a religious context, one meets Dharma teachers in the realm of artistic creation. Westerners can look to the great writers, artists, and musicians to show them the truth of impermanence.

Consider the portrait on the previous page. Is this man a bodhisattva? For me, he is. Wolfgang Amadeus Mozart (1756-1791) is among my most important Dharma teachers. By that, I mean that he shows me limitless reality. He has done so for the last forty-seven years, which is quite a long time for the truth to sink in. Even so, I am only beginning to appreciate him.

In speaking about Mozart, it's easy to run out of superlatives. The quantity of music that he composed during his brief life is so large that it's difficult to imagine how one man managed even to write it all down, much less to have thought through the composition. As a point of reference, the Beatles were very productive songwriters who created around 230 original songs. By comparison, Mozart's catalog contains over 600 compositions. Considering that his works are usually scored for many parts and that they are far longer than pop songs, we might estimate that the quantity of music that this man composed is 100 times more than the total output of the Beatles! Despite this astounding productivity, he was anything but a recluse. He spent much of his time enjoying the company of family and friends, often while writing music, or, more accurately, transcribing it, because he had already composed the new piece in his head!

Mozart's range was astonishing: symphonies, concertos, chamber music, solo keyboard pieces, operas, sacred music—in each of these forms, his works are among the supreme examples in Western music. His friend Joseph Haydn (1732-1809), who was likewise a musician of superhuman productivity, is reported to have declared to Mozart's father, "I tell you before God, and as an honest man, that your son is the greatest composer I know, either personally or by reputation: he has taste and moreover the greatest possible knowledge of the science of composition."

All of this is evidence that Mozart was a great genius, but was he also a teacher of the Dharma? I have no doubt that this is true, but to convince you of it using words is quite difficult. One of the verses of the *Jūnirai* says that the Dharma cannot be expressed by words. There is a story that Śākyamuni gave a sermon in which he wanted to express a truth that was beyond words. He did this by simply holding up a flower while saying nothing. It was the wordless transmission of the

Dharma from Śākyamuni's mind to the mind of his disciple. Mozart's music has just this quality—a direct transmission of voiceless truth from the composer's mind to the mind of the listener.

If I claim that truth is transmitted from Mozart to me, does that mean that he invented it? Not exactly. I believe that the message has always existed and that it was *discovered* by the composer, rather than being his invention. The Dharma fills and surrounds us continually, even if I perceive it only on rare occasions. But unlike me, Mozart seems to have been plugged into limitless reality pretty much all the time! That is what it means to be an awakened person. There is the Sanskrit word *tathāgata*, or the equivalent Japanese word *nyorai*. A *nyorai* is one who has come from the Dharma realm and who is now showing us the truth. He or she might use words, but a direct transmission without words can be more effective. A composer of genius does just that.

Quite often I become aware that Mozart's teachings are running through my mind. As a result of long familiarity, I can hear many of his compositions without there being any external source of sound. In the same way, through long familiarity, we might become conscious of Namo Amida Butsu running through our mind. Namo Amida Butsu, the six-character Name, is a form that the Dharma takes so that we can hear its command, "Take refuge!" Likewise, Mozart's music is the Dharma saying, "Jim, wake up!"

Mozart died of an illness at the age of thirty-five, at the height of his powers. No one knows for sure what caused his death, but it's not likely that he was done in by a rival composer, as one legend claims. In the 18th century, people could die suddenly from conditions that nowadays can be prevented or cured. Mozart probably figured on living longer than he did. Nevertheless, he was intimately familiar with sickness and death among the members of his family. In addition to losing his parents, he saw four of his children die in infancy.

A sharp awareness of mortality underlies much of Mozart's music. Through the perfection of musical form, he expresses "a peculiar kind of melancholy, a melancholy amounting almost to panic, which so often haunts the isolation of genius. Mozart felt it quite young."[203] A hallmark of his music is the effortless transition between light and darkness, between joy and grief. The transitions can be so subtle that we scarcely notice them taking place, yet once recognized they strike us as having been inevitable. Mozart is teaching that light and darkness are two aspects of one transcendent reality.

It may seem surprising, but the composer's *subjective* feelings are not important here. The music, I would say, is not a record of his immediate emotions or circumstances; rather, it is an *objective* expression of something timeless. Even if I knew nothing about W.A. Mozart (the finite human being), the same transcendent reality would still be conveyed by his music. The meaning supersedes his personality in a way that I encounter with very few composers. Ludwig van Beethoven (1770-1827) is another of my Dharma teachers, but most of his compositions are an expression of his subjectivity; they are about *him* (I mean this in a good way). But toward the end of his life, particularly in his final piano sonatas and string quartets, Beethoven achieved the objective expression of transcendent reality, just as Mozart had done.

It has been said that Mozart shows us what it means to be human, or in fact, what it means to be human in an absolute sense, to be human in a way that goes beyond any personal history.[204] He shows us what it means to become Buddha.

I hope what I've written provides some justification for saying that Mozart is my Dharma teacher. Recognizing that words can take us only so far, I will let the composer finish this essay. Please listen, for example, to the Adagio from the Piano Concerto no. 23, K. 488. The opening theme in F-sharp minor is printed on the next page. It is the Dharma saying, "You there! Wake up!"

SELF-AWARENESS

Birth and Death

The fatality of one's being cannot be divorced from the fatality of all that which has been and that which will be.... One is necessary, one is a piece of fate, one belongs to the whole, one is in the whole... [205]

—Friedrich Nietzsche

A few years ago, in a certain part of the United States, a ballot measure asked, Does personhood begin at conception? The question is viewed as a litmus test or wedge issue to be exploited by political factions. Hence, most voters may have considered their answers to be definitive, amounting to a choice between good and evil. But from a Buddhist perspective, it would not be possible to respond with a simple Yes or No.

It's commonly thought that the life of a human being begins once and ends once at fixed points called "birth" and "death," but Buddhism teaches that death and rebirth of the self are taking place in every moment. Our bodies appear to be about the same from day to day, but we are composed of cells that undergo continual death and regeneration. Likewise, we sometimes meet with difficult situations that can be described as spiritual death followed by renewal. As a consequence of biology and of life experience, time makes us into something different from what we were during childhood. Life is ending and beginning continually, as a person matures, grows old, and passes away.

What is a human being? Buddhism teaches that what "I" am is a combination of ever-changing physical and mental activities that may be categorized in five groupings called *skandhas*, meaning bundles or aggregates. They include familiar things such as the body's metabolism and the conscious activities of seeing, hearing, smelling, tasting, touching, and thinking. There is nothing mystical in the *skandhas*. Anyone who is willing to study the teaching can understand what they are and can recognize them in himself or herself.[206]

Gotama Buddha realized that these physical and mental activities are coming into existence and passing away in every moment of our lives. The self certainly exists, but its continual arising and passing away are dependent on everything else in the world. Each aspect of the self is "relative, interdependent, and interconnected, and nothing is absolute or independent."[207] The Buddha's awakening occurred when, after years of searching, he arrived at this answer to his question, What am I? The insight, called conditional arising, is at the core of his teaching.[208] What "I" am is not the intrinsic self that other religions identify as a person or a soul. No such intrinsic self came into existence when my parents' chromosomes were joined together at the time of conception, or when their son appeared in the hospital delivery room. No such intrinsic self will come to an end when my body is cremated. A modern commentary explains Gotama's insight this way:

> Human existence, human life, is produced by causes and conditions. These causes and conditions are limitless and unfathomable. They cannot be grasped by the finite wisdom or intellect of human beings. Although human beings think that they control and regulate everything that surrounds their all-important selves, their lives are actually shaped by reciprocal relationships among the unfathomable causes and conditions in this infinite world.[209]

It might be thought that a soul or personhood continues to exist after physical death. Christianity teaches that the soul is punished or rewarded through divine justice, while Hinduism teaches that the *ātman* is reborn as a different life-form in accord with the law of karma. On the other hand, it might be thought that the self, whatever it may be when we are alive, is entirely destroyed at physical death. When asked about such matters, Gotama refused to be drawn into "a thicket of views" concerning the *ātman* and rebirth, as in the following dialogue with the wanderer Vacchagotta:

"Master Gotama, when mendicants' minds are freed, where are they reborn?"

"*They're reborn* doesn't apply, Vaccha."

"Well then, are they not reborn?"

"*They're not reborn* doesn't apply, Vaccha."

"Well then, are they both reborn and not reborn?"

"*They're both reborn and not reborn* doesn't apply, Vaccha."

"Well then, are they neither reborn nor not reborn?"

"*They're neither reborn nor not reborn* doesn't apply, Vaccha."

"Master Gotama, when asked all these questions, you say: 'It doesn't apply.' I fail to understand this point, Master Gotama; I've fallen into confusion. And I've now lost even the degree of clarity I had from previous discussions with Master Gotama."

"No wonder you don't understand, Vaccha, no wonder you're confused.... It's hard for you to understand, since you have a different view, creed, preference, practice, and tradition. Well then, Vaccha, I'll ask you about this in return, and you can answer as you like.... Suppose a fire was burning in front of you. Would you know: 'This fire is burning in front of me'?"

"Yes, I would, Master Gotama."

"But Vaccha, suppose you were asked: 'This fire burning in front of you: what does it depend on to burn?' How would you answer?"

"I would answer like this: 'This fire burns in dependence on grass and sticks as fuel.'"

"Suppose that the fire were extinguished. Would you know: 'This fire in front of me is extinguished'?"

"Yes, I would, Master Gotama."

"But Vaccha, suppose you were asked: 'This fire in front of you that is extinguished: in what direction did it go—east, south, west, or north?' How would you answer?"

"It doesn't apply, Master Gotama. The fire depended on grass and sticks as fuel. When that runs out, and no more fuel is added, the fire is reckoned to have become extinguished due to lack of fuel."[210]

On another occasion, when the wanderer asked whether the self does or does not exist absolutely, the Buddha chose to remain silent.[211] The impression made by this silence proved to be illuminating: Vacchagotta's confusion abated, and he became an *arahant*.

Buddhism regards the physical and mental activities constituting the self as continually changing and interdependent with all life forms. Because the self exists in a web of reciprocal relationships, the question about when personhood allegedly begins and ends is seen to be wrongly framed. My ego asserts that I have an intrinsic self that is separate from things outside of me. I speculate that this self will either live on in an after-death world, or will disappear and leave no trace. Liberation is to recognize that the self is interdependent with all of life in a universal flow. The self arises from the flow, is sustained by it for a certain interval, and rejoins it at physical death.

> Briefly formulated, the universal doctrine teaches that all the visible structures of the world—all things and beings—are the effects of a ubiquitous power out of which they rise, which supports and fills them during the period of their manifestation, and back into which they must ultimately dissolve.[212]

This view of birth and death is not speculation about things that are unknowable. Rather, the Buddha relied on direct insight into what he truly was. We cannot appreciate his teaching apart from this understanding of birth and death.

Divine Messengers

In Greek mythology the little owl (*Athene noctua*) is a messenger of Athena, goddess of wisdom—the highest ideal of ancient Greece. Owls were considered to be divine messengers—creatures that will share wisdom with us if we are able listen to them. The Buddhist scriptures also speak about divine messengers, although they are not owls. I will come back to them shortly.

The Buddha's words may at times sound harsh, but he did not make judgments about his listeners or seek to punish them. His intent was to liberate them from suffering—not to inflict more of it. Our lives contain so many distractions that we may never have time for the things that are of greatest importance. Harsh-sounding words are a skillful means to help us out of this difficulty. To illustrate, here is a passage by the Russian novelist Fyodor Dostoevsky (1821-1881), whose books have meant a lot to me over the years. The author imagines

> ... what criminals feel when they are being taken to the scaffold. They have another long, long street to pass down and at walking pace, past thousands of people. Then there will be a turning into another street and only at the end of that street is the dread place of execution! I fancy that at the beginning of the journey the condemned man, sitting on his shameful cart, must feel that he has infinite life still before him. The houses recede, the cart moves on—oh, that's nothing, it's still far to the turning into the second street, and he still looks boldly to right and to left at those thousands of callously curious people with their eyes fixed on him, and he still fancies that he is just such a man as they. But now the turning comes to the next street. Oh, that's nothing, nothing, there's still a whole street before him, and however many houses have been passed, he will still think there are many left. And so, to the very end, to the very scaffold.[213]

SELF-AWARENESS

To produce great literature, an author must write about what he knows, namely, aspects of life that he has experienced personally. Hence, we might wonder if Dostoevsky was qualified to describe the psychological state of a man being taken to his execution. Amazingly, he did possess this qualification! At age twenty-eight, he was sentenced to death as a political criminal for opposing the policies of Czar Nicolas I. As one commentator describes it, Dostoevsky

> ... was led out, with twenty others, for execution by firing-squad in the Semenovsky Square in St. Petersburg. But then the sentences were suddenly commuted at the last moment: by prior arrangement and on the express instructions of the Czar himself.[214]

It was a cruel trick to break the will of the political dissidents. Dostoevsky spent the next four years with his hands and feet shackled, doing hard labor in a Siberian prison camp. He then performed compulsory service in the army and eventually returned to St. Petersburg, where he became a celebrated novelist and died of natural causes at the age of fifty-nine. His greatness as a writer was a product of his nightmarish experiences.

In the story, the condemned man feels that "he has infinite life still before him," because the streets are very long, and the cart is moving slowly. He thinks, "it's still far to the turning into the second street." The man clings to the idea that he is like the on-lookers, that he is "just such a man as they" who will be alive tomorrow and the next day. Upon reflection, each of us is just like that condemned man! Living in the world of delusion, we imagine that all eternity is still before us, even as the cart rolls on, passing house after house, rounding one corner, and then another. We neglect to focus on what could become our most important priority—meeting with a buddha and listening to the Dharma. Responsibilities pile up, one after another. We have duties at home and at work, duties of caring for family members, of supporting activities at the temple. We have aspirations for self-improvement, for hobbies, and for recreation. All of these activities demand our attention. Meanwhile, as in the story, the cart keeps rolling on, passing house after house, inexorably carrying us to the square. And before death comes, we may be physically disabled or lose our cognitive ability.

Is there a way to overcome the distractions in life that lead us to postpone Dharma listening? Gotama Buddha gave a wonderful teaching to help us. He said that there are three "divine messengers" in our midst, messengers who remind us not to put off the most important priority. He gave the teaching as a parable, told in a mythical context. Imagine a man who dies and is reborn in the hell realm, where he is brought before Yama, the Lord of Death.

> Then King Yama pursues, presses, and grills him about the first messenger of the gods: "Mister, did you not see the first messenger of the gods that appeared among human beings?"
>
> He says, "I saw nothing, sir."
>
> Then King Yama says, "Mister, did you not see among human beings an elderly woman or a man—eighty, ninety, or a hundred years old—bent double, crooked, leaning on a staff, trembling as they walk, ailing, past their prime, with teeth broken, hair grey and scanty or bald, skin wrinkled, and limbs blotchy?"
>
> He says, "I saw that, sir."
>
> Then King Yama says, "Mister, did it not occur to you—being sensible and mature— 'I, too, am liable to grow old. I'm not exempt from old age. I'd better do good by way of body, speech, and mind'?"
>
> He says, "I couldn't, sir. I was negligent."
>
> [Then follow similar exchanges concerning illness and death. Owing to his negligence, the man is subjected to the torments of hell.][215]

That is the parable. *Aging*, *illness*, and *death* are the divine messengers. Receiving their message is what enables us to focus on Dharma listening. If we have a comfortable life, and if the messengers stay in the background, then we have no need for the Dharma. Distractions and various urgent matters drown out their message. We may feel blessed with good fortune, but, from the Buddha's perspective, we are most unfortunate in not being able to hear the messengers. We are like the condemned man rolling along in his cart and thinking that the end is still far away. Dr. Hideo Yonezawa recounts a statement made by one of his patients, a young woman with a terminal illness: "Unless we human beings have our backs to the wall, we will not listen to the teachings. Because we feel that we will continue to live in the future, we do not listen earnestly."[216]

There is a legend about the boy Matsuwakamaru's entry to monastic life. Arriving at the temple in the evening, he was told that his ordination ceremony must be put off until the next day. In response, he composed a poem: *Cherry blossoms that are felt / To last till the morrow, / Might well blow away / During the night.* Struck by the boy's insistence, the priest conducted the ceremony that evening. Even at a young age, Matsuwakamaru heard the divine messengers clearly. He continued to hear them as an adult, when his name was Shinran. During Japan's Kamakura period, warfare and natural disasters were prevalent, so that he encountered death far more frequently than we do.[217] That helps to explain why Shinran was a serious Dharma listener. Likewise, Dostoevsky's experience of having faced a firing squad gave him a unique ability to hear the divine messengers. Teachers are urging us not to be distracted from the matters of greatest importance. Like Athena's owls, the Buddha's messengers will share wisdom with us if we pay attention.

Underground Man

When my wife and I first came in contact with Buddhism, our lives took a new direction. How was it that we were open to making a change? For one thing, the teacher's message was compelling. But there was also preparation on our part. Willingness to listen is the beginner's mind, brought about by a favorable karmic background—the inner cause or seed that germinates when the right external conditions are present. Because of teachers that I met earlier in life, I was able to listen to the Dharma when the opportunity arose.

At age thirty I encountered a book that greatly altered my perspective. I was struck by the ideas contained in Fyodor Dostoevsky's *Notes from Underground*, as in this passage:

> And yet I think man will never renounce real suffering, that is, destruction and chaos. Why, suffering is the sole origin of consciousness! Though I did lay it down at the beginning that consciousness is the greatest misfortune for man, yet I know man prizes it and would not give it up for any satisfaction.[218]

Written in the 1860s, *Notes* was unconventional in its form and content. Using a mixture of satire and tragedy, the author harshly criticized popular views that he disagreed with. This book announced his maturity as a writer, and he went on to produce the five great novels: *Crime and Punishment*, *The Idiot*, *The Possessed*, *The Adolescent*, and *The Brothers Karamazov*.

Notes from Underground introduces a fictional narrator whose name is never stated. We can call him "underground man." Underground in this case does not refer to a clandestine organization, but rather to the state of mind of a man who lives among us without being one of us. It's as though he has been crouching in a dark cellar for many years, listening to our words through a crack in the floor. He knows about our self-deceptions—how we tell lies to ourselves. He rails at us, his readers, for leading unexamined lives. He is equally critical of his own shortcomings and misdeeds.

SELF-AWARENESS

Underground man says that human beings will never renounce destruction and chaos, even though these actions cause us to suffer. We feel compelled to harm ourselves and to harm other people. It's not that we are tempted to do it by an external devil. Rather, we *choose* to commit destructive and self-destructive acts. A special consciousness arises through this type of suffering. It is to know the true nature of the ego self, to know one's own frailty and meanness.

Dostoevsky suggests that if life could be free from suffering, it would be impossible to know the self. Does that have a familiar ring?

Gotama, while living in his palace, is untouched by aging, illness, and death. In that environment he is incapable of knowing himself as he truly is. But after seeing at first hand an old person, a sick person, a dead person, and a renunciant, he reflects on his condition. He begins to suffer from the knowledge that someday his happiness will come to an end. Because of impermanence, the life he has been living appears to be meaningless. The shock awakens him from his dreaming. It is the start of the path that leads to Buddhahood.

Going out from the palace in four stages is a parable, a story that lets us grasp an important teaching.[219] Of course, life for us is not altogether free of suffering. We have plenty of *duhkha* to go around. Nevertheless, we try to stay inside our own mental palace by finding distractions—things that temporarily hide the reality of *duhkha*. Cocooned in this way, we are unable to know ourselves. Knowledge of suffering allowed Gotama to realize self-awareness. Or, as underground man says, suffering is "the sole origin of consciousness." From a Buddhist perspective, it is *knowledge of both happiness and suffering* that leads to self-awareness. The contrast between these emotional states induces us to look for meaning in our lives—to seek a way of transcending happiness and suffering.

Reading *Notes from Underground* long ago was a preview of ideas that I would encounter again in the teachings of Buddhism. However, Dostoevsky's book is not about receiving shinjin or becoming a buddha like Gotama. Underground man has attained heightened consciousness of the ego self, but he calls it a disease—a mental illness that sets him apart from people who lack this consciousness. He is sharply aware of his destructive and chaotic tendencies, but he does not transcend them.

Time and again his actions cause harm to himself and to others. He understands what is happening, but he is incapable of acting differently. Underground man admits that he is lost. He says that you, the reader, are lost too, but you won't admit it:

> I know that you will very likely be angry with me for that, and will begin shouting and stamping. "Speak for yourself," you will say, "and for your miseries in your underground holes, and don't dare to say all of us"—excuse me, gentlemen, I am not justifying myself with that "all of us." As for what concerns me in particular I have only in my life carried to an extreme what you have not dared to carry halfway, and what's more, you have taken your cowardice for good sense, and have found comfort in deceiving yourselves. So that perhaps, after all, there is more life in me than in you. Look into it more carefully![220]

In 19th century Russia there were those who believed that society could be perfected. They said that rational thought would eventually put an end to harmful behavior, and self-inflicted suffering would disappear. Dostoevsky disagreed. For him, there would never be an end to irrational and destructive behavior. Those who believed otherwise had failed to understand what they truly were. It's precisely what Shinran teaches:

> As expressed in the parable of the two rivers of water and fire, we are full of ignorance and blind passion. Our desires are countless, and anger, wrath, jealousy, and envy are overwhelming, arising without pause; to the very last moment of life they do not cease, or disappear, or exhaust themselves.[221]

By virtue of his psychological insight, Shinran was something of an underground man. He was conscious of his self-deception, of his inability to be other than a foolish being. And he criticized institutional Buddhism for being a masquerade.

Continuing in the psychological vein, here is Dostoevsky again:

> Every man has reminiscences which he would not tell to everyone, but only to his friends. He has other matters in his mind which he would not reveal even to his friends, but only to himself, and that in secret. But there are other things which a man is afraid to tell even to himself, and every decent man has a number of such things stored away in his mind. The more decent he is, the greater the number of such things in his mind.[222]

What are these things that I am afraid to reveal even to myself? They might be memories of frightening or shameful experiences residing in my unconscious mind. Underground man is probably speaking about repressed memories like that. But from a Buddhist perspective, my mind contains something that goes deeper than difficult memories. What I am afraid to reveal even to myself is the ignorance that lies at the root of my existence. It is the basic characteristic of life in samsara, our inheritance transmitted over millions of years of evolution. It means being confused about the nature of reality. It means thinking that I have an eternal, independent self and that satisfying the desires of this self will bring me happiness. What I am unwilling to recognize is that I have a false view of reality. Even though I hear the Buddhist teachings, I continue to engage in self-deception.

To live in the three lower realms of samsara is all suffering, and no liberation can occur there. We might think that the heavenly realm is the best one—heavenly beings experience only happiness, although it eventually comes to an end. However, the human realm is actually the most favorable, because here we experience a mixture of happiness and suffering that can open a path to liberation. The alternation of joy and grief inspires us to search for meaning.

Dostoevsky's *Notes from Underground* introduced me long ago to the idea that suffering can lead to consciousness of the self.[223] Without that background, I might not have been prepared to receive the Buddhist teachings when the opportunity came along. We can gain unexpected insights from all varieties of teachers. Indeed, the *Larger*

Sutra says there are "countless great sages as many as the sands of the Ganges" who help us on the Buddhist path. I hope we will continue listening to them.

Alone and Unknown

The *Larger Sutra* contains this bleak assessment: "In the midst of worldly desires and attachments, people are born alone and die alone, they come alone and go alone.... When they have gone to faraway realms, they will not see each other again." [224] These words came vividly to mind when I read a local news story.

By way of background, in the first half of the 20th century the Boyle Heights district of Los Angeles was an ethnically diverse community that included people of Japanese ancestry. Evergreen Cemetery, a prominent feature of Boyle Heights, holds the graves of many Japanese Americans, among them my wife's grandparents and uncles. We go there periodically to clean the grave marker and to place flowers in their memory. Since its establishment in 1877, Evergreen has also included a "potter's field" or public burial ground for indigent residents. And still today the County of Los Angeles maintains a crematory for this purpose at the east end of Evergreen, as seen in the photo below.

SELF-AWARENESS

Annually in December a special event takes place at the crematory, which usually garners a story in the *Times*:

Poignant Burial Ritual for the Poor[225]

They are the unidentified, the estranged, those whose loved ones just couldn't afford to bury them. In a simple yet poignant ceremony Wednesday near a busy Boyle Heights intersection, the ashes of more than 1600 people who had never been identified or whose bodies were never claimed were buried in a single grave.

… The chaplain said he has met and spent time with people who will someday probably be among those whose ashes are interred in the common grave. Many, he said, know that they will probably die alone.

… the county's cemetery caretaker said he's been to more than 30 of the annual burials. Each has an emotional tug. "It's hard, especially when you have to cremate babies," he said. "Off the top of my head, there are about 300 babies this year from hospitals around the county, with families who can't afford to bury them."…

"A lot of people who came to our soup kitchen—in poor health or estranged from their family—probably have ended up here," said [one attendee]. "You have the 1% at the top. This is the 1% at the bottom."

There are people now living, my wife being among them, who knew her grandparents and who occasionally visit their grave. Not so for the thousands of unidentified and unclaimed persons whose ashes go into the ground on the east side of Evergreen. For a moment, imagine the experience of someone dying alone and unknown in the midst of a crowded city. Then reflect: Am I really any different from those people? Most of us have family and friends who will remember us for a time, but the living memory will soon disappear, just as it has for those buried anonymously. Another passage from the *Larger Sutra* states,

"Furthermore, their bodies perish and their lives end in the midst of these agonies, they are forced to discard all that they have and leave this world with no one to accompany them. Even the noble and the wealthy have these worries; they are afflicted in this way by numerous anxieties and fears."[226]

My ego thinks, "I am separate from the unidentified and unclaimed persons who are buried at Evergreen. I am not them." In contrast, the Buddha taught that the true self is interdependent with all other life in a universal flow. My true self has no separate existence apart from others. It arises from the universal flow, is sustained by it during the brief interval of this life, and rejoins it at physical death. My true self exists in a reciprocal relationship with all living beings, including the ones who die alone and unknown.

'I Might Do Anything'

Shin Buddhism teaches a path to awakening that challenges the ideas that we have about ourselves, as illustrated in this statement by Shinran: "If the karmic cause so prompts us, we will commit any kind of act." Or, in a different translation, "Under certain karmic conditions, I might do anything."[227] Here Shinran is saying that there is no limit to the outrageous acts he might commit if the necessary conditions arose. He is confessing that he lacks the discipline to behave in an ethical manner.

I was reminded of Shinran's statement by a powerful story in the newspaper.[228] At a prison in Vacaville, California there is a facility that provides hospice care to convicts who are dying of terminal illnesses. The caregivers are convicted murderers who have volunteered and been given training for this role. It's remarkable that the men providing this assistance came to the role by having killed someone at an earlier stage of their lives.

The story focused on a murderer named John who had gone to an apartment with the intention of shooting a rival gang member. Because he misidentified the apartment, the victim was not the person he had intended to kill. As it turned out, the man who died was a 30-year-old Japanese American. John was tried and found guilty. At the sentencing, the judge read to the courtroom a letter by the victim's brother that implored him to consider deeply what he had done and to turn his life around. The news story described how John eventually took those words to heart and became a prison hospice worker.

I don't know if the murdered man grew up in a Buddhist family, but I was struck by what his brother had to say: "Nothing can bring [my brother] back. We miss him terribly. But after finding out about [the hospice worker], I'm glad he is doing what he is doing. He could have gone in a really bad direction in prison, worse than he'd been before, but he resisted that. It's gratifying that the letter I wrote had an impact, gratifying that he did change his life."

The brother said that he has never felt a need for angry, eye-for-an-eye retribution. Hatred has not consumed him. He doesn't believe that more hatred would do the world any good. The reporter asked him about redemption and forgiveness. "I think it is not up to me to forgive," he said. "It's not for my side to offer redemption—that has to come from within. He has to find it within himself. But I will say this. The path that he is on, that path is far from hopeless. It is a good path. Whether he is inside the prison or out, I want him to stay on that path. That is what I ask of him."

Often, I fail to consider the consequences of my actions. For example, I sustain my life by killing plants and animals; it seems that I have no choice in the matter. Even worse, as an American consumer I participate in the over-consumption of resources that has led to a mass extinction of plants and animals. The rate of species extinction caused by human activity is currently about 1000 times greater than the pre-human rate. Given current trends, the majority of recently-existing plant and animal species will disappear by the end of the 21st century, a permanent loss of perhaps 3 million unique life forms.[229] The last time the biosphere suffered a collapse of this magnitude and rapidity was 66 million years ago, when three-quarters of the plant and animal species were eliminated by the impact of an asteroid or comet.

Even so, I still don't see myself as a murderer of people. Yet, can I really say that I would never kill a human being? Am I not a citizen of a nation that during the course of my life has killed vast numbers of human beings for the stated purpose of allowing me to live here securely? A rough estimate is 2.5 million people killed by American actions overseas during my lifetime—1.5 million in southeast Asia (combat and dioxin poisoning, 1960-present); 0.5 million in Iraq (economic sanctions, 1990-2003); 0.5 million in Iraq, Afghanistan, and Pakistan ("war on terror," 2003-present). Reflecting on these matters, it seems more and more accurate to say, "I might do anything." Or, as Shinran is reported to have said,

> "We do not kill, not because our thoughts are good but because we do not have the karma to kill even a single person. Yet, even though we do not want to injure anyone, we may be led to kill a hundred or a thousand people."[230]

Unlike Judaism and Christianity, Buddhism does not speak of atonement or redemption. Whenever I cause harm (e.g., species extinction, killing of human beings) I cannot undo it, even if I could somehow know its extent. In Buddhist terminology, this insight is called the fruition of karma. My actions will inevitably cause suffering or perhaps alleviate it at some point in the future. Both of these outcomes are sharply illustrated in the story of the hospice worker.

The brother of the murdered man spoke well in saying that it is not for him to offer forgiveness. Instead, he said that John must find redemption within himself. Rather than redemption, Buddhism uses the words liberation or awakening to describe what may be taking place. After having been the cause of great suffering earlier in his life, John became a caregiver for people who are dying. No doubt he appreciates more deeply than I do the truth of Shinran's statement: "Under certain karmic conditions, I might do anything."

Interlude

Shinran's Uniqueness

*Lacking even small love and small compassion,
I cannot hope to benefit sentient beings.
Were it not for the ship of Amida's Vow,
How could I cross the ocean of painful existence?*[231]

—Hymns of the Dharma-Ages

Disciple of Śākyamuni

Jōdo Shinshū is defined by Shinran's teachings and life experience, through which he rediscovered the true heart and mind of Śākyamuni Buddha. Among the many names that Shinran went by, the foremost is Gutoku Shaku Shinran, where *Gutoku* means foolish stubble-haired one, and *Shaku* means disciple of Śākyamuni.[232] Therefore, to appreciate the uniqueness of Shinran, we must understand what was the core of Śākyamuni's teaching. Here, one might mention the Middle Way or the Four Truths or the Eightfold Path, but I would point to an aspect that is even more basic. The framework of the teachings is the idea of *sickness and cure*,[233] as in this passage from the *Nirvana Sutra*:

> "Further, good sons, the Buddhas and bodhisattvas are great physicians; hence they are called 'true teachers.' Why? Because they know sicknesses and the medicines to cure them, and they give the medicine appropriate to the disease...."
>
> "The Buddhas and bodhisattvas are like this. They know all the sicknesses of foolish beings, which fall into three types: greed, anger, and folly."[234]

If we have no awareness that we are spiritually sick, then we will have no desire to seek a cure, and the teachings given by the Buddha will not pertain to us. The indicator of sickness is dissatisfaction, the feeling that something is not right about our life. Usually, we interpret negative experiences in terms of external factors: *that* person or *that* group harmed me. Instead, the Buddha teaches us to look at the internal factors, the sickness within that gives rise to dissatisfaction. At the outset, it's impossible to do this, because we feel self-satisfied and healthy. We think that our difficulties must have an external cause.

Siddhattha Gotama's life as a prince in the palace is a model for the initial view of the self. Our mind is like his was, prior to meeting with impermanence. In the story, he sees that everything he has treasured will come to an end, and his self-satisfaction disappears. Then he meets a truth-seeker—an awakened person. Through this encounter, he becomes convinced that his sickness has a cure and that he will find it. Awareness of his sickness and its possible cure is the framework for all that comes after. We might say it is the basis of Buddhism.

Another way of expressing it is to say that human life has an underlying reality with two aspects: ignorance and awakening. Initially we live at the surface level, feeling confident and self-satisfied. We are not conscious of the underlying aspects of existence. The teachings of the Buddha are aimed at helping us to awaken this consciousness. We believe that we are healthy, like the prince in the palace. Going deeper within, we become aware that our apparent healthiness is an illusion. To recognize that we are seriously sick is the first stage of self-awareness; seeing this, we desire to be cured. The second stage is to receive the cure by gaining insight into the human condition, namely, to recognize that the world of ignorance and the world of awakening are not separate! Aging, illness, and death are transformed from being our enemies to being our teachers. There is just one underlying reality that might be called true healthiness or Buddhahood.

Shinran lived during a time of social chaos brought on by warfare and natural disasters. From age eight (1181) to age twenty-eight (1201) he engaged in rigorous study and practice as a Buddhist monk. He learned many teachings and practices, yet he did not find in them the authentic spirit of Śākyamuni. It seemed to him that the Buddha's teaching was nearly extinct. In spite of this, he could say eventually that *Jōdo Shinshū is the path to realization that is now vital and flourishing.*[235] I will mention four distinguishing features to indicate what is special about Jōdo Shinshū.

The first feature is that Shinran abandoned monastic discipline. When the government broke up Hōnen's sangha in 1207,

> ... [the teacher] and a number of his followers, without receiving any deliberation of their [alleged] crimes, were summarily sentenced to death or were dispossessed of their monkhood, given [secular] names, and consigned to distant banishment. I was among the latter. Hence, I am now neither

a monk nor one in worldly life. For this reason, I have taken the term *toku* as my name.[236]

Toku described "the hair of monks that had grown out longer than appropriate; it was employed as a term of derision for those who broke their precepts with no sign of repentance and indicated their essential criminality."[237] From the time of his exile, Shinran had no further connection with Buddhist institutions. He did not identify himself as a religious founder or organizer. To be "neither a priest nor a lay follower" (in the ordinary sense of those terms), concisely sums up his way of life. As one writer puts it, "To have this physical body and to live is to be a layman. But while I have this physical body and live, there is also the spiritual dimension that can be called the life of a priest."[238] Discovering the spiritual dimension within secular life is a hallmark of Jōdo Shinshū.

The second distinguishing feature is Shinran's stance toward the teachings of the Buddha, which he characterizes as being either "true-and-real" or "provisional."[239] At the outset, we are ill-equipped to appreciate the true-and-real teachings; it is unnatural for us to start there. Provisional teachings and practices are ones that the Buddha has skillfully disguised to lead us through this difficulty. Looking beyond the disguises for the deeper meaning, Shinran came to appreciate this distinction, which his contemporaries failed to recognize. He discovered in the provisional teachings a skillful means residing on the surface, pointing to the true meaning within. The distinction is not an academic one. He interpreted provisional teachings and practices as representing the stages of spiritual development that he experienced. It was by this process that he realized he was seriously sick.

The third special feature of Shinran's teaching is that recognizing our sickness and receiving the cure are simultaneous, as the darkness of the self is made visible by the light of the Dharma. Therefore, awakening includes both feelings of sadness and feelings of joy. Negative thoughts and experiences change from being our enemies to being our teachers. In some other forms of Buddhism, the cure is to be realized in a future existence where negative thoughts and experiences are eliminated. However,

> ...Shinran rejects notions of the Pure Land way as a future-oriented religion in which the moment of death, rather than the present, is crucial, and manifests it as a path fundamentally in accord with Mahāyāna thought.[240]

For Shinran, the cure is to receive self-awareness here and now by looking into the mirror of the teachings. On this path, the fulfillment of one's life is not contingent on any future attainment. Yet, because self-awareness is ever-deepening, there can be no end to our listening and learning.

The fourth special feature is that the cure is received through self-knowing, not through self-improvement—this is the difference between true-and-real and provisional realization. In the usual logic of spiritual seeking, I must perform various practices to bring about the sought-after awakening. My mind can readily grasp this logic. I strive to be an ethical person or a devout person, because I hope to eliminate my harmful thoughts, words, and deeds. I feel that my efforts deserve to be rewarded. Painfully, Shinran discovered that this comforting logic is not part of the cure. Instead, it is the aspect of our sickness that is hardest to overcome. Jōdo Shinshū challenges our customary reliance on ethical conduct and religious practices as a way of self-improvement.[241] Instead, the focus is on self-awareness, specifically, to know our own frailty, our inability to bring about a cure. Shinran expressed deep gratitude for the provisional teachings and practices that led him to recognize his sickness and thereby to receive the cure.

To recap, Śākyamuni Buddha taught a path of spiritual transformation which necessarily begins by recognizing that our apparent healthiness is an illusion. Initially we experience the human condition at the surface level like the prince in his palace, but the Buddha is pointing us toward the underlying reality where our sickness becomes evident and a remedy becomes available.

Shinran's achievement was to rediscover the spirit of Śākyamuni despite the corrupt religious climate of his day. Four distinguishing features of Jōdo Shinshū were noted. First, Shinran was a lapsed renunciant who sought the spiritual dimension within the struggles of everyday life. Second, he identified a model for the difficult spiritual development that he experienced, relying initially on provisional teachings as the natural starting point. Third, he came to understand that recognizing his sickness and receiving the cure are simultaneous. The cure is awareness of the self and awareness of the Dharma here and now, rather than future attainment. Fourth, Shinran found that spiritual self-reliance was part of his sickness rather than being the remedy.

Jōdo Shinshū arose in response to the social and religious crises of the Kamakura period, when the existing forms of Buddhism had lost touch with the heart and mind of Śākyamuni. Owing to the timelessness and depth of Shinran's insights, I believe that the path he identified is well adapted to our own troubled era. In our spiritual searching, can we too affirm that "Jōdo Shinshū is the path to realization that is now vital and flourishing?"

Part V

Our Rituals

It is impossible for us, who are possessed of blind passions, to free ourselves from birth-and-death through any practice whatever.[242]

—A Record in Lament of Divergences

What Is the Purpose?

Buddhism includes rituals such as offering incense, bowing, wearing a *nenju*, and chanting sutras—activities with no tangible benefit that would be discernible to a secularly minded outsider. But, if we gain no material advantage from such things, then what *is* the purpose? We might perform these actions automatically without pausing to reflect. However, in questioning the purpose we are brought to the heart of Shinran's teaching. In fact, his writings do not identify a positive role for *any* of the rituals we commonly perform at the temple. What might that tell us about Jōdo Shinshū?

Certainly, from religious practices one should not expect material benefits, such as curing an illness or becoming financially successful. Even so, in the spiritual dimension I might have a "gaining idea", such as, "I offer incense in order to purify myself," or "I recite Namo Amida Butsu in order to be born in the Pure Land." These are widely held religious views, but they are far removed from the teaching of Shinran. To recite the *myōgō* or Name of Amida is not the mechanism by which I become purified or attain Buddhahood. My relationship to the Name is that of a passive listener rather than an active reciter, as Shinran explains:

> It is the Name that is good, the Name that is the practice. When we speak [naïvely] of practice, we mean [our own good action]. The [*Hongan*] is clearly the Buddha's promise. When we have understood this, we see that the Vow is not our good, nor is it our practice.[243]

> Because Namo Amida Butsu arises wholly from *tariki* and is free of *jiriki*, it is neither a religious practice nor a good act on the part of the practitioner.[244]

Performing rituals at the temple may be seen as having a purpose, but it's always passive or indirect. Something happens to us, but this should not be seen as our achievement. Simply stated, the purpose is to prepare us to be better listeners. The only practice that is effective for liberating us is listening to the Dharma with self-reflection. Rituals are vital preparation, but when viewed as "good acts," they become a hindrance to understanding.

How does true listening take place? One way is by hearing a Dharma talk with a mind that is ready to reflect on the teachings. True listening is also the study and searching that we do on our own. Another way of listening is sharing our experiences with sangha members and learning from their life stories. The most significant words that we hear are "Namo Amida Butsu"—the command of limitless reality, telling us, "You there, wake up!" The Pure Land sutras and Shinran's writings are expanded versions of Namo Amida Butsu. For example, by chanting the words of the *Shōshinge* (i.e., *Kimyō muryōju nyorai / Namo fukashigi kō* ...) we may come to hear the Buddha's aspiration as an imperative. For Shinran, "to take refuge" (*Namo* or *Kimyō*) is "to be summoned by the *Hongan*; it is like the sovereign's command."[245]

A popular saying among Shin Buddhists is, "Reciting the Name is an expression of gratitude." In Shinran's writings, this refers to a person whose shinjin is "definitely settled (*ketsujō no shinjin*)" and who therefore recites the Name spontaneously to express gratitude for religious awakening.[246] Shinran gives only limited attention to the idea, but it was promoted by his descendants and is sometimes put forward as a stand-in for his entire teaching. A formula encoding it originated with Shinran's great-grandson, and it became a cornerstone of institutional doctrine.[247] This emphasis has drawbacks. First, it presupposes that the reciter is deeply familiar with Jōdo Shinshū, while leaving out the newcomer. Second, to express gratitude by recitation is actually a *consequence* of self-awareness, rather than a stand-in for it. For Shinran, the primary reason for saying Namo Amida Butsu is to hear and reflect on the meaning of the words telling us to wake up.[248] Foolish beings face a dilemma, in that the ego self is incapable of feeling genuine gratitude, which is necessarily spontaneous, not calculated. We cannot plan to be grateful, nor can we use recitation as a means to achieve it. Instead, we can allow our rituals serve their intended purpose, which is to prepare us for Dharma listening. Let's hear the meaning. *Namo Amida Butsu.*

The Chanting Experience[249]

Sutra chanting is given a place of prominence in Shin Buddhist services. The texts are in old-style Chinese or Japanese that cannot be deciphered unless one is familiar with the teachings of Pure Land Buddhism. Still, most people who participate in chanting would say that they experience something meaningful, even if they cannot articulate it clearly. The experience can be regarded as having a meditative aspect, a ritual aspect, and a learning aspect.

The *meditative* aspect of chanting is the same as the meditative aspect of sitting and breathing. Sitting quietly or chanting are ways of calming the mind and focusing on the present moment. Many people find these calming activities to be helpful before listening to a Dharma message. The meditative aspect of chanting is most evident when one does not know or think about the meaning of the text, but simply vocalizes each syllable.

Chanting also has a *ritual* aspect. Rituals are a way of bringing our views into alignment with a timeless message by reenacting events or stories that embody the teachings. Chanting before a Buddhist altar connects us with a continuous tradition going back to the time when the disciples of the Buddha preserved his sermons by memorizing and reciting them. We often chant *Sanbutsuge* and *Jūseige*, which are verses found in the *Larger Sutra*. The words are those of Dharmākara, the hero of the story told by Śākyamuni. Whenever these words are chanted, we are reenacting Dharmākara's story and establishing a link with the many disciples who transmitted this teaching down through the centuries. The ritual aspect of chanting includes a feeling of oneness that develops among the group of participants.

The *learning* aspect of chanting has to do with listening to the Dharma. Listening involves understanding the meaning of the words, despite the language barrier. If one tried to make an English translation suitable for chanting, it would be difficult to convey even a fraction of the meaning of the original text. Hence it is important for participants to gain a general awareness of the story by becoming familiar with an

English translation of the *Larger Sutra*. A further step is to study and appreciate the original Chinese text.

One of my teachers has said that to chant with no understanding is mysticism akin to the practices of tantric Buddhism. I tend to agree with him, although I think this is not necessarily true for newcomers—we encourage them to begin by experiencing only the meditative and ritual aspects. However, it would be a shame to stop there if one genuinely aspires to follow the Shin Buddhist path. For a person who has this aspiration, the learning aspect of chanting naturally follows from engaging with the teachings.

Why Meditate?

Twice I've been examined by Magnetic Resonance Imaging (MRI), a procedure that allows the doctor to check for health problems that would otherwise go undetected. The patient lies down and is slid inside the core of an electromagnet. Imaging can take up to thirty minutes, and you must lie completely still. It's close quarters in there and rather noisy, with machinery whirling around you. In some people, it can trigger claustrophobia. They find it unendurable and have to call off the exam or else be sedated. While I was in the apparatus, I closed my eyes, followed the breath, and kept still. Time passed quickly. Because I refrained from moving, the imaging took only twenty minutes. Upon emerging, I jokingly asked the technician if I made an *A* on the exam. He said, "You got an *A*+."

Having an easier time of it during MRI exams is a nice benefit of participating in meditation. Therapeutic benefits could be cited in connection with stress reduction and pain management, or in lessening the frustration of waiting in line. Not bad as far as utility. Given the benefits, the practice of sitting quietly seems to repay the modest effort that it costs us. However, thinking along those lines, i.e., calculating costs and benefits, is not the main reason to participate in meditation at a Shin Buddhist temple, nor is it likely to fulfill the deeper need that one may be feeling. A Zen teacher might make the same point, as indicated here:

> As long as one seeks some limited benefit from the practice, one simply uses it to enhance the very obstacle to true happiness, true peace, and true health. This obstacle is the sense of self, the personality, or, to use a much more familiar word, the ego. It is, in short, a selfish practice. To see the practice as useless is to see it as a gateway to liberation from the useful, to no longer be part of the machine.[250]

We might think that it is "useful" to sit quietly. We might seek some "limited benefit." But, if thinking in that way only enhances my ego, then my meditation would seem to be non-Buddhist in character.

On the other hand, we might choose to regard quiet sitting as a ritual, like bowing, chanting sutras, or offering incense. All of these are religious activities that cannot be explained in terms of usefulness. Clearly, they are not done in the hope of gaining a material reward, but we should go further and say that rituals like sitting or chanting are not techniques for self-improvement. Shin Buddhist awakening is not the result of my calculated efforts to perform religious practices. Rather, awakening occurs in spite of my calculations. I cease to be an active performer of practices, and I become a passive recipient of them.

The problem is not with religious practices themselves, but with what I am seeking from them. I chant, I meditate, I offer incense—I want a psychological reward for my effort. It's all I, I, I. But at some point, we may feel a need that is deeper than receiving a limited benefit, a need *not* to be distracted from matters of ultimate concern. We may have a desire to live authentically, to give up role-playing, to go beyond the idea of self-improvement. So, while it can be expedient at first to chant or meditate with the idea of being rewarded, we might eventually recognize this kind of thinking as provisional or temporary.

What ultimately concerns us and leads us to participate in Buddhist rituals is meeting with impermanence and doubting our secular values. If this does not occur, then we may never discover a spiritual dimension in life. Where is the spiritual dimension to be found? On the Shin Buddhist path, I do not look for an external means of transcendence. Rather, the path is to commit myself to a question, which can be expressed in various ways: What is impermanence? What is birth-and-death? What is Namo Amida Butsu? What am I? These are not everyday questions, for which I might be able to discover an answer. When I abandon the idea of self-improvement, I can commit myself to asking, What am I? Rituals like chanting and meditation help us, in spite of our calculated thinking, to embrace this path.

Reenactments

For it is a curious characteristic of our unformed species that we live and model our lives through acts of make-believe.[251]

—Joseph Campbell

Campbell's remark is not meant to be disparaging. As a student of mythology, he devoted his life to affirming the value of "acts of make-believe" that give structure to our lives.

Make-believe battles were part of my childhood. My friends and I pretended that we were cowboys or soldiers. We chased each other around the neighborhood, sometimes hiding in ambush, then suddenly leaping out, yelling, and aiming toy guns at each other. This was usually followed by an argument about which of us had "died" in the skirmish. Eventually, I gave up that sort of pretending. However, for quite a few adults, pretending to do battle is an ongoing interest. Their hobby is to perform *historical reenactments* while clad in replica uniforms and wielding armaments of a bygone era. Battle reenactments take place all over the world and represent many historical epochs from ancient Greece to World War II.

One time my wife and I were eating dinner at Stovepipe Wells in Death Valley with our friend Eileen. A man came into the restaurant and sat at the adjacent table. He was wearing the full uniform of a Roman legionnaire, and he proceeded to order his meal. After a while, Eileen could not contain her curiosity and blurted out, "Excuse me, but what's with the costume?" The soldier told us that he was part of a legion reenacting the Battle of Masada (73-74 CE), and he was preparing to go on a night march in Death Valley. Evidently, the non-authentic meal was allowed prior to curtain time.

Historical reenactments are not limited to military engagements. Often there is a religious theme such as the death of Jesus. Great attention is devoted to reproducing the gruesome details of what is said to have happened long ago. People seek meaning in their lives, and vivid reenactments enable them to find it. The more historical accuracy, the more meaningful the event becomes.

Another type of make-believe event is the *symbolic reenactment*, which aims to evoke timeless values rather than to achieve historical fidelity. The Olympic Games are a modern sports festival inspired by the ideals of ancient Greece. However, faithful replication of Greek athletic contests is not the goal. Religious rituals can be viewed similarly. For Christian believers the ceremony of Holy Communion reenacts the last supper of Jesus and his disciples, but it does not use historical stage sets or period costumes. That level of detail is unnecessary, because the meaning is conveyed through symbols, and not through literal replication of the original story line. This is the essence of a ritual; it is an acting out of a story that conveys a timeless idea. It serves very effectively to bring the minds of the participants into alignment with a universal message. Here are examples of symbolic reenactments practiced in the Buddhist Churches of America:

Hanamatsuri. To commemorate the birth of Siddhattha Gotama, the Flower Pavilion or *Hanamidō* is placed before the altar to display a small statue of the infant. In some temples, the pavilion rests on the back of a white elephant, which recalls the legend of the Buddha's miraculous conception. In addition to offering flowers, everyone attending may come forward and pour sweet tea over the statue to represent the soft rain that is said to have bathed the infant. By participating in the reenactment, we gain an appreciation for the importance of this birth. "How rare and wondrous it is to be able to listen to the Buddha-dharma, and now we are able to hear it." We would not be reciting those words if the Buddha had not been born.

Chanting. In the symbolic reenactment of sutra chanting, we join in a ritual that has been repeated countless times over 2500 years of Buddhist history. It brings to life the moment when the Buddha gave a particular teaching such as the *Amida Sutra*: *Nyo ze ga mon / ichi ji butsu zai / sha e koku / gi ju kik-ko doku on....* Chanting this text reenacts the moment when Śākyamuni first described Amida and the Pure Land to his disciples, and it signifies the transmission of the teaching from person to person over the centuries. To participate in chanting is to form a connection with the teacher Śākyamuni and with innumerable followers who preserved the teaching and who carried it throughout Asia and to the West.

Sutras begin with the statement, *Nyo ze ga mon,* "Heard this way by me." It's usually understood that the first person to make the statement was the disciple Ānanda whose prodigious memory allowed him to mentally record all of Śākyamuni's teachings as they were given. "By me" in *Nyo ze ga mon* also refers to each person who subsequently has received and transmitted the teaching. Joining in the ritual of chanting makes it our own *Nyo ze ga mon.*

Meditation. By sitting quietly before a Buddhist altar, we reenact the pivotal moment when Siddhattha Gotama took his seat beneath the Bodhi Tree, as depicted in this photo, taken at Shwedagon Pagoda in Yangon. Appearing behind Gotama is the tree trunk that signifies the "midpoint of the universe,"[252] the place of perfect equilibrium where all previous buddhas sat, the seat that he was worthy to occupy because of merit accumulated in his past lives. The ritual of quiet sitting also connects us with the story of Dharmākara's meditation in the *Larger Sutra* and with Shinran's one hundred days of seclusion at Rokkakudō. Meditation reenacts these timeless stories that can serve as a basis for our lives.

Here I have interpreted various symbolic reenactments, but to explain rituals in this manner may be unnecessary. The act of make-believe alone is often sufficient for the participant, without the need for a verbal explanation of what the reenactment means. For Campbell, the ceremonial sights and sounds have the power to speak to us at the level of the unconscious, where mythological themes originate.

> The characteristic effect of mythic themes and motifs translated into ritual, consequently, is that they link the individual to trans-individual purposes and forces.[253]

We become connected to purposes that go beyond our narrow self-centered concerns. We intuit the forces that link us with a universal human experience.[254] It is the Dharma reaching into our lives and illuminating the darkness of our egocentric minds.

> A ritual is an organization of mythological symbols; and by participating in the drama of the rite one is brought directly in touch with these [symbols], not as verbal reports of historic events, either past, present, or to be, but as revelations, here and now, of what is always and forever.[255]

Devotion and Morality

Religious belief systems generally entail claims that are unsupported by evidence, as for example, "The world was created in seven days," or "Good karma leads to a fortunate rebirth." Acceptance of such claims is based on *faith* rather than on empirical findings. While some adherents are untroubled (or even attracted) by a lack of evidence, it does tend to discourage secularly-minded people from accepting religious conversion. Hence, for religion to thrive, there must be strong motivating factors at work—factors that overcome skepticism toward its speculative claims.

British historian Edward Gibbon (1737-1794) was a freethinker and a shrewd observer of Abrahamic and pagan religions. He identified two principal characteristics that account for the enduring popular appeal of religious faith. The motivating factors are *practices of devotion* and *moral duties*:

> Every mode of religion, to make a deep and lasting impression on the human mind, must exercise our obedience by enjoining practices of devotion for which we can assign no reason; and it must acquire our esteem by inculcating moral duties analogous to the dictates of our own hearts.[256]

The first factor is to "exercise our obedience by enjoining practices of devotion." Believers are urged to perform reverential practices such as praying, worshiping, chanting, offering incense, and making donations. These actions are understood to be a manifestation of sincere religious feeling or commitment. Becoming obedient to the form of the practices will enhance our self-worth and will allow us, through a public display of devotion, to make a positive impression on the minds of fellow adherents. As Gibbon noted, "we can assign no reason" for devotional practices in terms of tangible benefits, but the psychological rewards are considerable.

The second factor by which religion impresses the human mind is to "acquire our esteem by inculcating moral duties analogous to the dictates of our own hearts." We look to religion to provide a stamp of moral goodness on our actions, whatever form those actions might take. History shows that religious morality lacks any absolute standard, and thus it encompasses both feeding the hungry and burning the heretics—and everything in between. We are drawn to the moral standard that corresponds most closely to our natural impulses ("the dictates of our own hearts"), whether such impulses are benevolent or cruel.[257]

Edward Gibbon never encountered Shinran's ideas, but if he had, he might have questioned whether Jōdo Shinshū can be categorized as a religion. (Here I equate Jōdo Shinshū with Shinran's teaching and life experience, and not with institutional Shin Buddhism, which clearly *is* a religion.) Shinran's teaching does not rely on the factors mentioned above. It overturns devotion and morality as methods of spiritual self-enhancement.

Beyond Devotion. In some forms of Pure Land Buddhism, Amida is portrayed as a divine savior. Reciting Amida's Name is understood to be a devotional practice, through which one attains birth in the Pure Land after death—whatever such a "birth" might mean.[258] However, to conceive of Amida as a personal savior (or any type of substantial entity) is not part of Jōdo Shinshū.[259] Concretely, Amida is the *words of teachers*—words such as "unhindered light" and "wisdom itself"[260]—that point to limitless reality or *dharma-kāya*. Therefore, Namo Amida Butsu is "neither a religious practice nor a good act on the part of the practicer."[261] For Shinran, there is no personal practice or good act that can liberate us from samsara. The *Larger Sutra* taught him the path of "hearing the Name" and reflecting on its meaning.[262] Hence, Amida's Name is not a devotional practice, but rather a command extending from limitless reality toward sentient beings via the words of teachers like Shinran. In plain English it means, "You there!" [*Namo*], "Wake up!" [*Amida Butsu*].

Beyond Morality. Religious morality divides the world into goodness and evilness, with the presumption that goodness is on the side of one's own religion. Shinran's teaching negates this notion. He admonishes us "to abandon the conviction that one is good, to cease relying on the self, to stop reflecting knowingly on one's evil heart, and further to abandon the judging of people as good and bad."²⁶³ He confesses, "I am such that I do not know right and wrong and cannot distinguish truth from falsehood. I lack even small love and small compassion, and yet, for fame and profit, I enjoy teaching others."²⁶⁴ And he upends our usual conceptions of moral judgement: "Even the good person is born in the Pure Land, so without question is the person who is evil."²⁶⁵ In the light of the Dharma, the duality of good and evil is made to disappear, and with it the capacity of religion to certify the moral goodness of our actions.

At the core of most religions (institutional Buddhism included), one finds a belief system based on factually unsupported claims about the world, reinforced by practices of devotion and by moral duties. Shinran's teaching is breathtaking in its rejection of these familiar attributes. What he experienced and articulated is a path to liberation through awareness of the self and awareness of *dharma-kāya*. On this path, we might take up devotional practices and moral duties, but by carefully examining our motives, we might see our self-centeredness more clearly. We might experience the limitations of the self and the limitlessness of *dharma-kāya*. This is the content of awakening in Jōdo Shinshū.²⁶⁶

'Meditation Is Not Part of Our Tradition'

Each temple in the Buddhist Churches of America has a unique style as far as customs that are observed. A custom that I particularly enjoy is to begin the service with incense offering and quiet, sitting meditation to musical accompaniment. Devoting a few minutes to self-reflection while taking in the sound and fragrance of the ceremony is an excellent way to begin. It helps us to focus on why we are there. No one would find this experience frustrating or difficult.

Let me suggest that, with only a slight adjustment, one can envision sitting quietly when nothing else is going on—no incense offering or musical accompaniment—simply sitting before a Buddhist altar. Although that adjustment might seem inconsequential, it is enough to cause concerns for some people. The experience might be perceived as frustrating and difficult. Services that include sitting quietly are offered at a number of temples in the BCA. However, the custom is not universal, and for some BCA members it is unacceptable.

Have you encountered this statement? "Meditation is not part of our tradition." I've heard it expressed by Shin Buddhist ministers and lay people. However, those making the statement have not offered specific interpretations that would enable me to understand their view. Here I will suggest some possible interpretations, and I will question the validity of the idea that "meditation is not part of our tradition." As I see it, meditation, when defined appropriately, has always been an aspect of the Shin Buddhist path, and it must continue to be so.

Consider what takes place at our meditation services. After finding a posture that is comfortable and alert, we sit quietly for ten minutes. We switch to standing quietly for five minutes, followed by another ten minutes of sitting. Then there is sutra chanting and a Dharma message by the minister or the assistant. The service concludes with incense offering. Quiet sitting and standing are a prelude to chanting and to hearing a Dharma talk. For this kind of meditation, there is no skill to be taught or acquired, and no prior experience is needed. Ministers and assistants trade off in leading meditation; no one becomes a guru for the participants.

Away from the temple, we are exposed to a popular culture that emphasizes speed and intensity. Hence, we attach value to a new experience if it is faster and louder than anything which preceded it. However, the speed and the intensity are *all artificial*; they are not the basis for an authentic way of living. Sitting quietly before the altar allows us to connect with what is authentic in our lives. It is an excellent way to prepare for listening to the teachings. When sitting quietly, we are not striving to accomplish anything—it is a respite from striving. Americans (being reward-minded) can readily understand meditation in a non-religious context, and thus they meditate to achieve results such as reducing stress and managing pain or addiction. However, to gain tangible benefits is not the idea behind sitting quietly before a Buddhist altar.

Our framework for meditation is well-suited to the needs of a Shin Buddhist sangha, yet, there may be objections from those who say that "meditation is not part of our tradition." Why would someone object? Let me offer three possible reasons.

Doctrine. One might object to meditation on doctrinal grounds: "It's not what Shinran teaches." This is a dubious objection. Much of what we do in the BCA is not "what Shinran teaches." He rejected established customs such as ordaining priests and chanting sutras.[267] He did not endorse placing a human-like image of Amida on the altar.[268] He had nothing to say concerning *bon odori*.[269] However, no one today insists that these customs should be discarded.

As a monk on Mt. Hiei, Shinran diligently followed the path of Tendai Buddhism, including austere practices such as continuous walking meditation and repetitively circling the mountain. After years of practice and study, Shinran reached an impasse. He then abandoned *all* religious practices, as they were understood in his day. According to Eshinni's letter, Shinran left the mountain "to seclude himself for a hundred days in the Rokkakudō temple. There he prayed concerning his next life."[270] Certainly, he was finished with austerities. Through quiet reflection on what his path should be, Shinran engaged in the first Jōdo Shinshū meditation. After this period of seclusion, he was ready to become the first Jōdo Shinshū Dharma listener. Sitting quietly to prepare for listening to Hōnen was good enough for Shinran. So, without a doubt, to sit quietly is an excellent way for us to prepare to receive the teachings. It is entirely consistent with Shinran's life example and is on more secure ground doctrinally than nearly all of the customs that are common in the BCA.[271]

Shinran's actions closely echo the story of Gotama, who became the historical Buddha. After practicing austerities for six years and reaching an impasse, Gotama abandoned all religious practices and sat quietly under a tree. His fellow practitioners believed that he had given up the quest, but what he had done was to transcend the limitations of his former approach. The same can be said of Shinran. He transcended the limitations of the religious practices of his day.

Institution. Another basis for objecting to meditation is institutional: "It's not what Hongwanji does." Hongwanji is the headquarters in Japan for our sect of Shin Buddhism. And it's true that Hongwanji does not emphasize sitting quietly to prepare for listening. On this basis, one could say that "meditation is not part of our tradition." However, institutional Buddhism in Japan is, by and large, a response to the needs of a time and culture far removed from 21st century America. Hongwanji leaders recognize the need for Shin Buddhism to adapt to American culture, and they are generally supportive of our efforts to do that.

Then there is Shinran's radicalism to consider. His meditation at Rokkakudō established a new direction—he broke from the Buddhist institutions of his day. Significantly, he did not identify a role in Jōdo Shinshū for the rituals that his descendants adopted and popularized. This follows a pattern noted by historians: after the founder of a movement dies, it's necessary to show that the founder's authority has been transferred to the institution.[272] And so, in the centuries after Shinran's passing, a need was discovered for impressive buildings and ceremonies,[273] which might be seen as contradicting Shinran's life example. Here in the BCA we perform rituals, but we have no need to assert the authority of the institution. The purpose of our rituals is always passive rather than assertive. In America we are on firm ground in not trying to replicate "what Hongwanji does."

Experience. Objections to meditation might reflect personal history: "It's not like when I was growing up." Many BCA members enjoy the recollection of childhood experiences at the temple. Some might prefer to see services being conducted in the same manner as was done decades ago. Those childhood experiences probably did not include sitting quietly before the altar. Hence, someone might say that "meditation is not part of our tradition."

I was given a non-Buddhist religious upbringing. Going to church entailed activities that were quite different from what is done in the BCA. However, I abandoned those practices long ago. That has been my path to spiritual growth. In Buddhism, spiritual growth, or engaging with impermanence, is mandatory. Different levels of appreciation for the teachings apply during childhood, during our years of maturity, and during old age. Our life experiences let us discover greater depth in the teachings. Inevitably, we fall into distorted views of Buddhism and distorted views of the self, so the path involves discarding each of our former views in turn. Rather than holding on to our childhood view, I think it's advisable to be open to experiences that differ from what was done when we were growing up. That is my suggestion.

I have mentioned three possible reasons why someone might claim that "meditation is not part of our tradition." I don't find any of these reasons compelling, but there might be others that I am unaware of. For now, however, I will continue to think that meditation—sitting quietly as a prelude to Dharma listening—is appropriate for Shin Buddhists in America, and that it is consistent with the teachings of Shinran.

'I Am Incapable of Any Other Practice'

In the Buddhist Churches of America, we benefit from a diversity of views concerning the teachings. Often in organized religion the opposite situation prevails, namely, the exclusion of certain ideas in the interest of doctrinal uniformity. It's tempting to think, "Only my idea is valid; anything that disagrees with it is false," or, "Only one religion can be true, and mine is the one." We take an absolutist view about ideas to which we are deeply attached. However, this kind of thinking is contrary to the spirit of Mahāyāna Buddhism, which encourages us to question fixed ideas, rather than cling to them.

When we hear contradictory views concerning the teachings, instead of causing discomfort, it should be an opportunity for reflection. Are my ideas about Buddhism justified? Am I deepening my understanding if I only encounter teachers who say things that I agree with? This is an excellent reason for paying attention to teachers from Buddhist traditions other than our own. In so doing, we are better able to place Shinran in the context of Buddhism as a whole and to appreciate his uniqueness. Or, we may find that Shinran's teaching is not for us. Shinran, on two occasions, came to a turning point and concluded that the path he had been on would not lead him to liberation. Twice he made a complete change of direction.[274]

I once attended a lecture by a nun of the Tibetan Buddhist tradition, in which the key ideas are quite different from what is taught in Shin Buddhism. The teacher made a statement that really struck me: "As the end of our life approaches, only our spiritual practice will be of any benefit." If I might interpret, in the last days or hours of our life we are faced with giving up everything that has been of value to us— everything, that is, but the spiritual practice that we have cultivated. Only this practice will benefit us. I suspect that people with non-Buddhist views would disagree with this way of thinking. They might say that, on the contrary, having strong ties to family and friends will be of benefit at the end of one's life.[275] Or they might point to personal accomplishments that will provide a sense of fulfillment. Each person must ask what will be of benefit at the end of life, and then strive to cultivate it. This is a matter that should be of ultimate concern for us, whether or not we pursue a spiritual path.

The statement by the Tibetan teacher leads to the topic of rebirth. Within Buddhism there are traditions that teach practices leading to a *favorable rebirth* into a future existence. For the moment, I am putting aside any metaphorical interpretation of rebirth, and I am speaking about literal transmigration. That is how many Buddhists around the world understand repetitive birth and death in samsara, the world of suffering. It is cyclic existence as a deluded being on an endless treadmill. Rebirth, taken broadly, cannot be considered an advantageous outcome. But in a narrow sense, "favorable rebirth" means to avoid being born in one of the three evil realms of hell, hungry ghosts, and animals. The other three realms, considered to be good, relatively speaking, are the fighting demons, human beings, and heavenly beings. The objective of spiritual practices is to be reborn in one of the good realms, especially that of human beings. And within the human realm, the best outcome is to be born as a person who becomes a follower of a buddha. Eventually, assuming this favorable trend continues over many lives, one can hope to become a buddha oneself, and to be forever liberated from birth and death in samsara.

"As the end of our life approaches, only our spiritual practice will be of any benefit." The Tibetan teacher was referring, in part, to practices leading to a favorable rebirth. What is the spiritual practice that might lead, after many lives, to the most favorable outcome of becoming a buddha? For a lay person, it is to follow a meritorious way of life. The layperson's practice is to cultivate thoughts, words, and deeds that are wholesome, while avoiding thoughts, words, and deeds that cause harm. However, a monk or a nun is considered to have the best opportunity to cultivate such a life by, among other things, subsisting on alms-food, studying the scriptures, and meditating. These are the Buddhist practices that will be of benefit as death approaches; they define one type of answer to the question that should be of ultimate concern.

How might we evaluate the practices recommended here? First, consider whether the idea of transmigration from physical death to rebirth is literally true. This is the bedrock of Indian spirituality, but for most Westerners, it is far from obvious. From my perspective, the question of literal rebirth is speculative and unanswerable. The same can be said regarding the effectiveness of practices for a favorable rebirth: I cannot determine whether the practices do, in fact, lead to that outcome, in accord with the principle of karmic recompense. However, there is a different question that I can answer without resorting to speculation: Am I capable of performing the practices recommended for a layperson, namely, to embrace that which is wholesome and to avoid that which is harmful? Very likely, given my background, the answer is No. I cannot prepare myself for death and for the next existence in the manner prescribed. So, I do not need to answer speculative questions concerning literal rebirth. And rebirth, favorable or otherwise, is *not* the final goal. Instead, the aim of the Buddhist path is liberation from repetitive birth and death in samsara.[276]

The literal view described here represents, at least in part, the perspective of a cross-section of Buddhists around the world. For them, it establishes a suitable path that provides a direction for their lives. However, their path is not one that I can access, and it is quite unlike the Buddhism that I learn from Shinran. For me, Jōdo Shinshū is the most suitable path, and in fact, the *only* Buddhist path that I can follow. Eight centuries ago, Shinran reached the same conclusion:

> ... if I were capable of realizing Buddhahood by other religious practices and yet fell into hell for saying the nembutsu, I might have dire regrets for having been deceived. But since I am absolutely incapable of any religious practice, hell is my only home.
>
> ... In brief, such is the [shinjin] of this foolish one. Now, whether you accept the nembutsu, entrusting yourself to it, or reject it, that is your own decision.[277]

This statement demonstrates what it means to be an authentic teacher of Buddhism. An authentic teacher does not take an absolutist view, saying, "Only my idea is valid; all others are false." In fact, Shinran does not portray himself as a teacher, but rather as a student, as a person whose views are provisional and subject to error. From Shinran I receive an understanding of Buddhist practice that is quite different from what I described earlier. Yet, I think the statement cited above is still appropriate: "As the end of our life approaches, only our spiritual practice will be of any benefit." Shinran might say much the same thing.

What is a spiritual practice? It is that which brings about a transformation of our minds. Generally, it is understood to be an activity that "I perform," and, quite naturally, it's referred to as "my practice." I bow, I offer incense, I meditate, I chant sutras, I donate my time and money. Outside of Shin Buddhism, this is how a spiritual practice is usually construed, namely, volitional actions performed in a religious context. Exerting effort in this way becomes the mechanism for realizing the transformation of our minds. This easy logic applies to the everyday tasks that I face: if I make efforts in the right direction, then I can control the outcome so that things turn out in my favor. *Your Results, Your Way*—says a recent advertisement for a health club. Or applied in a Buddhist context, "If I perform meritorious actions, then I will have a favorable rebirth"—my spiritual self-reliance is thereby rewarded. In Shin Buddhist terminology, this is the mind of *jiriki* or self power.

Shinran, having made such efforts over many years, concluded that he would never achieve liberation in that manner. He recognized that there are *no* practices he might perform that would be the mechanism for transforming his mind:

Now, amid the five defilements in the last dharma-age,
Sentient beings are incapable of practice and realization;
Hence the teachings that Śākyamuni left behind
Have all passed into the naga's palace.[278]

For foolish beings in the last Dharma-age it's necessary to have the steps reversed: self-awareness, the transformation of the mind, comes first, which establishes the framework for actions that are reflective of the transformation. The spiritual practice set forth in the *Larger Sutra* is not an activity that I perform, it is an understanding that I receive. So, it's not accurate to call it "my practice" or "my understanding."

> True-and-real practice and shinjin are the accomplishment of the inconceivable Vow, the ocean of absolute reality and true suchness (*ichijitsu shinnyo kai*). This accords with the teaching of the *Larger Sutra*—the authentic meaning of *tariki*'s true essence.[279]

Limitless, formless reality breaking in on me is known as *tariki*. On the path identified by Shinran, this breaking in takes place through "hearing the Name"—Namo Amida Butsu. It is to receive a command by way of Buddhist teachers who are performing "the great practice."

> The great practice is to [praise] the Name of the Tathāgata of unhindered light. This practice, embodying all good acts and possessing all roots of virtue, is perfect and most rapid in bringing them to fullness. It is the treasure ocean of virtues that is suchness or true reality (*shinnyo ichijitsu kudoku hōkai*). For this reason, it is called great practice.[280]

This passage is from Shinran's commentary on the fulfillment of the 17th Vow of the *Larger Sutra*, known as "the Vow that all the Buddhas praise the Name." It's evident here and in other passages that he ascribes "the great practice" to countless Buddhas, rather than to foolish beings who recite the Name.[281] The metaphorical depiction in the 17th Vow is actualized in historical teachers ("all the Buddhas") who elucidate the meaning of the *Larger Sutra* ("praise the Name"). Nevertheless, self-power recitation of the Name, as a provisional practice, may still lead foolish beings to the true hearing of the Name expressed in the 18th Vow.[282]

In simple English, *tariki* is the command, "You there, wake up!" The Pure Land sutras and all of Shinran's writings are translations and elaborations thereof. The scriptures are stating in various ways what it means to have self-awareness, what it means to be a foolish being burdened with blind passions. Recognizing one's foolishness and awakening to *Hongan* is liberation in Shin Buddhism. This awareness is not brought about by actions that I perform. Rather, it is an understanding that arises unexpectedly when the Dharma breaks in on me and as I respond to what life itself is teaching. In the Shin Buddhist life of awakening there is no need for rebirth into a future existence. The present life ends in perfect completion or Buddhahood.

For Shinran, *tariki* is none other than the power of Amida's *Hongan*.[283] It is the command coming from limitless reality that negates our spiritual self-reliance and leads to the transformation of our minds. And, I suspect that as the end of life approaches, as we give up everything else that we have valued, only this transformation will be of benefit.

> No matter how loving of a parent or spouse we may be, since we are alone at our birth, we will also be alone at our death. Each one of us must die alone. Yet when each one of us dies alone, bringing along nothing else with us, there will still be one single treasure that we will surely have: the nembutsu.[284]

Part VI

Our Community

"Just as the Ganges river slants, slopes, and inclines towards the ocean, and keeps pushing into the ocean, in the same way Master Gotama's assembly—with both laypeople and renunciants—slants, slopes, and inclines towards nibbāna, and keeps pushing into nibbāna." [285]

—Mahāvaccha Sutta

Becoming a Truth-Seeker

During services at the temple we often recite the Three Treasures text, which contains a call to action: *If I do not transcend the world of delusion in this life, when will I ever attain spiritual liberation?* Liberation is the aim of the Buddhist path, and to follow this path we must find a gate or point of entry. Without it we will continue to live unexamined lives, putting up with our troubles or complaining about them—experiencing moments of happiness, but mostly just running out the clock on our brief existence. Entering a Dharma gate can be the turning point, the moment when we begin to find meaning in all things.

One of my teachers has identified two levels at which we may approach Buddhism, the first being the *practical level*.[286] Here, listening to the teachings can help us respond to difficulties like work-related stress, parenting, elder care, or a death in the family. By reading Buddhist books or by joining a sangha, we learn to cope with our troubles and to arrive at a greater level of happiness. Receiving this kind of help may be a point of entry to the path. It is described as the stage of "practicers who pray for worldly benefits."[287] We hope to experience less unhappiness and more happiness as we become attuned to ethical conduct and religious practices. This is a necessary stage, but we may come to see it as provisional or incomplete.

The second way of approaching Buddhism is at the *truth-level*. Truth-seeking can be metaphysical (What, ultimately, is true?), but for Shinran it is always psychological (What, truly speaking, is my motivation? What is my deepest wish?). Here the Dharma awakens the aspiration for Buddhahood, the perfect fulfillment of one's life. It is to realize something that goes beyond worldly benefits, namely, to meet with impermanence and to learn what I truly am. Shinran calls this aspiration *hikkyō-e*—that which can be relied on when nothing else works—that which remains when our other aspirations are gone.

Seeking the truth about myself is different from pursuing happiness and avoiding unhappiness. If I'm happy or unhappy I tend to view these mental states as absolutes. I cling to ideas that are reassuring and turn away from those that are troubling. However, these impressions are not inevitable or absolute. They are projections based on the judgments I make about people and events. By approaching Buddhism at the truth-level, I begin to transform this limited view. I start to appreciate the Buddha's all-encompassing wisdom which finds value in all experiences, including things that formerly I saw as being negative and meaningless.[288] Thus, everything in life can become a source of insight.

Regarding the practical level, it is sometimes said that we can learn "to apply Shin Buddhism in our lives." The phrase suggests that we *make use* of Shin Buddhism, a teaching we regard as external to us. Certainly, we can instrumentalize Buddhistic ideas from *other* traditions, but with Jōdo Shinshū our assumptions are upended. Rather than applying it for some limited benefit, Shinran's teaching is concerned with the transformation of one's entire being, or in Rev. Gyodo Haguri's phrase, a "mind and body revolution."[289] At first, such a transformation seems remote from my concerns. I feel attracted only by the prospect of practical results. I am satisfied with trying to live a more ethical life, and I may have no interest in what Shin Buddhism teaches at the truth-level. Nevertheless, the Dharma is still able to reach me if I am not totally closed off. An indication that this is happening is that I come to feel dissatisfied with my approach.

Shinran tried to become an ethical person and then to become a devout person, but dissatisfaction led him to recognize the provisional nature of his goals.[290] Through seriously questioning his motivations, he encountered Jōdo Shinshū. His phrase describing this transformation is *tennyū gankai*, "to turn and enter the ocean of the Buddha's Vow." It's a wonderful metaphor for Shin Buddhist awakening. Shinran devoted his life to seeking the truth, because he met a teacher who embodied the Dharma:

> *Through countless kalpas and innumerable lives,*
> *We did not know the [powerful condition] of liberation;*
> *Were it not for our teacher [Hōnen],*
> *This present life also would pass in vain.*[291]

Let me personalize the thought. Were it not for the Buddhist teachers I have met, my present life too would pass in vain. May we continue to reflect on the Three Treasures text and its call to action: if I do not become a truth-seeker in this life, when will I ever attain spiritual liberation?

Creating a Favorable Environment

I learned about creating a favorable environment for Dharma listening from an experience while visiting Japan. My wife and I were in Kyoto with a tour group to attend the 750th memorial service for Shinran. The photo shows our arrival at Nishi Hongwanji, at which time we were met by a man wearing a minister's robe who promptly *scolded* Janis and me for being members of Orange County Buddhist Church, a temple that offers meditation services. We were taken aback, because the critic had never seen us before and knew nothing of our Buddhist path, apart from our temple affiliation. He seemed to be speaking as a representative of Nishi Hongwanji, but I suspect that he was voicing his own opinion under color of authority. The critic then announced that we were deceived in our views (evidently, he was a mind-reader), and that it was imperative for us to adopt *his* belief system, which he proposed to explain. We declined the offer.

While an out-of-the-blue reprimand for visitors seems to have nothing to do with the path of Śākyamuni, we as Buddhist followers become attached to views. The critic's claim was that offering meditation services is not a legitimate activity for a Jōdo Shinshū temple, that is, a temple that professes adherence to the teachings of

Shinran. I think this claim was based on ignorance of the framework for meditation that we use, and on a view of Shinran's teachings that is quite different from mine. In fact, our meditation framework is very much in keeping with Jōdo Shinshū and with Shinran's life example.[292]

The critic implied that there is a litmus test against which temple activities can be measured for conformity with Shinran's teaching. Let's take him up on that! If I held a doctrinaire view, I would conclude that *many* aspects of life in BCA temples get a failing grade. According to Eshinni, Shinran rejected the practice of chanting sutras. There is no suggestion that he observed Tendai-derived rituals such as the *raiban* ceremony. In the BCA a human-like image of Amida is generally placed on the altar, which differs from Shinran's preference for a scroll showing the *myōgō* in Chinese characters. He lamented the popularity of the term *Hotoke*, which is still heard today as a nickname for Amida Buddha. Most strikingly, Shinran did not advocate having temples or priests on the Jōdo Shinshū path. I offer these observations to demonstrate that the critic's idea of a universal litmus test for temple activities was misguided. One should not be too judgmental about activities that our sangha members find to be helpful.

We are able to convey only a hint of Shinran's teaching to seekers who have just begun to encounter Buddhism. Learning to appreciate Jōdo Shinshū is the work of a lifetime. The Buddha-dharma and Shinran's understanding of it can never become stale. Always there is something new to challenge us, something that says we must go still deeper on this path of self-awareness. When I first came to Orange County Buddhist Church, I was in no position to appreciate the Pure Land sutras or Shinran's writings. Fortunately, there was an introductory class on Buddhism that inspired me to keep coming back. It was my gateway or point of entry to the sangha. For some people who come to our temple, meditation services have been the point of entry.

Shinran expressed his appreciation for "provisional" teachings that serve as a necessary stage on the path leading to the "true" teaching.[293] The various customs that are observed at the temple can be viewed in this way—as an expedient means to create a setting in which true Dharma listening is possible. Even so, there is no guarantee that listening will take place; the decision to engage rests with each person, and many choose not to.[294] But meditation services and other activities do help to foster a favorable environment for Dharma listening. At our temple all of these gateways are open for people who choose to walk through them.

Our brush with the critic caused me to feel disconnection and alienation, especially because it took place in a Buddhist context. It was unlike any other experience I have had in Japan. However, in day-to-day encounters with American popular culture, my feeling of disconnection is numbingly familiar. In America, the situation where I feel most connected is in our Buddhist sangha. It's why I am deeply grateful when we can gather at the temple to hear the Dharma.

Remembering Our Predecessors

What is the Buddhist Churches of America? Principally, it's us. The BCA consists of the ministers and members of temples and affiliated sanghas, and the headquarters organization that owns some buildings and employs a few staff people. At present, there are about sixty active (or semi-active) groups within the US mainland. Here, I will reflect on the path followed by our predecessors who created the BCA.

Starting in 1899, Shin Buddhist groups began to be established in the US and Canada under the *Hokubei Bukkyōdan* (Buddhist Mission to North America), a propagation arm of the Nishi Hongwanji sect in Japan. In the early decades of the 20th century, the sanghas were composed mostly of people of Japanese ancestry, that is, first-generation immigrants, the *issei*, and their children, the *nisei*. Most of the ministers were born and educated in Japan, and the teachings were transmitted primarily in the Japanese language. To the extent that there was outreach by the ministers to European-Americans, it was by teaching Theravāda-style general Buddhism,[295] for the reason that Jōdo Shinshū was seen as a Japanese ethnic religion.

World War II brought dramatic changes, as most of the membership was imprisoned in camps such as Manzanar, Heart Mountain, and Tule Lake. With ties to Hongwanji cut off, the path forward would have to be set by the US members. In 1943-1944 the sanghas were reincorporated as a new organization—the BCA—with an elected governing board of *nisei* Japanese Americans.[296] Changing the name of the organization to the Buddhist Churches of America was a way of announcing that this is Buddhism *of* America, and no longer just Buddhism *coming to* America. The word "churches" was introduced with the same intent, to indicate that Shin Buddhism is an American religion. Nowadays, some of us might prefer not to call ourselves churches, but in the context of the incarceration it's apparent why the name BCA was adopted. Considering the predicament of those in camp, establishing the new organization was an amazing expression of optimism. The people who took this step anticipated that they would have a future outside of the barbed wire, that their rights under the Constitution would be recognized, and that eventually the government would view them as Americans entitled to due process. At the time, there was no assurance that these hopes would be fulfilled.

Hope for the future was the outward-directed message conveyed by the name change. There was also an inward-directed message for sangha members. To call the organization the Buddhist Churches of America was an assertion that Shin Buddhism would become part of the broader culture. It marked a generational change for the sanghas, and a shift toward transmitting the teachings in English. Americanization of Buddhism was already underway in the pre-war years, but it accelerated in the camps with the introduction of "sermons at Sunday services and the adoption of Christian-originated terms such as 'minister' and 'reverend' to refer to Buddhist priests."[297] Other adaptations were the singing of Protestant-style hymns on Buddhist subjects (*gāthās*) accompanied by piano or organ, and the printing of service books containing chanting texts, as well as Buddhist invocations, creeds, scripture passages, and benedictions, all in Biblical-style archaic English.[298]

The world is continually changing, despite our wishing that certain things would stay the same. It must have been difficult for *issei* Shin Buddhist followers to accept the evolution of their tradition here in the US. The religion of their ancestors was being transformed into something Americanized and seemingly foreign. It was becoming less and less like what they grew up with.

In Japan as well, Shin Buddhism had been undergoing a painful transformation that was long in the making.[299] In 1603 the Tokugawa shogunate was established, initiating the Edo period when Japan was closed to the outside world. It was an era of social stability in which the political and religious authorities were closely connected. Shinran had lived centuries earlier, but the dynamism of his path was still enough to cause concerns, and to promote his writings would not do at all, owing to his vehement criticism of the Imperial Court and the Buddhist monks.[300] Hence, in the Edo period the creative spiritual content of Jōdo Shinshū was deemphasized, and Shin Buddhist institutions became doctrinally frozen. Shinjin was portrayed as dualistic faith rather than self-awareness. Jōdo Shinshū, so conceived, served to ease anxiety about the afterlife and had no value in this life:[301]

> It goes without saying that shinjin was never considered to be an experience of awakening, or a way of life in which one's old self is cast off and one realizes the growth of a new self. Instead, shinjin became a form of intoxication, for it encouraged people to close their eyes to the real contradictions present in their lives and submissively obey the prevailing political system.[302]

Consequently, Shin Buddhism did not run afoul of the government:

> By preaching to their followers to practice perseverance in hardship (even though such suffering was caused by the social structure itself) and to long for a better afterlife, Honganji leaders reinforced the existing social order. The theory of the "two truths" [ōbō-buppō] thus served as an ideology of Shin Buddhism by which its authorities separated mundane rules (the laws of this world) and spiritual principles (salvation in the afterlife), and demanded that followers understand and accept their social positions.[303]

The Meiji Revolution of 1868 brought the shogunate to an end and started Japan's transition from a pre-modern society to a technological one. In the rush to modernize, Buddhism was seen by some as an archaic foreign religion, a relic that should be abolished and replaced with Japan's original spirituality of Shintō and with ideas from Western thinkers.[304] In the early years of the Meiji period, Buddhists were subjected to persecution, but eventually, rather than attempting to abolish Buddhist institutions, the government chose to negotiate for their support. Shin Buddhists, for their part, "sought to reach a compromise with heterogeneous religious traditions by advocating the theory that Buddhism, Shintō, and Confucianism essentially taught the same thing."[305] Acceptance of the "conformity among the three teachings" restored the tight connection with the government that had existed in the Edo period, and in so doing, it devalued Shinran's path to liberation.[306]

At that time there were Buddhist teachers who believed that going back to the Edo framework was impossible. They attempted the difficult task of reforming Shin Buddhism from within. A pioneer in this effort was Rev. Manshi Kiyozawa (1863-1903).[307] Although he died young, having been mostly unsuccessful in his reform movement, he inspired a group of successors who became influential in the 20th century. Consistent with Shinran's actual teachings, they brought a renewed focus on the Indian origin of Buddhism and on the individual experience of awakening, to be felt here and now. Their most significant contribution was the idea that Jōdo Shinshū, as lived by Shinran, is a universal path to spiritual liberation.[308] When Japan was shut off from the outside world, there was no reason to think of Shin Buddhism in that manner, and so the tradition took on the flavor of a folk religion.[309] Rev. Kiyozawa and his students sought to overturn that view.

Now let's return to the founding of the BCA and the process by which Shin Buddhism was taking a new form as an American religion. I consider it extremely fortunate that a handful of reformers in Japan had rediscovered the universality of Shinran's teachings. If this rediscovery had not taken place, and if those ideas had not been nurtured at our temple, then my wife and I would never have encountered the Buddhist path. America's technological and multi-ethnic society is utterly different from Japan under the shogunate. Impermanence has accelerated, and cultural changes occur with dizzying speed. The blended form of Shin Buddhism was suited to the Edo period. For me, practice and realization on that path "died out long ago," just as Shinran said in his day regarding the Path of Sages.

Shinran lived and wrote in 13th century Japan. Yet, in reflecting seriously on his words rather than on institutional forms, we will find that his teachings resonate powerfully in our present circumstances. As with Gotama before him, Shinran's teachings are not limited to a specific historical period or locality. The psychological depth of his experience speaks to us directly in 21st century America. This is what enables Shin Buddhism to take its place as an American religion, in accord with the aspiration of the BCA's founders.

In remembering our predecessors, let's reflect on the BCA sanghas that no longer exist. Although many temples and affiliated groups are doing well, others are in decline. Around thirty sanghas that once gathered in central and southern California have become inactive or extinct, as is the case in the Imperial Valley, an agricultural area that extends from the Salton Sea to the Mexican border. Prior to World War II, the cities of Brawley and El Centro were home to thriving Japan towns. The history of those pre-war communities is documented at the Imperial Valley Pioneers' Museum in El Centro, which includes the beautifully curated Japanese American Gallery. One of the items on display is a *kanshō*, or Buddhist calling bell which, sadly, has not been rung for service since 1942. The text embossed on it says, *Bu-Ro-Re Bukkyō Kai* (Brawley Buddhist Church). The bell was dedicated on the occasion of Hanamatsuri in 1933, when there were sanghas in Brawley and in El Centro. Most of the members spent the war years at the Poston and Gila camps in Arizona, and their temples never re-opened. Because of hostility toward Japanese Americans, very few former residents returned to the Imperial Valley when they were released from camp. The Brawley temple building was demolished long ago, while the one in El Centro is now a Sikh temple. The altar furnishings from El Centro Buddhist Church are in use today at the Buddhist Temple of San Diego, after the original San Diego furnishings were destroyed by an arson fire in 1943.[310]

Everything in the world is continually changing. Our predecessors made the Shin Buddhist path available to us, but our path is not identical to the one that they followed. I will conclude with a quotation from Chinese master Tao-ch'o which Shinran copied out on the final page of his *Kyōgyōshinshō*:

> My wish is that those who have attained birth may lead those who come after them and those who aspire for birth may follow their predecessors, thus following one after another endlessly and uninterruptedly until the boundless sea of birth-and-death is exhausted.[311]

Institutional Buddhism

Given that impermanence is our most basic teaching, you might imagine that change would come easily for Buddhists, but that is not the case. I recognize impermanence in the world around me, and often I can be persuaded to accept it, but I protest when impermanence barges into my comfort zone. Extend the thought to a religious organization, and change becomes extremely difficult. Buddhists are often resistant to change, despite the respect that they accord to the truth of impermanence.

Sociologists have identified a recurring pattern in the history of religious organizations.[312] Generally, a new movement is associated with a founder who has extraordinary personal qualities. Gotama, Jesus, Mohammed, Martin Luther, Joseph Smith, Jr.—these are leading examples. The founder's charisma is so compelling that the new path gains momentum. As disciples spread the message, it starts to have mass appeal. But the movement faces a crisis when the founder exits history. Indeed, the sutras predict that the Buddha's teachings will die out, as the memory of his life example fades in succeeding generations.[313]

Religious movements can be perpetuated if institutional authority takes the place of individual charisma. Thus, an organization arises that is understood to be the authentic representative of the founder. The longevity of the organization is not limited by the life span of any one person. Its authority is supported by a hierarchy of priests and by monumental architecture as a symbolic expression of power. As for the teachings, no matter how creative they may have been during the founder's lifetime, they must now be codified in doctrines, which are selected and ratified by the founder's immediate successors. For good measure, the founder may be elevated to divine status. Such are the steps in a recipe for extreme resistance to change by religious organizations.

The pattern for the evolution of religious movements has played out many times in the history of Buddhism. A founding teacher, whether it be Gotama or Shinran, is succeeded by an official hierarchy, and his teachings become encoded in articles of faith. Yet, the pattern is a source of tension, because the authentic spirit of the Buddha is at odds with any attempt to capture it in fixed doctrines.[314] Impermanence or continual change negates our attachment to such views. The dilemma is that Buddhism cannot remain authentic if it is institutionalized, yet we would never receive the teachings if they had not been transmitted down through the centuries by the institutions.

In this regard, Shinran is as much of a paradox as Gotama. Upon leaving the monastery, and for the remaining sixty years of his life, he was an utterly non-institutional person.[315] Shinran never accommodated himself to the factions that had persecuted his teacher's sangha. In a category-defying statement, he declared, "I am now neither a Buddhist monk nor a lay follower (*hisō hizoku*)."[316] He did not see himself as the founder of a sect, but as a student of Hōnen and of Jōdo Shinshū, the tradition transmitted by the Pure Land masters.

> But if you imagine in me some special knowledge of a path to birth other than the nembutsu or of scriptural writings that teach it, you are greatly mistaken. If that is [your thought], since there are many eminent scholars in the southern capital of Nara or on Mt. Hiei to the north, you would do better to meet with them and inquire fully about the essentials for birth.... For myself, I do not have even a single disciple.[317]

Although many regarded Shinran as their teacher, he saw himself as a student, no different from his "fellow practicers" (*dōgyō*) or "fellow Dharma-friends" (*dōbō*). Not being content with a fixed understanding of the teachings, his path was a continual search for new meaning in the sutras and commentaries. Yet, after his death, Shin Buddhism became hierarchical and authoritarian—the same outcome as had taken place in Gotama's community. The most surprising of the changes made by Shinran's descendants was hereditary leadership succession, introduced in the 1330s by Kakunyo to cement his authority.[318] As far as I'm aware, no basis for this custom is to be found in any prior Buddhist teaching. When Gotama was asked who would lead the community after his passing, he declined to answer, saying, "I do not think in these terms."³¹⁹ Nor does it appear that Shinran named a successor, having disowned his ambitious son Zenran.³²⁰

We would have great difficulty finding the path without organizations to preserve and transmit the teachings. Yet, their nature is to preserve the teachings to the point of fossilization. The essential spirit of creativity becomes hidden: "The pure dharma is concealed in dormancy."³²¹ Still, Buddhist history shows that stagnation does not continue indefinitely. Around the 1ˢᵗ century BCE, Mahāyāna Buddhism emerged to revive the spirit of Gotama's life and teachings, eventually to undergo its own period of decline. During the 12ᵗʰ and 13ᵗʰ centuries in Japan, a number of charismatic monks, including Hōnen and Shinran, abandoned traditional forms of Mahāyāna to establish new directions. With the passing of time, each of the new paths became institutionalized and even fossilized.³²² In the 19ᵗʰ and 20ᵗʰ centuries, "new religions" emerged in Japan to supplant forms of Buddhism that were poorly adapted to modern society, and Shin Buddhism experienced turmoil as reformers tried to revive Shinran's spirit of creativity, with only limited success.

What message should we draw from this? The first bit of advice is to take heart. Our teachers are Gotama and Shinran—the two most creative truth-seekers of whom we have any record. If we feel stagnation, either personally or institutionally, their words have the power to keep us from being satisfied with our fixed views and organizations. Second, as individuals and as a sangha, we must "appreciate the tradition and realize creativity."³²³ Shinran's life exemplified this way of being. He listened deeply to the Pure Land masters so that he could give new expression to what historical teachers were pointing toward. We honor the tradition by listening deeply to Shinran and to our contemporary teachers. Realizing creativity means giving new expression to what teachers are saying. Whenever a sense of satisfaction arises ("Now I understand Jōdo Shinshū."), I ought to hear Shinran saying, "You need to go deeper."

How hard it must be to guide a Buddhist organization like the BCA! The leadership is faced with the task of maintaining continuity amid ever-changing social conditions, and in contradiction to the essential spirit of Gotama and Shinran. We are deeply indebted to those who have taken on this difficult role, particularly when circumstances allow them to help us appreciate the tradition, while realizing the spirit of creativity that the tradition has given us.

Merit-Making

Jōdo Shinshū is the consummation of Mahāyāna Buddhism; the provisional gateways of expedience include the other Mahāyāna and Hīnayāna teachings, accommodated and real.[324]

—Gutoku Shinran

Shinran explains Jōdo Shinshū by contrasting it with various forms of Buddhism that were prevalent in his day, which he refers to, collectively, as the Path of Sages.[325] That path encompasses the "Hīnayāna" teachings as well as teachings and practices of Mahāyāna schools such as Zen, Shingon, and Tendai.[326] In the 13th century, Jōdo Shinshū was not a school at all, yet Shinran had the audacity to claim that *it* is "the consummation of Mahāyāna Buddhism." He challenged the establishment by saying that authentic practice and realization on the Path of Sages had died out long ago.

If one is to appreciate Jōdo Shinshū, it's essential to gain a perspective on the traditional Path of Sages. Currently, the best place to do this may be in southeast Asia, rather than in Japan. Few modern Japanese have any personal affiliation with a Buddhist sect; they are affiliated by family custom. However, in southeast Asia the Path of Sages is a way of life for more than a hundred million people. When my wife and I traveled there we received a vivid impression of Buddhism in those lands.

Myanmar (also known as Burma) may be the most devoutly Buddhist nation in the world. It shares a border with India, and according to legend, missionaries sent by Gotama Buddha arrived there in the 5th century BCE. A major transition took place around 1060 CE when the Irrawaddy valley became unified politically and was ruled from the city of Bagan (or Pagan). At that time, the king converted to Theravāda Buddhism and made it the state religion. Bagan was for a time the main stronghold of Theravāda, which was in serious decline elsewhere. Although several ruling dynasties in Burma have come and gone over the centuries, Theravāda remains the spiritual path for 90% of the population.

Today Myanmar has an emerging economy with widespread poverty, yet the people devote a large portion of their resources to religious practices, such as making offerings to the Buddha, donating food to the monks, and adorning religious statues and buildings. Spending time and money in this way is the essential Buddhist practice for the Burmese. By performing *meritorious deeds*, they acquire good karma leading to a favorable rebirth along with incremental progress toward Buddhahood.[327] Merit-making is also said to bear fruit in the present life, in the form of material prosperity and warding off misfortune. Lay people in Myanmar are diligent in praying to the Buddha for such benefits.

During the Bagan Dynasty there was a surge of merit-making that led to the construction of temples and stupas by the thousands, including Shwezigon Pagoda shown here. The size and the sheer number of surviving structures inspires wonder: how could the society have mustered the resources to build them all? Bagan's imperial power and its building boom reached a peak in 1174-1235, fueled by the merit-making aspiration of the monarchs. Soon thereafter, the dynasty went into decline owing to resource depletion and an apparent lack of interest in civil governance, coupled with an invasion by the Mongol empire. By 1300 the city of Bagan had lost its ruling authority, and most of its population had dispersed. Yet, the spiritual path established in those days continued without alteration and can be observed in Myanmar today.

In Myanmar, to live as a monk is the best route for becoming an awakened person or *arahant*. It means renouncing family life, begging for food on the alms-round, eating one daily meal, and devoting the rest of one's time to study and meditation. A devout lay person strives to become a monk in a future life by acquiring good karma through meritorious deeds. Every Burmese boy receives ordination as a novice monk and spends several months obeying the precepts and studying the teachings. Later he may choose either to continue on the monastic path or to reenter secular life. Adult laymen will, at intervals, temporarily return to the monastery to study and meditate with the monks.

The overriding message for lay people is that good actions bring good consequences, and bad actions bring bad consequences, both now and in future lives.[328] The imperative for merit-making is a teaching that can be understood by anyone. It resolves life's big questions and provides followers with a sense of control over the future. Buddhism in Myanmar has changed very little in the last 950 years, demonstrating that it is well adapted to life in that part of the world. However, considering the attributes that I've described, Theravāda is not easily exportable to Western societies.

Shinran's lifetime (1173-1263) coincided with the period of Bagan's imperial greatness and decline, but he may not have been aware of what was taking place there. His direct experience of the Path of Sages was limited to Japan during an era when Buddhist institutions suffered from internal corruption and from external political intrigue and violence. Shinran saw this as confirmation that Japan was in the declining Dharma-age (*mappō*), when the teachings remained, but practice and realization were impossible on the Path of Sages. Would his perspective have been different if he had visited Bagan, where the Path of Sages was vital and flourishing? Indeed, the Mahāyāna concept of *mappō* does not exist in Theravāda. Monks see themselves as direct successors of Gotama and faithful followers of his path.

Many of the visible differences between Jōdo Shinshū and the Path of Sages are culturally derived, but there is also a fundamental difference in regard to one's intention, as Shinran explains:

> Those who follow the Path of Sages all take the mind of self-power as essential.[329]
>
> Self-power is the effort to attain birth… by endeavoring to make yourself worthy through mending the confusion in your acts, words, and thoughts, confident of your own powers and guided by your own calculation.[330]
>
> "Self-power" characterizes those who have full confidence in themselves, trusting in their own hearts and minds, striving with their own powers, and relying on their own various roots of good.[331]

"Various roots of good" are ethical and religious practices which, in the practitioner's view, will lead to good consequences. There are said to be "gateways numbering 84,000 and more… suited to the capacities of beings,"[332] from which practitioners pick and choose according to their own conception of merit-making.

The traditional form of the Path of Sages is found mainly in southeast Asia, but a contemporary form of it is the most prevalent Buddhistic path in America today. I'm referring to the secularized way of meditation and mindfulness that dominates the shelves of our bookstores and the pages of magazines for Western converts.[333] This way is well-suited to "those who have full confidence in themselves, trusting in their own hearts and minds, striving with their own powers, and relying on their own various roots of good." To aim for self-improvement on the Path of Sages conforms with the Western ideal of individualism and agrees with the expectations of Americans seeking a spiritual path. By contrast, Pure Land Buddhism aims to *overturn* our expectations.

*To awaken aspiration and perform practices in this world
Is the Path of Sages and is termed self-power.
The present is the last dharma-age; it is the world of the five
   defilements;
The Pure Land alone affords passage.*[334]

According to Shinran, the teachings and practices of the Path of Sages were true and real in former days, but they are ill-suited to the capacities of people living in the present age of *mappō*.[335] He abandoned Mt. Hiei Buddhism when he saw that merit-making was bringing him no closer to the goal of becoming a buddha. His outer appearance was meritorious, but his inner reality was quite the opposite. Eventually, Shinran saw himself as a foolish ordinary person, as someone who admits, "Under certain conditions, I might do anything." Rather than meritorious deeds, the only practice we are urged to perform is to hear and reflect upon the teachings. The path leading to a favorable rebirth through ethical and religious merit-making is not part of Jōdo Shinshū.[336]

Shin Buddhism is inherently non-monastic. A distinctive feature is that ministers are at the same level as lay people with respect to following the path. Shinran's term for this is *dōgyō*, or equal practitioners—a community of fellow Dharma listeners. To identify oneself as a master is not done; teachers are themselves students. Ministers receive special training, and they go to Japan for ordination, but when serving in the United States their way of life is not substantially different from that of lay people. We honor teachers because they connect us with the Dharma, not for their having gained merit.

Shin Buddhism, although a product of medieval Japan, is remarkably well suited to the conditions of our own day. However, American converts to Buddhism tend to be drawn not to the Pure Land but to the Path of Sages. Their focus is less on achieving a favorable rebirth and more on finding personal happiness through self-improvement—a laudable goal. That is the contemporary form of merit-making. But I wonder if the right questions are being asked. Spiritual self-reliance might never be subjected to scrutiny. Is liberation more likely to take place through a teaching that confirms our expectations or through a teaching that overturns them?

I feel fortunate to have encountered the Dharma gateway of Jōdo Shinshū. If teachers had not introduced me to Shinran's ideas, I would certainly have remained a secular person. Being temperamentally unsuited to merit-making on the Path of Sages, I would not have adopted the version of it that one finds in America. This was brought home to me when I encountered the form of Buddhism that is especially suited to the cultures of southeast Asia.

Your Island

In reciting the Three Treasures text we proclaim our reliance on the Buddha, Dharma, and Sangha. The first two Treasures exist in the realm of ideas and are ever-present. The timeless Sangha is also an idea, but its embodiment is a contingent, historical group of finite human beings—a sangha (with a small *s*). What does it mean to take refuge in a sangha?

As the Buddha's life was drawing to a close, he instructed his disciple:

> "Therefore, Ānanda, dwell making yourself your island, making yourself, not anyone else, your refuge; making the Dharma your island, the Dharma your refuge, nothing else your refuge."[337]

The expression used by Gotama is sometimes translated as "make of yourself a light." However, in this context the Pāli word *dīpa* does not mean lamp or light, but rather island or support.[338] This instruction was in response to a question from Ānanda, who was distraught over what would become of the community after the death of the Buddha. Surely, Ānanda thought, a successor would have to be named, but Gotama refused to do so:

> "If there is someone who thinks, 'I shall take charge of the community,' or 'the community should refer to me,' let him make some statement about it, but I do not think in these terms."[339]

The Buddha offered the metaphor of an island, a bit of habitable ground in the midst of the ocean of birth and death, to explain how disciples should see themselves and the Dharma.

The word Dharma refers to the teachings given by the Buddha, and it also refers to limitless, formless reality, the refuge to which all the teachings are pointing. When Gotama speaks of taking refuge in yourself and the Dharma, he means that we must make the Dharma so much a part of ourselves that we take refuge in both simultaneously. That marks an important change in us. In the Pāli suttas, this stage of discipleship is called *stream entry*. It is not the attainment of *nibbāna*, but it is to have gained "lucid confidence" in the Buddha, Dharma, and Sangha. Stream enterers, Gotama stated, are men and women

> "…who carry out my instruction, respond to my advice, have gone beyond doubt, become free from perplexity, gained intrepidity, and become independent of others in the Teacher's dispensation."[340]

That means internalizing the teachings and becoming secure enough to stand on your own two feet. In Jōdo Shinshū this sense of having found the path, despite our human frailty, is called shinjin or true settlement.[341] It denotes that the fulfillment of our lives is certain to be realized, even as we continue to live as foolish beings. As Gotama stated,

> "By realizing [the Dharma] for yourselves here and now through direct knowledge, you will soon enter and dwell in that supreme goal of the holy life."[342]

No one else can have the experience for us—this realizing, knowing, and dwelling.

The ideas that I'm sharing may seem jarring to Shin Buddhists. It might be asked, "What's this about making yourself your island and becoming independent of others? Aren't we liberated by the power beyond the self? Doesn't Shinran teach us to abandon the mind of self-power?" Sometimes the pendulum of our understanding can swing too far in one direction and needs to be nudged back. The island metaphor from the Pāli suttas may be a useful corrective.

If we can hear the teachings of Gotama and Shinran today, it is thanks to teachers and to the environment created by the temple, by the Buddhist Churches of America, and by Hongwanji in Japan. Nevertheless, relying on the sangha has limits. We cannot place ultimate reliance on contingent things, such as individuals and organizations. Ministers may retire or be re-assigned. The temple and the BCA, if not for the continued efforts of many people, may cease to exist. Undoubtedly, that would be very upsetting, but I trust that our Dharma path would go forward in spite of adversity. This is one implication of making yourself your island, and making the Dharma your island. The corollary is not to be overly reliant on one personal teacher. Shinran deflected that kind of attention away from himself.

The manner in which we regard Shinran should be guided by his life example. He did not take refuge in his own teacher Hōnen, although he felt deep gratitude for what the teacher had conveyed to him. Shinran took refuge in the Dharma, just as the Buddha had instructed. Therefore, we must not take refuge in Shinran, the finite human being. His whole life-example argues against doing that. His role is to be the person who points us to the Dharma, but in regard to his "fellow practicers" he disavowed any master-disciple relationship.

After six years as Hōnen's student, Shinran was forcibly separated from his teacher and his sangha when the community was dissolved by the ruling authorities. Banished to a life of hardship in rural Echigo and cut off from the sangha he had known, Shinran was thrown back on his own resources. The seven years he spent there in semi-isolation enabled him to find a new direction, as described in a modern commentary:

> …with his exile and experience in Echigo, Shinran had begun to probe a dimension of Pure Land thought in which he could expect no further guidance from Hōnen.[343]
>
> Letting go of the final remnants of his monastic practice, he delved to the roots of religious life, reaching beyond the ordinary conceptions of wisdom and ignorance, moral rectitude and wrong-doing, into the fundamental nature of human existence as illuminated by the Buddha's wisdom.[344]

If not for his Echigo experience, it's safe to say that there would be no Shin Buddhism. This formative period in Shinran's life ended at age forty-one when he began his work in the Kantō region, where he lived for twenty years, choosing

> ...to remain away from the world of academic Buddhism and to deepen his own self-awareness and his insight into the dharma by sharing it with the people of the countryside.
>
> Shinran settled in Hitachi and actively spread the teaching there and in neighboring provinces, eventually building a large following. He established meeting places called *dōjō*...[345]

Here one can perceive an echo of Gotama Buddha's career: a period spent in isolation, then awakening, culminating in the decision to spread the teaching. For the rest of his long life, Shinran made himself and the Dharma his island. Living as "neither a priest nor a lay follower," he continued to listen deeply to the teachings through his reading and writing. He avoided institutions and remained visible only to a small community of fellow practicers. But, in the centuries after his death, his influence was strongly felt:

> He was not a major actor in the public events of the times.... Nevertheless, through his thought he decisively altered the landscape of Japanese religious life, and his teaching remains one of the peaks of the Mahāyāna Buddhist tradition.[346]

A more recent example of making yourself your island was Rev. Haya Akegarasu (1877-1954), a Shin teacher with a turbulent personal history.[347] He began as a conventional minister and might have remained so, but devastating experiences forced him to abandon the mind of self-power. That was the beginning of his appreciation of Jōdo Shinshū, as he had seen it in the life of his teacher, Rev. Kiyozawa. Having placed his reliance on *tariki*, or the power beyond the self, Rev. Akegarasu nevertheless called himself a *doku-ritsu-sha*, literally an alone-standing-person or, as we might translate it, an independent person. A basic teaching of Buddhism is that all things are interdependent. You and I, the universe—nothing exists independently.

So, what is meant by *doku-ritsu-sha*? One of my teachers suggested that the alone-standing-person is "neither controlling others nor being controlled by others."[348] That is a good description of Shinran, a person who embodied the Buddha's instruction to make yourself your island. The alone-standing-person avoids becoming overly reliant on individuals and organizations, avoids a state of co-dependency. That type of over-reliance on specific things prevents us from seeing the interdependence of all things, as expressed in the following verses from the *Suttanipāta*:

> *One who is independent is not vulnerable,*
> *But one who is dependent and grasping,*
> *In this form of existence or some other,*
> *Does not escape transmigration.*
>
> *Knowing this danger,*
> *That dependencies are the great fear,*
> *Independent, not grasping,*
> *Mindful, a bhikkhu would go forth.*[349]

Part VII

What Nature Teaches

There is grandeur in this view of life, with its several powers, having been originally breathed into a few forms or into one; and that, whilst this planet has gone cycling on according to the fixed law of gravity, from so simple a beginning endless forms most beautiful and most wonderful have been, and are being, evolved.[350]

—Charles Darwin (1809-1882)

Bugs, Germs, and People

We encounter bugs frequently, even if we would rather avoid them. Although individually tiny, they exist in huge numbers, and their influence is pervasive. The weight of all of the termites on earth is estimated to be 500 million tons, which is more than the weight of all seven billion human beings. This might lead us to ask, Are humans really the dominant life form on this planet?

Our judgments about bugs depend on whether they appear to be beautiful or ugly, and whether they have economic value or are viewed as pests. The ladybug is an ideal insect—not only are ladybugs harmless to humans and darned cute, they prey on crop-destroying aphids. Honeybees might be perceived as dangerous rather than cute, but their economic value as pollinators is immense; bees are crucial to our food supply. Butterflies delight us with their beauty and with their life-cycle of metamorphosis from caterpillars. And, who hasn't been inspired by the amazing architectural creations of spiders?

Only a few kinds of bugs are viewed in a positive light. For most of the others, our negative reactions include fear, annoyance, and disgust. We may attempt to avoid killing bugs that are beautiful or beneficial, while not hesitating to kill those seen as ugly and harmful. As Buddhists, this should lead us to reflect. Perhaps we can pause before killing other life forms, even the ones that we view as dangerous or disgusting. Around the house I try to catch and release the crawlers that I find, but capturing becomes difficult if they are airborne. If I see a bug indoors that could pose a danger, then I usually end up killing it, while feeling regret. Furthermore, countless bugs are being killed to keep me supplied with life's necessities. The least I can do is to be mindful of the sacrifices that are represented in the food on my plate, in the clothes that I wear, and in the buildings that shelter me.

Now consider microorganisms—popularly dubbed "germs"—the tiny life forms that exist on us and in us.[351] Well before the coronavirus pandemic, one of the most effective ways of selling a product to Americans was to claim that it "kills germs." The advertising slogan has long been effective because of the widely held view that microorganisms are all "bad" and must be destroyed.

Yet, science has revealed that the microorganisms living on us and in us play an essential role in keeping us healthy. The human body is home to myriads of bacteria—far more than I would have guessed—amounting to about three pounds of our body's weight. These resident bacteria, comprising some 10,000 different species, perform many crucial functions for us, such as making vitamins, preventing infections, fortifying the immune system, and helping us to digest food. Rather than wanting to do away with our body's "germs," we should learn how to cultivate those that are beneficial.

> Looked upon in this way, the human body turns out to be a vast, highly mutable ecosystem—each of us seems more like a farm than like an individual assembled from a rulebook of genetic instructions. Medicine becomes a matter of cultivation, as if our bacterial cells were crops in a field.[352]

Of course, some types of bacteria cause serious illnesses like cholera, plague, and tuberculosis, but those are rare exceptions to the favorable interactions that we have with most of them.

I would like to think that this body is all *mine* in some sense, but it is home to tiny life forms that do not share my DNA. This body is able to live only because it incorporates countless microorganisms that perform functions necessary for my survival. By the same token, these life forms could not exist if I did not find food and water, get adequate sleep, and drive safely on my way to and from the temple. Given the reciprocal relationship, it's wrong to think that I have a self that could exist independently of the microorganisms. In light of this beautiful mutualism, it would be more accurate to describe *me* as *us*.

We have a much harder time accepting that we are interdependent with microorganisms that cause diseases, but I think that is where the teachings of the Buddha lead us. In my ignorance, I divide the world into dualities like friend and enemy, sickness and health, germs and me. Buddhism teaches the transcendence of all dualities. A scientific understanding of the role of microorganisms did not exist in ancient

India, but the Buddha perceived correctly that the self is sustained by unseen causes and conditions. He realized that the arising and perishing of the self reflects a deep connection with the whole of existence.

In matters of medicine and public health, it is proper to rely on what science can do to repair the body and to save lives. But in terms of a spiritual path, one can envision two ways of responding to an illness.[353] Either we can imagine doing battle with it, or we can become one with it. To take the first approach is to see the disease as an outside enemy, which might help in certain situations, but it may amplify our distress if the disease proves to be incurable. Taking the second approach of becoming one with the disease means accepting the reality of illness and not seeing it as something foreign. Then there is no conflict between the sick self and the healthy self. Gotama Buddha exemplified this teaching during his final illness, which may have been caused by microorganisms in the food that he was given. He told his disciple Ānanda that no one should blame the cook for his death, and that it was an act of great merit to give a buddha his last meal before his parinirvana.[354] The Buddha realized oneness with all living things. The existence of microorganisms, both beneficial and harmful, was unknown in his day, but I believe that his sense of oneness with all of life would have included "germs."

Where Do We Come From?

One of the most beautiful works of Paul Gauguin (1848-1903) is a huge painting of an imaginary landscape in Polynesia. A detail from it is shown here. The painting symbolically depicts the trajectory of human life from birth to death. In a corner of the canvas the artist wrote the words *Where Do We Come From / What Are We / Where Are We Going*. These questions are universal; to ask them is an inherent human need.[355] By way of an answer, the symbolic story-telling in many cultures includes creation myths and predictions about the end of the world.

Another way to address the three existential questions is through the careful observation of nature, as was done by Charles Darwin. He found that plant and animal species are continually coming into being and going extinct in response to causes and conditions in their environment, especially through interaction with other species. He concluded that life forms *co-originate and co-extinguish through evolution by natural selection*, a principle that became the basis of modern biology. In the "economy of nature" there is no central planner. Species arise and perish naturally through (1) random variation of heritable traits and (2) non-random survival of traits based on reproductive fitness in a particular environment.

> ... I can see no limit to the amount of change, to the beauty and complexity of the co-adaptations between all organic beings, one with another and with their physical conditions of life, which may have been effected in the long course of time through nature's power of selection, that is, by the survival of the fittest.[356]

There is overwhelming evidence in support of this idea, but it continues to challenge our preconceptions. We may be persuaded to accept evolution by natural selection as an objective fact, but to feel its truth *subjectively* is difficult because it conflicts with our narrow, self-centered view of the world. Darwin's *Origin of Species* (1859) is

> ... a radical work, which argues that the fundamental forces driving life on this planet occur on timescales that render the span of a human life insignificant. Furthermore, although the effects of natural selection are there for all to see, its daily operation is almost completely hidden from view. Both our life spans and our five senses are inadequate to the task of comprehension. The most powerful mechanism of organic change lies well beyond our everyday experience.[357]

Darwin and his successors gathered objective evidence to account for the existence of our species, *Homo sapiens*, but science cannot account for the subjective experience of individual humans. Thus, we may find the objective answers to be insufficient. We may feel compelled to ask the three questions subjectively: Where did I come from? What am I? Where am I going? The desire for self-understanding takes us beyond science and into philosophy and religion. From a Buddhist perspective, the dawning of self-awareness is to recognize that my life is *duhkha*; it is bound up with sorrow. That is Buddhism's "noble" response to the question, What am I? Knowing subjectively that my life is *duhkha* is different from knowing objectively that all living things participate in "the struggle for life" that drives the evolution of species. Darwin makes a similar point:

> Nothing is easier than to admit in words the truth of the universal struggle for life, or more difficult—at least I have found it so—than constantly to bear this conclusion in mind. Yet unless it be thoroughly engrained in the mind, the whole economy of nature, with every fact on distribution, rarity, abundance, extinction, and variation, will be dimly seen or quite misunderstood.[358]

Likewise, the human condition is quite misunderstood if we are ignorant of the noble truth that life is *duhkha*.

Animals feel physical pain, and they have mental states that we may call fear or anxiety, but they do not perceive that life is sorrowful in the way that humans do. Natural selection has provided them with certain drives and with a brain that formulates responses to satisfy those drives, but they live primarily in the moment and are free of inherent sorrow. I, on the other hand, brood over difficult experiences, and I anticipate the inevitability of old age, sickness, and death. My life is *duhkha*, because I feel regret for the past and fear about the future. It is an endless cycle of dreaming about where I came from and where I am going. When the Buddha examined the self to its ultimate depth, he discovered that everything in it is continually turning and evolving. He realized that the conventional self is impermanent and without intrinsic substance. He awakened to the Dharma—limitless reality—and he became one with it. By following the path of the Buddha, we can devote less time to self-centered dreaming about the past and the future.

The religious response to Gauguin's questions typically takes the form of origin myths and prophecies about the future. Such stories fulfill a deep human need, but when taken as fact, the stories are in conflict with the findings of science, causing skeptics to question the value of religion and believers to reject the scientific method. However, as Joseph Campbell observed, literalist claims and the ensuing criticisms are both off base:

In fact, the famous conflict of science and religion has actually nothing to do with religion, but is simply of two sciences: that of 4000 B.C. and that of A.D. 2000.[359]

Does Buddhism make claims that are refuted by contemporary science? I think not. To walk the Dharma path is to see the limitations of any fixed or literal understandings of religion. Buddhism's basic ideas—impermanence and interdependence—are not imagined narratives, nor are they static doctrines that we can grasp and codify. The same can be said of their manifestation in the arising and perishing of species by natural selection. As Darwin noted, we are unable to grasp

> ...the action and reaction of the innumerable plants and animals which have determined in the course of centuries the proportional numbers and kinds of [life forms]... This ought to convince us of our ignorance on the mutual relations of all organic beings; a conviction as necessary, as it is difficult to acquire.[360]

Evolution Is Buddha-dharma

The word "dharma" means the teachings of the historical Buddha. In another sense of the word, "Dharma" means the law of the universe, true reality, or suchness, as embodied in the world around us. Nature cannot be other than true reality—it is suchness taking form. To observe and to understand the natural world is one aspect of being open to the Dharma. I want to suggest that nature is echoing what the Buddha teaches.

Occasionally we are inspired to wonder about the amazing variety of plants and animals that share this special world with us. Where did these countless life forms with all their complexity come from? Where, for that matter, did human beings come from? The principle that *species arise and perish by natural selection* provides a coherent, factual explanation for much of the diversity of life on earth.[361] This explanation is supported by overwhelming evidence from many scientific fields. The complexity of life forms arose through a natural process that continues even today. To appreciate this fact can inspire a feeling of awe, just as origin myths were an inspiration to people who lived in ancient times.

How might the teachings of Buddhism connect with the evolution of species? In the Pāli suttas very little attention is given to creation stories.[362] Rather, Gotama construes the human condition as having no beginning or ending.

> "Monks, this samsara is without discoverable beginning. A first point is not discerned of beings roaming and wandering on hindered by ignorance and fettered by craving."[363]

Instead of focusing on the past and the future, we are taught to awaken to limitless reality in the present moment. Awakening is to understand that everything in the world is interdependent and is continually changing. The natural arising and perishing of species can be seen as embodying these basic teachings.

Evidence from all fields of science has shown that (1) the earth is 4.5 billion years old, (2) there has been life on earth for at least 2 billion years,[364] and (3) the genetic information, or DNA, from those early life forms has been propagating and evolving in new ways ever since. These are astounding facts to contemplate! If we could hear them as if for the first time, it ought to take our breath away. Another breathtaking insight is that all true classification of species is *genealogical*—its fundamental basis is community of descent from extinct ancestor species, a demonstration of interconnectedness that should inspire us.[365]

> When I view all beings not as special creations, but as the lineal descendants of some few beings which lived long before the first bed of the Cambrian system was deposited, they seem to me to become ennobled.[366]

Without being aware of it, we are immersed in a dynamic reality that extends far beyond our everyday experience. Here on planet earth, the "voiceless voice" of the Dharma is manifested, most concretely, in the continual origin and extinction of species, as played out over vast stretches of time. Plants and animals are still evolving today, and will continue to evolve in the future, governed by the principle of natural selection. Human beings are part of this oneness of life, having arisen from a line of extinct predecessors. The scientific understanding of evolution is a beautiful illustration of the Buddha's teachings of interdependence and continual change.

As far as human origins, fossil evidence shows that in Africa 300,000 years ago there were people whose bones were anatomically indistinguishable from ours.[367] We and they belong to the species *Homo sapiens*. When did these ancestors first have a mind that was just like ours? Clues start to appear between 300,000 to 100,000 years ago, in the form of cultural artifacts.[368] By 30,000 years ago the evidence includes human-like figurines, bone flutes, and cave paintings of prehistoric animals, such as those from Lascaux Cave in France estimated to be 17,000 years old. The sensitive artistry of these renderings suggests that the creators had minds that were indistinguishable from ours. The key point is that starting sometime between 300,000 and 30,000 years ago, there were people who had the same bodies and minds that we have.[369]

One of the hallmarks of the human mind is to ask Gauguin's questions: Where do we come from? What are we? Where are we going? Throughout almost the entire span of human history, the three existential questions were answered subjectively, based on desires and fears. The first objective answers came from Darwin's discovery of the origin and extinction of species by natural selection.[370] It was a revolution in humanity's long quest for self-awareness. No advanced technology was needed to make this discovery. What was required was a willingness to look very closely at the world and to think about the observations with the mind of a beginner. In the 19th century many naturalists assumed that each life form had come into existence through an act of special creation and was immutable thereafter. After examining a vast array of evidence, Darwin concluded that the ideas of immutability and special creation are false:

> I can entertain no doubt, after the most deliberate study and dispassionate judgment of which I am capable, that the view which most naturalists until recently entertained, and which I formerly entertained—namely, that each species has been independently created—is erroneous. I am fully convinced that species are not immutable.[371]

Why did it take so long for this to happen? Why a hundred thousand years of questioning by our ancestors before objective answers, based on the evidence from nature, emerged 150 years ago? Throughout most of human history, it would have been infeasible for any one person to examine the worldwide diversity and distribution of plant and animal species, as Darwin did.[372] Furthermore, it's very difficult for humans to comprehend nature's timescale, sometimes called "deep time."[373] With our typical attention span, we are equipped to understand events lasting from a few seconds to a few decades. But as Darwin noted, nature's timescale is much, much longer.

> The mind cannot possibly grasp the full meaning of the term of even a million years; it cannot add up and perceive the full effects of many slight variations [of life forms], accumulated during an almost infinite number of generations.[374]

> We see nothing of these slow changes in progress, until the hand of time has marked the lapse of ages, and then so imperfect is our view into long-past geological ages, that we see only that the forms of life are now different from what they formerly were.[375]

The idea that the world is extremely old is not generally taught in Western religions. However, this idea was inherent in the spiritual traditions of ancient India, where time is measured in kalpas. One kalpa is pretty close to a gazillion years, and the world is said to have existed for innumerable kalpas. By using figurative language to express an insight about the world, people in India were on the right track long before Western scientists quantified deep time.

Nature is our first and best teacher—all else is a human contrivance. A basic premise in Mahāyāna Buddhism is that truth transcends our contrivances, that is, our words and images. Therefore, we are obliged to reflect carefully on what nature teaches us. I contend that the evolution of species by natural selection is Buddha-dharma, nature's manifestation of the basic teachings of the Buddha. Did Gotama know all about evolution 2500 years ago? No, not in its scientific details, but he realized the essentials. Through deep *awareness of the self*, the Buddha saw the truth of interdependence and impermanence. Through deep *awareness of the world* around him, he understood intuitively that these truths are universal—that interdependence and impermanence are the basis for all life on earth.

Buddhism teaches me to abandon the idea that I have a permanent, essential self. It teaches that I should awaken to interdependence, and that I should see myself as one with the flow of life. Based on the findings of Darwin and his successors, we can go further and say that our species, *Homo sapiens*, is without any permanent essence:

Judging from the past, we may safely infer that not one living species will transmit its unaltered likeness to a distant futurity. And of the species now living, very few will transmit progeny of any kind to a far distant futurity; for the manner in which all organic beings are grouped, shows that the greater number of species in each genus, and all the species in many genera, have left no descendants, but have become utterly extinct.[376]

Homo sapiens is a temporary container for genetic information received from countless predecessor species. Humans may in turn transmit their genetic information to successor species in the distant future. Given that all life forms are co-adapted and undergoing change, there is no independent self and no permanent human species. This recognition is pointing us toward Buddhist awakening.

What Doesn't Go Away

A good definition for "reality" is that which doesn't go away, even if I don't believe in it. A nightmare produces anxiety or fear, and although it seems real, it disappears when I wake up. Or I may worry about some future event, but the event never actually takes place. When my worry or my nightmare goes away, I am relieved to find that it was not reality.

Suppose I have a negative experience, such as being seriously injured, which makes me say, "I cannot believe I did something that dumb!" I refuse to believe what happened, but it does not go away. I desperately wish that I had not been injured, but my desires are brought up short by reality. This is how we grow from childhood into adulthood. We recognize that our desires are in conflict with a reality that does not go away. We learn as well that the future cannot be influenced simply by wishing for a certain event to happen.

At times I refuse to believe in an idea because it conflicts with my desires. It's fine to be skeptical, but when there is a preponderance of evidence in favor of that idea, I ought to accept it for the time being. Take the idea that life forms, including humans, have arisen by evolution through natural selection, and that they will eventually go extinct as new species arise. Today there is so much evidence for the evolution of species that it ought to be as obvious as the law of gravity. Yet, 44% of Americans reject this explanation of life on earth.[377] They want the reality of nature to go away, because nature manifests a truth that undermines their illusions. In like fashion, the Church put scientist Galileo Galilei (1564-1642) on trial for presenting evidence contradicting the doctrine that the earth is the center of the universe.

As another example of desires in conflict with reality, there is the belief that society should take a hands-off approach on the issues of human over-population and over-consumption. In the 1980s this became the official policy of the U.S. government, namely, that population growth and resource consumption should not be constrained.[378] However, as Darwin noted, there is a delicate balance that determines population size:

WHAT NATURE TEACHES

> In looking at Nature, it is most necessary... never to forget that every single organic being may be said to be striving to the utmost to increase its numbers; that each lives by a struggle at some period of its life; that heavy destruction inevitably falls either on the young or old, during each generation or at recurring intervals. Lighten any check, mitigate the destruction ever so little, and the number of the species will almost instantaneously increase to any amount.[379]

According to credible projections, the human population will reach a maximum around the middle of the 21st century, followed by a major decline in our numbers owing to resource depletion, environmental degradation, and the resulting social chaos.[380] The reality is that a less hospitable climate and a collapsing biosphere will not accommodate the desire for our species to grow and to consume without limit.

Buddhism teaches us about realities that don't go away, even though we want things to be otherwise. We cling to people and possessions that we know and love, and we want them not to change. When the Buddha says that all conditioned things are impermanent, we are brought face to face with reality. Even if I refuse to accept it, the world continues to evolve and change without my approval. Shinran's teaching, too, is one I would rather not accept. As he stated,

> ... we are full of ignorance and blind passion. Our desires are countless, and anger, wrath, jealousy, and envy are overwhelming, arising without pause; to the very last moment of life they do not cease, or disappear, or exhaust themselves.[381]

I would like to think that Shinran was describing himself but not me. However, the Shin Buddhist path is one of recognizing that his statement *does* apply to me, of recognizing that my greed, anger, and ignorance are a reality that does not go away.

I might think that greed, anger, and ignorance are standing in the way of liberation, and so I desire to eliminate them. In Shinran's terms, this desire arises from the calculating mind or the mind of self-power. This mind seeks to deny a reality that does not go away. Shin Buddhist teachings are pointing us toward a path on which our desires are recognized and transcended. The poisons of greed, anger, and ignorance remain intact, but they are no longer an obstacle to liberation. The reality of our passions is what teaches us to be humble.

Looking for the Self

On the Buddhist path, the central question is, What am I? or What is the self? To guide us, there is the teaching of *anātman*, taken to mean "non-self," but this calls for an explanation. Does Buddhism teach that the self does not exist?

I tend to make false assumptions about the self. I imagine there is a "me" that persists from moment to moment, from birth to death—a perpetual spectator residing in my brain, a personal frame of reference that never changes, that supersedes my identity as "Jim." The self-as-spectator watches this life unfold but somehow is detached from my experiences. Before his awakening, Gotama's assumptions may have been like that. He considered the self to be a permanent identity, an individual essence, perhaps a spectator such as I've described. However, he discarded these ideas when he failed to discover any frame of reference that was independent of his sense faculties. He could find no essence that existed apart from his experience.

How did Gotama proceed to search for the self? One does not usually hear that the Buddha followed a *method*—i.e., an orderly procedure for investigating or teaching something—but the term is appropriate. As an illustration of method, I will share a scientific example. Sound waves are carried by the medium of the air; without the air to carry the sound, there would be only silence, as in the vacuum of space. Unlike sound, light waves travel freely through a vacuum. Thus, we receive light from the sun millions of miles away. Is there a medium in the vacuum of space that carries the light waves? One hundred forty years ago it was natural for physicists to assume that a light-carrying medium called the "aether" fills the universe. However, in 1887 a celebrated experiment cast serious doubt on this assumption.[382] The result was hard to fathom, until 1905 when Albert Einstein (1879-1955) explained why the idea of the aether is unnecessary![383] This illustrates how careful observation and analysis can disprove our favorite assumptions. Gotama's method of looking for the self was something like the physicists' search for the aether.

In ancient India, spiritual teachers were expected to offer their views on speculative matters, that is, questions for which no clear answer could be found. Is the world eternal or not eternal? Is the world finite or infinite? Gotama rejected such speculation and focused instead on what he could actually observe, namely, his own body and mind. To make careful observations prior to drawing firm conclusions is what defines scientific investigation. On the other hand, to draw conclusions without gathering the data is speculation. Not to over-interpret, but the Buddha's method of self-examination was more akin to science than to the revelations that are the basis of other religions. In revealed theology, truth is said to come from the divine realm. There's no role for observations or experiments. Not so in Buddhism, where fact-checking applies. Gotama is the rare exception to Nietzsche's complaint regarding religious founders:

> One form of honesty has always been lacking among founders of religions and their kin:—they have never made their experiences a matter of the intellectual conscience. "What did I really experience? What then took place in me and around me? Was my understanding clear enough? Was my will directly opposed to all deception of the senses, and courageous in its defense against fantastic notions?"—None of them ever asked these questions...[384]

Science is continually advancing the frontier of knowledge. Questions on which one could only speculate in ancient times, can now be investigated empirically. For example, there is no need for speculation on whether the earth is or is not eternal. It came into existence 4.5 billion years ago. But the Buddha, in his day, had no access to the necessary data, and he was right to refrain from answering this question.

At the corporate laboratory where I once worked, a colleague had an amusing sign on his door: *In God we trust. All others must bring data.* Which is to say: show me results from the test lab. As far as the Buddha was concerned, even God (to be considered trustworthy) must bring data. Nature is our first and our best teacher, and moreover, an unforgiving teacher when we deceive ourselves. We might have desires and opinions about how the world should be, but nature is completely indifferent to our views. Grim proof of this is seen today in pandemic denialism, a distorted view that has led to thousands of unnecessary deaths and incalculable suffering. Unlike humans, nature cannot be fooled.[385]

I ought to be willing to abandon my opinions if nature teaches me that they are false. Likewise, I ought to distinguish my opinions from ideas that have been verified by careful observation and analysis.[386] The scientific world-view is grounded in the empirical method, as expressed here by Richard Feynman: *The test of all knowledge is experiment. Experiment is the sole judge of scientific "truth."* [387] One does not become attached to scientific truth. It is always provisional, pending the next clever experiment.

Gotama's initial assumption about the self was that it contained a permanent essence, a spectator that was independent of his experience. In carrying out the difficult work of self-examination, he did not seek answers from heavenly gods or earthly gods. He examined his body and mind looking for a permanent self. And what did he find? That everything in him, without exception, was turning and evolving in response to his experiences. He could find no evidence for a permanent spectator, an essence that existed apart from his experience, a self that might survive his physical death:

> "But self and what belongs to a self are not acknowledged as a genuine fact. This being so, is not the following a totally foolish teaching: 'The self and the cosmos are one and the same. After death I will be permanent, everlasting, eternal, imperishable, and will last forever and ever'?"[388]

It was the first stage of awakening, the realizing of *anātman*, the negation of the permanent and independent self.[389] Perhaps it was not the outcome Gotama had hoped for. In recognizing the ever-changing nature of the self, he was forced to abandon ideas that he had once relied on, just as physicists had to discard their notion of the aether.

The Buddha's search went beyond the stage of negation. The Pāli suttas contain three descriptions of what he found after giving up the idea of a permanent spectator self.[390] The need for more than one description points up the limitation of using concepts to explain a self that is continually evolving. I view these descriptions as provisional ideas that can be used for the time being, similar to the way scientific findings are treated; none of them can be taken as an ultimate explanation of the self. In them, the Buddha enumerates *aspects of experience*, the physical and mental activities that constitute a human being. The description called the "five aggregates" is a list of physical and mental activities, grouped into the broad categories of physical forms, feelings, perceptions, inclinations, and consciousness.[391] It includes, among other things, the sense faculties of eye, ear, nose, mouth, body, and brain, and various responses like appreciating, cringing, wanting, and calculating. There is nothing mystical about these activities. They are aspects of experience that every human being is familiar with, even if we haven't taken the trouble to categorize them. To the extent that anything about the self can be considered to be *real*, these ever-changing aspects of experience are it. We ascribe reality to the flow of physical and mental activities from moment to moment, but this continuity of experience should not be mistaken for a perpetual identity or unchanging perspective.

Note how the focus of Gotama's inquiry shifted. Initially he asked, What, ultimately, is the self? which can be addressed only through speculation.[392] At some point he began to ask, What is being experienced, here and now? This question is not speculative. Any human being can respond to it. It has to do with comprehending the human condition, with developing a practical response to one's situation, with finding one's path in life. Responding to this question was the second stage of the Buddha's awakening, the stage of affirming the ever-changing and interdependent self. The five aggregates are a provisional description of what is experienced here and now, as the interdependent self is manifested. It is not an ultimate description, which might be mistaken for a permanent identity. The self cannot be reduced in that manner. As the *Heart Sutra* declares, "Even the five aggregates are empty of intrinsic existence." They are not an "essence" that arises independently of external circumstances.

I've suggested why we should question our assumptions about the self. The Buddha's method of looking for the self has traits in common with science but very little in common with revealed religion. After negating the idea of a permanent self, the Buddha went on to describe aspects of what the ever-changing self is experiencing here and now—provisionally, the five aggregates of attachment—while acknowledging that the self is not ultimately findable within these aspects.

Some of the ideas that I've shared here come from the writings of Stephen Batchelor, who sums it up this way: "For not only are we not identical with what makes up our experience, we are not something different from it either."[393]

The Mind of a Beginner

I have no special talents; I am only passionately curious.[394]

—Albert Einstein

To follow the Buddhist path, it's essential to awaken the mind of a beginner.[395] Although this mind may not contain a lot of knowledge, it has a broad view of what is possible. It sees the world as ever-expanding. It seeks meaning in all things. The expert's mind, on the other hand, contains some knowledge, but its view of what is possible is narrow and is constrained by what is already known. Holding such a view, the Buddhist path is very hard to encounter. By way of illustration, let me mention a notable scientific discovery.

Today, in popular culture, Einstein personifies the brainy guy. But rather than his cultural persona, it was his scientific work that made news in 2016. One hundred years earlier he published a remarkable result based on his newly developed theory of gravity. The theory implied that the universe is full of gravitational waves.[396] At the time there was no evidence for such waves, and Einstein was reluctant to conclude that they existed. Six decades later, in the 1970s, astronomers looking deep into space found the first indirect evidence for gravitational waves. Then it was announced in 2016 that an experiment here on earth had confirmed Einstein's idea in spectacular fashion.[397] For the first time, there was direct detection of gravitational waves produced by the merging of two black holes in a distant galaxy.

The experimental result was a cause for rejoicing among physicists. Most of them had felt for a long time that Einstein's prediction was correct, and thus they were not surprised to see it confirmed. But why the great fanfare over the announcement? One reason is that the measurement was *extremely* difficult—it was achieved at considerable expense after fifty years of work by thousands of highly talented people. There was a justifiable feeling of accomplishment, of having met a supreme challenge. There was also the expectation that future observations of gravitational waves would be even more revealing.[398]

The second reason for celebrating has to do with the nature of Einstein's theory of gravity, which changed humanity's understanding of the universe. Also known as the general theory of relativity, it describes much more than gravitational waves. Several of its predictions were confirmed by observations during Einstein's lifetime, which made him a scientific saint. Humans could never again look at the world in the way they had done before he came along. And still today, the discovery imparts a sense of wonder, a feeling of amazement that humans can touch something eternal. It's a feeling that transcends our individual complaints and worries, a feeling that reconnects us with the beginner's mind that we possessed as children. All scientific findings do this to at least a small degree, if only for the few people directly involved. But it's rare that a discovery alters the whole picture of the universe.

As far as gravity is concerned, the only person to have made a discovery comparable to Einstein's was Isaac Newton (1643-1727). The everyday force of gravity does not surprise us, but what Newton accomplished 350 years ago was astonishing. He proved that the force of gravity that causes an apple to fall also governs the motions of the sun, the earth, the moon, and the planets. Celestial motions are not controlled by inscrutable powers, as humans of earlier eras had believed. Rather, it is everyday gravity that governs the universe, and Newton was the first person to demonstrate this convincingly. As a poet wrote at the time, *Nature and Nature's laws lay hid in night: / God said, Let Newton be! and all was light.*[399] The older world-view had to be discarded. Even so, Newton realized that his theory was incomplete. He explained the *effects* of gravity but not its *cause*. Newton said,

> I have not yet been able to discover the cause of these properties of gravity from phenomena, and I contrive no hypotheses [about it].... It is enough that gravity does really exist and acts according to the laws I have explained, and that it abundantly serves to account for all the motions of celestial bodies.

Einstein's contribution was to take a fresh look at the problem and to probe at a deeper level than was possible in Newton's day. Einstein explained the origin or cause of gravity, and in doing so, he completed what Newton had begun.

This example from physics illustrates what it means to have the mind of a beginner. Here is a statement by Einstein that describes his way of working:

> However we try to explain the laws of nature, in no case will the theoretical treatment be forever appropriate. Newton's theory was eventually proved to be wanting, and mine has taken its place. But the day will come when my theory, too, will have to yield to another one, for reasons which at present we do not yet surmise. I believe that this process of deepening the theory has no limits.[400]

To follow the Buddhist path or to make a great discovery in science, one must have the mind of a beginner. Such a mind has a broad view of what is possible and sees everything in life as offering an opportunity for learning. It believes that the process of deepening our understanding has no limits. The beginner's mind is not attached to any fixed ideas or concepts. On the other hand, the expert's mind sees life as being limited to what is already known and understood. It is attached to fixed views and preconceptions, and to a comfortable view of the self. At one time or another, each of us sees the world with the eyes of a beginner. And, at one time or another, each of us sees the world with the eyes of an expert. Which view do we adopt when it comes to the Buddha-dharma? Which view will it be when we look for the true self? Is it deepening endlessly or remaining in our comfort zone?

Two hundred years after Newton, many physicists thought there was nothing fundamentally new that could be discovered concerning gravity. Einstein was, of course, highly knowledgeable, but his beginner's mind led him to tackle problems that the expert's mind would have ignored. And so, he changed our understanding of the universe. For the rest of his life, the beginner's mind led him to ask questions that ran against the grain of contemporary physics, and thus his scientific quest became a lonely one.[401] A genuine truth-seeker does not need a lot of company. In distinctive fashion, Einstein cited a religious dimension to his truth-seeking:

> Everyone who is seriously involved in the pursuit of science becomes convinced that a spirit is manifested in the laws of the Universe—a spirit vastly superior to that of man, and one in the face of which we with our modest powers must feel humble. In this way the pursuit of science leads to a religious feeling of a special sort, which is indeed quite different from the religiosity of someone more naïve.[402]

He rejected the notion that this universal "spirit" involves itself in any way with human affairs. The "spirit manifested in the laws of the Universe" is what Buddhists call *dharma-kāya* or the flow of voiceless truth.

One of Einstein's friends described him this way: "He was the freest man I have ever known."[403] He was liberated by becoming a truth-seeker, by perfecting his beginner's mind. This is identical to what is meant by liberation in Shin Buddhism—to become a truth-seeker and to perfect the mind of a beginner.

At our temple I once gave a tour of the Hondō to a group of true beginners. They asked many questions and wanted to understand everything that I was saying to them. They showed a remarkable level of interest in the objects I pointed out on the altar. This was a group of nine-year-old Cub Scouts. Each of them entered the Hondō with boundless curiosity. As teenagers and adults, do *we* come to the temple with such an open mind? Unfortunately, it is very difficult for us to do. In growing beyond childhood, we lose access to the natural spontaneity that we once possessed. As we mature through adolescence and into adulthood, the mind of the beginner is replaced by that of the expert: "There's nothing more I can learn from Buddhism. I refuse to listen deeply." Among temple members, this secularized mind is quite prevalent.

However, the time may come when we encounter something that our minds cannot grasp. We may be compelled to face questions that go beyond our expertise. Why is there suffering? What is death? What am I? The expert's mind turns away from such questions. On the other hand, we might be prompted to reawaken the beginner's mind; to see everything in life as offering an opportunity for learning; to realize that the process of deepening self-awareness has no limits. The basis of Shin Buddhism is to rediscover the beginner's mind and to deepen it endlessly. That spirit is expressed in the *Larger Sutra* in these verses:

> *Even though there are zillions of Buddhas*
> *And great sages as many as the sand grains of the River Ganges,*
> *I will visit all of them and study under them.*
> *Nothing is greater than seeking the way,*
> *Continuously advancing and never retreating.*[404]

May we awaken the mind that sees many possibilities, that finds meaning in all things.

Cause and Effect

So that is how the wise see action as it really is—seers of dependent origination, skilled in action and its result.[405]

—Suttanipāta

When the forces of nature take the form of violent events like tornados and earthquakes, people are understandably fearful. Should nature therefore be seen as hostile to us? Is there a menacing power behind the forces of nature? Or, to take a different view, are human beings the lords over creation? Can we squander nature's resources and ignore the consequences? In the view of some, the natural world has no value when left unexploited by humans. Nature gains value only when it lends itself to resource extraction and to displays of barbarian prowess, such as trophy hunting. From a Buddhist perspective, all of these are distorted views. The natural world is not our adversary, nor is it our slave to be exploited. Buddhism teaches that *the whole of existence is interdependent*. The forces of nature contain both creation and destruction. All living things arise from the natural world. They are sustained by it for a certain season and then revert to raw materials when life ends. However, human beings are attached to ideas that confuse the natural order of the world. They see the environment as an adversary or a slave.

As an example of humans at war with nature, consider an historical incident from 2500 years ago. Xerxes, king of Persia, aimed to conquer the fiercely independent Greeks. The Persian army needed to cross the Hellespont, a narrow ocean strait separating Asia from Europe, and the king ordered the construction of a pontoon bridge. When a storm destroyed the bridge, Xerxes was enraged. To take revenge on nature, he commanded that the ocean be whipped 300 times and branded with hot irons. "Bad ocean! Baaaad!"[406] Eventually Xerxes crossed over the strait and attacked Greece. Although the Persian forces were more numerous, they were defeated by the superior tactics and foresight of the defenders. From the perspective of Greek values, Xerxes was guilty of *hubris* or overweening pride, the sin of thinking himself the equal of the gods.

In Greek mythology the gods were subject to the same passions as human beings—love, anger, jealousy, pride, and so on. The gods were said to be capricious; their actions could be unpredictable and arbitrary. When disputes arose between them, they would take it out on human beings through the forces of nature. That was the explanation given when humans experienced good fortune or bad fortune, apparently at random. The poet Homer imagines what Zeus might say in response:

> "What a lamentable thing it is that men should blame the gods and regard *us* as the source of their troubles, when it is their own wickedness that brings them sufferings worse than any which Destiny allots them."[407]

However, the traditional way of thinking gradually gave way to a different view of the world. Philosophically minded Greeks came to venerate the goddess Athena, who symbolized wisdom or divine intelligence. They made wisdom their highest ideal. Civilization owes a tremendous debt to the Greeks for establishing new ways of thinking. They bequeathed to us the idea that man and nature should be objects of systematic study and that one should seek rational explanations for natural phenomena. The long transition leading from superstition to science made a great step forward in ancient Greece.[408]

Like the traditional gods, nature might seem to be capricious. An earthquake or a volcanic eruption can happen without warning. But in fact, natural disasters (sometimes called "acts of God") are not entirely random. There are patterns in nature, such as atmospheric circulation and tectonic plate motions, that can be discerned through careful observations. Unvarying laws of nature underlie seemingly random events. Darwin reminds us that these laws are inferred and verified by the observation of causal sequences:

> It is difficult to avoid personifying the word Nature; but I mean by Nature, only the aggregate action and product of

many natural laws, and by laws the sequence of events as ascertained by us.[409]

Even when the forces of nature are beyond our powers of prediction, humans can learn how best to prepare and to respond through understanding of nature's lessons. We don't have to rely on the gods' commands or on the commands of a tyrant who believes he is a god. To realize the Greek ideal of wisdom, we must view nature as a teacher rather than an adversary or a slave. But if, like Xerxes, we are in denial about what nature teaches us, there is no limit to the wrong views that we might adopt.

Today, around half of America has chosen to discard the heritage of the Greek thinkers. They reject the methods and findings of science concerning the age of the earth, the origin of species, and human effects on the environment. Ignoring what nature teaches, they put their faith in Biblical literalism, pseudoscience, and crackpot conspiracy hoaxes.[410] Many are led to deny that human activity is warming the earth's climate, to deny the efficacy of medically-proven vaccines, and to deny the present reality of the coronavirus pandemic. They choose to live in what Carl Sagan called "the demon-haunted world." It is not a recent development, as shown by opinion polls going back several decades.[411] However, since 2016 the polls have noted an upsurge in the fear and loathing of higher education.[412] Some Americans feel justified in rejecting certain fields of natural science and medicine while accepting others, but this is a fallacy. The interconnectedness of scientific disciplines means that to deny the validity of one field is to deny the validity of all. Rather than venerating Athena—symbol of sound judgment informed by what nature teaches—about half of America chooses to embrace the irrational.

To give the natural world an irrational interpretation is superstition, one aspect of which is *magical thinking*, the notion that fervent beliefs can turn wishes into reality or can make disagreeable facts go away. Religion becomes magical when believers ask the supernatural powers to provide them with blessings and to protect them from harm. The hallmark of superstition is the denial of causality, the principle of cause and effect in the natural world. In medieval Europe, to investigate causality was treated as heresy, because it would lead people to doubt God's will and the authority of the Church. "The priest knows only one great danger," says Nietzsche, "and that is science—the healthy concept of cause and effect."[413]

Empirical science holds that knowledge comes from the careful observation of causal sequences in everyday reality.[414] By contrast, magical thinking asserts that the causes are whatever I imagine, and the effects are whatever I desire: *When you wish upon a star / Makes no difference who you are / Anything your heart desires will come... to... you.* I might choose to believe that random events, like a throw of dice, have a mysterious cause called *luck*. Success or failure in gambling is often interpreted in this way—today I was unlucky and lost, but next time my luck will change. I have invented an imaginary cause that controls what will happen:

> The sporting man's sense of luck... implies the possibility of propitiating, or of deceiving and cajoling... the apparatus and accessories of any game of skill or chance... [It] is a more or less articulate belief in an inscrutable preternatural agency.[415]

Magical thinking also means believing that real phenomena can produce supernatural effects. Astrology proposes that the sun, moon, and planets have uncanny agency, such that their positions at the moment of my birth will influence my character and life events.[416] But the evidence from physics has completely refuted this claim; there is no physical mechanism or agency by which distant heavenly bodies could affect the make-up of a human being.

Believing in imaginary causes and supernatural effects is a basic attribute of superstition, and there can be no room for it on the Buddhist path. Why so? *Conditional arising* (or *dependent origination*) is the idea that everything in the world arises and perishes by causes and conditions. To see clearly the connection between each action and its result is what led to the Buddha's awakening, and all of his teachings flow from it.[417]

"A learned noble disciple carefully and properly attends to dependent origination itself: 'When this exists, that is; due to the arising of this, that arises. When this doesn't exist, that is not; due to the cessation of this, that ceases.'"[418]

The affirmation of causality sets Buddhism apart from magical religions. Shinran, founder of Jōdo Shinshū, understood the truth of conditional arising. Although he lived in a time and place when magical beliefs and practices were prevalent, Shinran denied the value of such practices, including deathbed rituals, fortune telling, and praying to the gods for material rewards.[419] Therefore, in Shin Buddhism we make a ritual offering of incense and bow in *gasshō* as an expression of reverence and gratitude. The meaning is psychological. There is no expectation that we will be purified or receive a material reward.

Religious practices may seem magical, but a closer look might lead us to change our opinion. A favorite place for sightseeing near Kyoto is Fushimi Inari Taisha, a shrine that includes hundreds of orange *torii* gates that have been donated by businesses to ensure their success. Japanese businesspeople also pray at shrines for prosperity in the year ahead. If company employees genuinely believe that these practices are effective, this could, in itself, give employees the motivation to succeed. Donating *torii* and praying at a shrine may appear to reflect magical thinking, but looked at psychologically these actions could have a real effect on how the business performs.

In evaluating religious practices, there is a strong element of subjective experience to consider. Yet, the process of mental transformation on the Shin Buddhist path involves only true causes and real effects, consistent with the Buddha's original insight. If we find something in Shin Buddhism that seems to deny causality, that means we need to look more deeply for the symbolic or psychological meaning.

To sum up, people tend to see the natural world as something to be feared or exploited, which is contrary to the teachings of Buddhism. An antidote to wrong views was provided by the ancient Greeks, who sought to learn from nature. Contrast that with magical thinking, in which the world is given a supernatural interpretation. Affirming the principle of cause and effect is the Buddha's basic teaching, so by my definition, Buddhism is not a magical religion. Neither do the teachings of Shinran support a magical view. Finally, in following the Shin Buddhist path, we experience a psychological transformation based on true causes and real effects. Coming to understand that we are interdependent with the whole of existence is the Shin Buddhist life of awakening.

Part VIII

What Shinran Teaches

"To abandon the mind of self-power" admonishes the various and diverse kinds of people... to abandon the conviction that one is good, to cease relying on the self, to stop reflecting knowingly on one's evil heart, and further to abandon the judging of people as good and bad.[420]

—Notes on 'Essentials of Faith Alone'

The Teaching for Our Era

Ignorance and blind passions abound,
Pervading everywhere like innumerable particles of dust.[421]

—Gutoku Shinran

There are a great many Buddhist teachings, described as eighty-four thousand gateways to the Dharma.[422] This reflects the uniqueness of each human being and of each time and place where the Dharma is shared. From out of these many teachings, how can we find the right path? Shinran confronted this question eight centuries ago. As a monk he practiced on Mt. Hiei for twenty years but could not discover a way to liberation that was suitable for his era. Embracing a path that lay outside of institutional Buddhism, he declared that Jōdo Shinshū is "the teaching and practice for our latter age; devote yourself solely to it."[423] To appreciate Shinran's teaching, we must have an awareness of the historical era in which he lived. What led him to call it the "latter age" of the Dharma?[424] Could it have anything in common with our own strife-filled era?

Shinran was born in 1173 during the waning years of the Heian period when Japan's capital city was Heian-kyō, or Kyoto as it's known today. Political stability and flourishing culture had been the norm for almost four centuries, but the final decades of the Heian period were a time of conflict, the result of which was the transfer of political authority from the Imperial Court in Heian-kyō to the shogunate in Kamakura. This turning point is memorialized in a literary classic, the *Tale of the Heike*. The word "Heike" refers to the Taira clan, whose story it is. The *Tale* draws on a cast of historical figures who gained legendary status as warriors and rulers. It takes impermanence as its theme, as expressed in the opening lines:

> The sound of the bell of Gion Shōja echoes the impermanence of all things. The hue of the flowers of the sal tree declares that they who flourish must be brought low. Yea, the proud ones are but for a moment, like an evening

dream in springtime. The mighty are destroyed at the last: they are as dust before the wind.[425]

Thus, the *Tale* goes on to describe the rise and fall of the Taira clan. I will focus on a specific historical figure—the man whose actions propel the drama of this story—Taira no Kiyomori (1118-1181). Earlier in the Heian period the Emperor served as the head of state, while much of the actual authority resided with leaders of the nobility, mainly the Fujiwara family. Political disputes in the capital were settled without bloodshed. However, in the 1150s the winds of impermanence swept through Japan. Rival factions in the palace squared off, and as the conflict escalated to open violence, the warrior clans were called in. Taira no Kiyomori ended up on the winning side, and the leaders of the losing side were all executed. Kiyomori had surmised that by beheading his own uncles, his temporary ally and main rival, Minamoto no Yoshitomo, would be forced to behead his own father and brothers. In the events that followed the bloodbath, the Taira clan (or Heike) gained the advantage over their rivals, the Minamoto clan (also known as the Genji).

For the next twenty years, the ruling power resided with Kiyomori, an autocrat lacking any trace of humility. His arrogance was boundless, and his impulsive behavior provoked resentment, as when he ignored palace seniority and promoted his sons to high-ranking positions. He arranged for his daughter to marry to the Emperor, and when a son was born, he forced the sovereign to abdicate.[426] Kiyomori's infant grandson became the new Emperor. Kiyomori acquired and discarded beautiful women, and he fathered around twenty children. He had one virtuous advisor, his son Shigemori, who prevented his father from harassing the retired Emperor and from executing more of the nobles. But after the son's early death, Kiyomori was unrestrained in his cruelty, which was seen as hastening the end of Taira supremacy. As the *Tale* declares, "The proud ones are but for a moment."

In 1180, angered by provocations from the monks in Nara, Kiyomori ordered his forces to attack. This resulted in the burning of the famous temples of Nara, including Tōdai-ji with its Great Buddha

Hall. If you have visited Nara, you saw buildings and statues that were reconstructed after the fire. This act was regarded as Kiyomori's most terrible crime, for which he would suffer karmic retribution. And within a few months he was gravely ill. Legend tells that he was so overheated with fever that water brought to cool him boiled away, and smoke filled the room. He was defiant to the end, demanding the head of his enemy, the leader of the Minamoto clan.[427] But that desire went unfulfilled. After Kiyomori's death the Taira suffered losses on the battlefield, leading to their final destruction in 1185 by the Minamoto. "The mighty are destroyed at the last: they are as dust before the wind."

The turmoil of the late Heian period was not only political. In the years leading up to 1185, the capital Heian-kyō suffered heavy damage from a series of disasters, including a great fire, a great whirlwind, and a great earthquake.[428] Added to these were famine and plague, and corpses were piled up in the streets. Two teachers from our tradition were on hand for these terrible events. Hōnen had become famous by sharing Pure Land Buddhism with people in the city; he even makes an appearance as a character in the *Tale of the Heike*.[429] Meanwhile, a boy monk named Hannen was diligently studying and practicing on Mt. Hiei. As an adult, he would leave the mountain to become a student of Hōnen and a follower of Jōdo Shinshū. Eventually, Hannen would take the name Gutoku Shinran.

What was it like to practice Buddhism on Mt. Hiei? Monasteries in those days were quite different from what we might expect. Monks were organized into armed goon squads, which enabled the Mt. Hiei and Nara monasteries to do battle with rival sects and with the warrior clans. There were instances when the monks executed their prisoners. It was not unusual for a member of the nobility, even a retired Emperor, to take monastic vows while continuing to engage in political intrigues. Absurd as it might seem, Taira no Kiyomori at the height of his power "renounced the world" (allegedly) and received ordination as a novice, in the hope that it would cure his illness.[430] Hence, the sculpture of Kiyomori shown on the next page depicts him in the garb of a priest! Given these travesties, it's apparent why Hannen came to doubt the validity of the monastic path.

WHAT SHINRAN TEACHES

If that was the character of monastic Buddhism in medieval Japan, then what was the layperson's religion? In those days it was a belief system based on imaginary causes and supernatural effects, in other words, magical thinking. As with Kiyomori's ordination, religious practices were performed to bring good fortune and ward off bad fortune, an idea that pervades the *Tale of the Heike*. Monasteries inspired fear not only through acts of violence but through a popular belief in evil spirits or demons, which the monks could supposedly control. Another popular belief was to see the Buddhist Pure Land as a place of refuge after death, which one could attain through religious practices, especially through deathbed rituals to prepare for Amida's coming (*rinjū no raikō*). The idea became increasingly prevalent as social conditions in Japan deteriorated.

Such was religion in Shinran's era, the "latter age" of the Dharma. Buddhist institutions had lost all validity, and the layperson's belief system was superstition and escapism.

> *How lamentable it is that monks and laypeople*
> *Select "fortunate times" and "auspicious days,"*
> *And paying homage to gods of the heavens and the earth,*
> *Engage in divination and rituals of worship.*[431]

Other teachings applies to those who incline toward the Path of Sages or non-Buddhist ways, endeavor in other practices, think on other Buddhas, observe lucky days and auspicious occasions, and depend on fortune-telling and ritual purification. Such people belong to non-Buddhist ways; they rely wholly on self-power.[432]

Those who believe the deluded teachings of evil maras, non-Buddhists, or sorcerers foretelling calamity or fortune may be stricken by fear; their minds will become unsound. Engaging in divination, they will foretell misfortune and will come to kill various sentient beings. They may make prayers to gods or invoke spirits to beg for good fortune and wish for long life, but in the end these will not be obtained.[433]

In rejecting religion as he found it, Shinran discovered an authentic Buddhist path. He taught that ritual purification cannot bring rewards or prevent bad fortune, that evil spirits cannot obstruct the path of a person of the nembutsu, and that for a nembutsu person there is no need for deathbed rites to prepare for Amida's coming.[434] These are notable departures from the commonly held views of his day. It was necessary, he felt, to reject such misconceptions in order to encounter Jōdo Shinshū, the true essence of the Pure Land.

Shinran identified the teaching and practice suited for his era when warfare and natural disasters led to social chaos. It was a time of limitless greed, hatred, and ignorance, of which Taira no Kiyomori was emblematic. What about 21st century America? Is Shin Buddhism the teaching and practice for our own era? Do present-day conditions resemble the demon-haunted world of medieval Japan? Not entirely, but similarities are increasingly evident. We can anticipate devastation from earthquakes and from the consequences of climate warming, including wildfires, flooding, plagues, warfare, and mass migration. Perversely, around half of America's adults have chosen to reject the findings of science and medicine and to rely instead on their own desires and superstitions.[435] They take a pre-scientific, medieval view of the world, despite this being the 21st century. As an analog to the Kamakura warrior clans, we have America's political factions. In our poisoned public life, there are slander and diatribe instead of dialogue, reaction instead of reflection, and escalation of disagreements to limitless hatred and acts of violence. Most ominously, the Kiyomori for our own era has emerged.[436]

Allow me to suggest that Shin Buddhism is applicable in any era, including 21st century America, because it does not depend on finding favorable conditions for performing Buddhist practices. Thus, even in the Kamakura period when the Dharma was mostly extinct, Shinran could say that Jōdo Shinshū is "the path to realization that is now vital and flourishing." He saw it as a universal way to spiritual liberation that speaks to the human condition regardless of locality or historical era. Śākyamuni is said to have taught eighty-four thousand Dharma gateways, which Shinran understood to be the Buddha's expedient means that can lead us eventually to Jōdo Shinshū:

> Encouraging and guiding all sentient beings with various means through [the provisional gateways], the Buddha teaches and encourages them to enter "the great treasure ocean of true and real virtue—the [*Hongan*], perfect and unhindered, which is the One Vehicle."[437]

For Shinran, the Buddha appeared in the world solely to teach *Hongan*, the true essence of the Pure Land.

His Path to Realization

At the end of a life man notices that he has spent years becoming sure of a single truth. But a single truth, if it is obvious, is enough to guide an existence.[438]

—Albert Camus

Near the conclusion of the *Kyōgyōshinshō*, Shinran delineates the trajectory of his life in one brief sentence.[439] Whenever I read the passage—Shinran's single truth—I am struck by how personal it is and by its universal implications. It begins this way:

Reflecting within myself,

The words emphasize that Shinran's path is one of self-examination, and that the statements to follow are autobiographical.

I see that in the various teachings of the Path of Sages, practice and enlightenment died out long ago,

This discovery marked the death of Shinran's ambitions for self-improvement, that is, practices leading to enlightenment. As a monk he was devoted to the Path of Sages, which in Mt. Hiei Buddhism includes extreme physical and mental disciplines reminiscent of the asceticism followed by Gotama prior to his awakening. The first part of Shinran's life came to an end when he, like Gotama, reached an impasse, and he felt compelled to discard his former approach and to leave Mt. Hiei. Regarding the second part of his life, Shinran says,

while Jōdo Shinshū is the path to realization now vital and flourishing.

He does not construe the words "Jōdo Shinshū" as the name of a Buddhist sect. Rather, the words are an assertion that the Pure Land teaching is the true essence of Buddhism. Shinran embraced the Pure Land by listening to his teacher Hōnen, who embodied the timeless truth of the Dharma. In so doing, he stopped relying on his religious ego, and became a seeker like Dharmākara, the hero of the story told in the *Larger Sutra*. Shinran continued to revere Hōnen as his great teacher, but his exploration of the scriptures went beyond what Hōnen taught. By continuing to deepen his appreciation of Jōdo Shinshū, Shinran's path to realization remained vital and flourishing.

Teacher and Poet

Wisdom-light in its brilliance wakens wisdom-eyes,
And the Name is heard throughout the ten quarters.[440]

—Gutoku Shinran

Shinran's spiritual seeking was a great advance for the Buddha-dharma, owing to the psychological depth of what he found and to the unstable era in which he lived. Eight centuries later, we are just beginning to appreciate his accomplishment. Shinran put forward a thorough "revaluation" of Buddhist values amid the social and religious disintegration of the Kamakura period. Soon after his death the spirit of his teaching was compromised by a blending with secular values,[441] and it fell further into obscurity during the Edo period (1603-1868) when religious institutions were closely allied with the central government.[442] What about our own era? Amid the instability and alienation of 21st century America, could the Dharma-gate of Jōdo Shinshū have opened again? Perhaps Shinran's greatest impact on Buddhist history *has yet to be felt*.

If we aspire to learn about the path that he followed, it's crucial to understand what, exactly, was his Buddhist practice. Notably, by around age forty, he had abandoned all religious practices, as they were understood in his day.[443] While living in the Kantō region, Shinran was part of a community of Buddhist laypeople. They gathered at *dōjō*, or meeting places, which could be any ordinary residences that were suitable. There were no officially sanctioned temples for Jōdo Shinshū followers, and when the sangha gathered, their activities did not involve priests performing rituals. One practice that we can be certain they emphasized was Dharma listening. To the extent that we listen to the teachings as they did, we will be on the right track as Shin Buddhists.

The final thirty years of Shinran's life were spent in Kyoto, mostly out of the public eye. So far as one can tell, his sole focus during this time was hearing and reflecting on the Dharma ever more deeply.[444] Specifically, his Buddhist practice was *reading and writing*. He does not mention any sort of practices beyond this. It appears that he did not aim to establish a new sect of Buddhism or to record his own ideas for posterity's sake. Rather, his reading and writing were for the purpose of asking What am I? in light of the teachings he had received. Yet, the ripples spreading outward from the life of this truth-seeker would eventually give rise to some of the most powerful religious organizations in Japan!

Shinran drew inspiration from the sutras and from commentaries by his predecessors, the Pure Land masters. Most of his writings are reflections on these ancient texts, set down for the purpose of clarifying his understanding. The sutras and commentaries contain a great deal of poetry, that is, verses such as *Sanbutsuge*, *Jūseige*, and *Jūnirai*. From these examples Shinran was inspired to compose his own poems, most significantly the *Shōshinge*, which he produced during the middle part of his life. The 120 lines are a summary of Shinran's entire teaching, written in a highly compressed poetic form with seven Chinese characters per line. Here is the opening stanza:[445]

Kimyō muryōju nyorai
In the Tathāgata of Immeasurable Life, take refuge!

Namo fukashigi kō
In the Light that surpasses all thoughts and ideas, take refuge!

Hōzō bosatsu inni ji
Dharmākara, while on the bodhisattva path

Zai sejizaiō bussho
And under the guidance of the Buddha, Spiritual-King-Who-Lived-Freely-in-Samsara,

At the outset, there is the command for refuge taking, leading immediately into the story of the truth-seeker Dharmākara. Stanzas 1 through 5 of *Shōshinge* convey core teachings from the *Larger Sutra*; stanzas 6 through 11 describe the Shin Buddhist life of awakening; while stanzas 12 through 30 pay homage to the Pure Land masters. Every line requires considerable decoding if one is to grasp the meaning.[446] Such a poem could only have been composed by a literary genius—an underappreciated aspect of Shinran's achievement. Centuries later, chanting *Shōshinge* became a popular practice for Jōdo Shinshū followers. However, Shinran said nothing to advocate doing this, which suggests that he wrote the verses for his own study and reflection.[447] His writings contain a second (possibly earlier) version of the 120-line poem with variants that add to our understanding, such as the epigraph at the head of this essay.[448]

Shinran continued to read and write with great energy until the end of his life, with poetry being the main literary form that he employed in his old age. He composed the *Nyūshutsu nimonge*, a Chinese-language poem in 148 lines, reflecting on the teaching of Vasubandhu and the Chinese masters.[449] In the four-line Japanese-language poems called *wasan* he found a way to make the teachings available to laypeople who could not understand Chinese. His *wasan* poems dealing with Amida Buddha, the Pure Land, and the masters of India, China, and Japan were circulated among the members of the community. Here is the most famous of them:

Such is the benevolence of the Tathāgata's great compassion,
That I must strive to repay it even if my body turns to dust.
Such is the benevolence of the masters and true teachers,
That I will thank them until my bones have crumbled.[450]

Popularly known as *Ondokusan*, the poem is from a collection called *Hymns of the Dharma-Ages*, which contains some of Shinran's sharpest reflections on the age when the Dharma is ending (*mappō no jidai*).

The three pillars of Buddhism are teachings (sutras and commentaries), practices (transforming activities), and realization (awakening), which are seen as diminishing in sequential eras after Śākyamuni's passing.[451] In the *right age* of the Dharma, the Buddha's influence is strongly felt. All three pillars are sturdy, and many people attain realization. Then follows the *semblance age* when true teachings and practices still exist, but no realization can occur by the route taken previously. In the *ending age* of the Dharma the teaching remains, but neither practice nor realization are possible on the Path of Sages.[452] Here is how Shinran—at age 84—responds to the spiritual climate of his era:

> In 1257, on the night of the ninth day of the second month, during the hour of the tiger, I was told in a dream:
>
> *Entrust yourself to Amida's [Hongan].*
> *Through the benefit of being grasped, never to be abandoned,*
> *All who entrust themselves to the [Hongan]*
> *Attain the supreme enlightenment.*[453]

He admonishes us to be mindful of conditions in the present era, lest we overestimate our spiritual capabilities.

> *It is now more than two thousand years*
> *Since the passing of Śākyamuni Tathāgata.*
> *The right and semblance ages have already closed;*
> *So lament, disciples of later times!* [454]
>
> *Sentient beings' wrong views grow rampant*
> *Becoming like thickets and forests, bramble and thorns;*
> *Filled with suspicion, they slander those who follow the nembutsu,*
> *While the use of violence and the poison of anger spread widely.*[455]
>
> *With the advent of the semblance and last dharma-ages, and this world of the five defilements,*
> *The teachings left by Śākyamuni entered into concealment.*
> *Only the compassionate Vow of Amida becomes widely known,*
> *And attainment of birth through the nembutsu spreads.*
>
> Know that the teachings that were left by Śākyamuni have been distorted and lost, and have entered [into concealment].[456]

Shinran came to see himself as embodying both *mappō* and the necessity for transcending it, an understanding that he called the true essence of the Pure Land. His *Hymns of the Dharma-Ages* are a characteristic expression of his teaching: a deep reflection on the impossibility of a foolish being attaining liberation, and a deep sense of gratitude for the Pure Land teaching by which this does, in fact, take place.

To Liberate All Sentient Beings

On seeing a bodhisattva perform various practices, some give rise to a good mind and others a mind of evil, but the bodhisattva embraces them all.[457]

—Garland Sutra

Mahāyāna Buddhism teaches the path of the bodhisattva, a being striving for enlightenment who defers final nirvana until all sentient beings have been liberated. A bodhisattva has the aspiration to save everyone, with no exceptions, an idea that is difficult for us to embrace. I once heard a temple member ask, "Why should I try to become a buddha if even [a notorious murderer] will be liberated too?" This question derives from certain views that we might adopt at one time or another. Consider the following examples.

Work Ethic. I may think that my effort to follow the Buddhist path is wasted if a murderer can be saved by a short-cut approach. "It's unfair for me to work hard at being a good person, while he becomes a buddha without doing the virtuous things I've done. Why should he be rewarded without putting in the effort?" The error here is that I am making an invidious comparison between my path and the path that others have followed. In Jōdo Shinshū, Buddhahood is attained in spite of my calculated efforts, rather than because of them.

> Great compassion illuminates everyone at all times, but any contrivance to attain enlightenment by cultivating one's own virtues or capabilities—whether through moral action or religious practice—will blind one to it, making sincere trust (shinjin) impossible.[458]

Sin and Judgment. I may think that Buddhahood is a reward for moral and ethical accomplishments, and that a virtuous person is more deserving of becoming a buddha than is the criminal. In some religions, the gods reward virtuous actions and punish harmful actions. By contrast, Shin Buddhist liberation means understanding that I am a foolish being who wrongly believes he is capable of sound moral judgments and virtuous actions, and who is for that very reason "incurable." Shin Buddhist liberation is not a reward for moral goodness.

> A foolish being is by nature possessed of blind passions, so you must recognize yourself as a being of karmic evil. On the other hand, you should not think that you deserve to attain birth because you are good. You cannot be born into the true and real fulfilled land through such self-power calculation.[459]

> ...people who rely on doing good through their self-power fail to entrust themselves wholeheartedly to [*tariki*] and therefore are not in accord with Amida's [*Hongan*], but when they overturn the mind of self-power and entrust themselves to [*tariki*], they will attain birth in the true and real fulfilled land.[460]

Tariki is power beyond the self; it is the expression of *Hongan*, the universal wish to become a Buddha.[461] The *akunin* or "evil person" (better rendered as the obstinate or unfortunate person), awakens this deeply hidden aspiration through listening to the Dharma.

> It is impossible for us, who are possessed of blind passions, to free ourselves from birth-and-death through any practice whatever. Sorrowing at this, Amida made the Vow, the essential intent of which is the evil person's attainment of Buddhahood. Hence, evil persons who entrust themselves to [*tariki*] are precisely the ones who possess the true cause of birth.[462]

History and Prophecy. I may take a Biblical perspective, which is to believe that history is guided by the divine will and that prophecies in scripture are fulfilled by historical events. However, the bodhisattva ideal is unlike the teaching of Biblical religions. All people can be liberated, but the causes and conditions are such that many are not. The bodhisattva's vow that all people will be saved is not a prophecy, but rather an aspiration, the focus of one's entire being. A bodhisattva realizes the wisdom that makes no distinction between self and others. Therefore, liberation for oneself is possible only by seeking liberation for everyone.

The *Contemplation Sutra* tells the story of Ajātaśatru, a prince who seizes power from his father, King Bimbisāra, and tries to starve him to death in prison. He attempts to kill his mother, Queen Vaidehī, before locking her in prison as well. Parricide is among the grave offenses that make a person unsavable, and Ajātaśatru is the model for the *icchantika* or incurable person.[463] Remarkably, Shinran saw his own deeds as no different from Ajātaśatru's and no different from the crimes of Devadatta, the disciple who attempted to overthrow and kill the Buddha. In Shinran's startling interpretation, the story in the *Contemplation Sutra* is "a cosmic drama produced by Śākyamuni with a cast of actors and actresses made up of incarnated sages, i.e., enlightened ones, who acted out the play in order to make us aware of our own grave offenses and evils."[464]

> Thus it is that when conditions for the teaching of birth in the Pure Land had matured, Devadatta provoked Ajātaśatru to commit grave crimes. And when the opportunity arose for explaining the pure act by which birth is settled, Śākyamuni led Vaidehī to select the land of peace. In their selfless love, these incarnated ones—Devadatta, Ajātaśatru, Vaidehī—all aspired to save the multitudes of beings from pain and affliction, and in his compassion, Śākyamuni, the great hero, sought indeed to bless those committing the five grave offenses, those slandering the Dharma, and those lacking the seed of Buddhahood.[465]

Shinran did not regard Devadatta, Ajātaśatru, and Vaidehī simply as historical figures, but rather as characters in a timeless story. Could that also be how he regarded Śākyamuni, the great hero?

Shinran interpreted the bodhisattva's vow to save everyone, with no exceptions, as having been made expressly for him, a person who was unsavable, like the archetypal villains of Buddhism. Rather than resenting the idea that a murderer can become a buddha, he revered these "incarnated sages" for their role in establishing the Pure Land teaching by which the unsavable person can attain Buddhahood.

A Narrow Road to the Interior

Would you go into solitude, my brother? Would you seek the way to yourself? Tarry yet a little, and listen to me.[466]

—Friedrich Nietzsche

Shin Buddhism emphasizes just one element of the Eightfold Path: *shōken*, or right view. Realizing all eight elements is the goal on the Path of Sages. From a Shin Buddhist perspective, right view is bound up with *jaken*, or distorted views. These two seeming opposites (right view and distorted views) are realized simultaneously! Right view means to become aware of my deeply seated wrong views. I do not overcome *jaken*, and therefore I am unable to follow the Eightfold Path in the manner of the early disciples. I have a distorted view of the self and wrong ideas about Buddhism. Through reflection on what we truly are, the Shin Buddhist path brings about the transformation of our minds to realize *shōken* through the awareness of *jaken*.

Shinran experienced this transformation. The path he followed can be described metaphorically as a narrow road to the interior (*oku no hoso michi*).[467] In pursuing it, he encountered three stages of spiritual seeking, which came to be called *sangan tennyū* ("three-vows-turning-entering").[468] Shinran's search led him to Jōdo Shinshū, the true essence of the Pure Land, but before reaching that stage, he twice came to recognize his distorted views of Buddhism.[469]

Early in life he tried to attain enlightenment through monastic discipline. As an ambitious Tendai practitioner, he sought to become a buddha by "performing meritorious acts," which likely included the austere practices of continuous walking meditation (*jōgyō zanmai*) and repetitively circling the mountain (*kaihōgyō*). At age twenty-eight (1201), he abandoned that approach when he understood the depth of his ego and the impossibility of acquiring merit through his own effort. In one sense, Shinran had failed, but in so doing he transcended the limitations of the Path of Sages. He saw that self-improvement through meritorious deeds rests on a distorted view or *jaken*. Shinran realized one aspect of right view or *shōken*. He had gained a clearer awareness of the self.

Then, having met his teacher Hōnen, he adopted the view that he would attain birth in the Pure Land through "cultivating the root of virtue" by reciting Namo Amida Butsu. This seemed to be what Hōnen was teaching and what the members of Hōnen's sangha were practicing. The idea was popular in China and Japan: recite Namo Amida Butsu in order to be born in a land of extreme happiness after death. Shinran committed himself to attaining Pure Land birth through religious practices. Rather than being an ambitious person, he now aspired to be a devout person. After a few years, though, he started to have doubts about what he was doing. He wondered if he had misunderstood his teacher. The path of devotional practices leading to a heavenly afterworld seems far removed from the teachings of Gotama Buddha. Through his careful study of the sutras and commentaries, Shinran concluded that he had again adopted a distorted view of the Buddhist path:

> Sages of the Mahāyāna and Hīnayāna and all good people make [the *Hongan's*] auspicious Name their own root of good; hence, they cannot give rise to shinjin and do not apprehend the Buddha's wisdom. Because they cannot comprehend [Dharmākara's intent] in establishing the cause [of supreme enlightenment], they do not enter the fulfilled land.[470]

This change of heart seems to have occurred by or during 1205, a year of significant events in his studentship with Hōnen.[471]

Shinran's great insight was to see that to be an ambitious person and to be a devout person are provisional forms of Buddhism that rely on the ego-centered notion of self-improvement.[472] They are distorted views that were, for him, necessary stages leading to the true Pure Land teaching. Henceforth, he saw himself only as a foolish person with no capacity for spiritual advancement through meritorious deeds and religious devotion. Given the level of his commitment, we can assume that, outwardly, he was an exemplary practitioner. Yet, inwardly, he saw that his actions were lacking in truth and sincerity; they were false and empty.

Shinran's word for the mind of self-improvement is *hakarai*, or calculated thinking. It is to formulate a plan for attaining religious awakening by relying on one's own perceived goodness. Calculated thinking, arising from the religious ego, is the most basic type of distorted view. Shinran's relentless self-examination led him to doubt his calculating mind, a realization that he expressed with a vivid metaphor:

> The ocean of the Vow does not keep within it the dead bodies of various good practices performed by *śrāvakas* and *pratyekabuddhas*. How, then, can it accommodate the corpses of deluded and deceitful good deeds arising from our poisoned and mixed-up minds?[473]

Yet, his perspective is not one-sidedly negative. He advocates a middle way between the extremes of being ignorant of one's limitations and being obsessive over them. He admonishes priests and laypeople "to abandon the conviction that one is good" and, simultaneously, "to stop reflecting knowingly on one's evil heart."[474] To have a perverse pride in one's failings is another manifestation of egotism.

None of us has the same personal history as Shinran. Yet, if we aspire to follow the path, we will go through stages that are analogous to what he experienced. We have confidence in our ability to act in an ethical manner, and we find satisfaction in appearing to be religious. These are necessary stages, by which we may come to doubt what we are doing. This kind of doubt is a basic characteristic of the Buddhist path. Once we experience doubts about our approach, we are in a position to receive the teachings at the level of the foolish, ordinary person. Such a person ceases to feel confident in his or her ability to act in an ethical manner. Such a person becomes aware of the ego-centered desire to appear devout. This person can admit, "Under certain conditions, I might do anything."

It can be said that there is a cycle with positive feedback.[475] I embrace various distorted views, and consequently, I come to experience my limitations. Then there is the onset of doubt—Is my approach mistaken?—as a result of which, I can listen to the teachings at a deeper level. Moving through these stages is not a one-time occurrence. It happens repeatedly. This, I believe, was Shinran's experience throughout his life.

From a Shin Buddhist perspective, right view is the awareness of my firmly held wrong views. I do not eliminate *jaken*, and therefore I am unable to follow the Path of Sages. Nevertheless, we may transcend, or cease to be limited by *jaken*. Our views are negated and affirmed at the same time, as has been expressed by Takamaro Shigaraki:

> Thinking deeply about it, I see a sharp contradiction, where my life is completely affirmed on the one hand and completely negated on the other. I live with the tension of harsh opposites, joy and pain, negating each other. To embrace a lofty aspiration through deep inner reflection is truly difficult for foolish beings like us. Through everyday activities and at the risk of my life, I must select and keep, living sincerely and earnestly while recognizing the falsity and emptiness. Painfully, I come to know with my whole heart the harsh tension of my life, while continuing to live with that tension. Experiencing this, a path opens for the first time. It turns me from the reality of what I am toward the ideal of what I aspire for—from a life of delusion to a life of awakening.[476]

Is Life Refuted?

Friedrich Nietzsche (1844-1900) describes his life's work as a "revaluation of all values." He takes aim primarily at the values of the West, but also at those of the East. His words may cause us discomfort—hitting, as they do, close to home:

> There are preachers of death; and the earth is full of those to whom denial of life must be preached. Full is the earth of the superfluous; marred is life by the all-too-many. May they be decoyed out of this life by the "life eternal"!...
>
> They meet an invalid, or an old man, or a corpse—and immediately they say: "Life is refuted!" But only they are refuted, and their eye, which sees only one aspect of existence. Shrouded in thick melancholy, and eager for the little casualties that bring death: thus do they wait, and clench their teeth....
>
> "Life is only suffering": so say others who do not lie. Then see to it that *you* cease! See to it that the life ceases which is only suffering! And let this be the teaching of your virtue: "You shall slay yourself! You shall steal away from yourself!"...
>
> Everywhere resound the voices of those who preach death; and the earth is full of those to whom death has to be preached. Or "life eternal"; it is all the same to me—if only they pass away quickly![477]

Gotama Buddha taught the reality of *duhkha*, often translated as "suffering." Does that make him one of the "preachers of death" that Nietzsche criticizes? Did Gotama teach that life is refuted because aging, sickness, and death are inevitable? Surely, he did not. And Nietzsche, judging from his later writings, does not conclude that the Buddha was a preacher of death.[478] But what about those who came after Gotama? Could they have misunderstood him? As time passed, Buddhism developed an afterworldly mentality that devalued the present life in favor of a distant future existence when Buddhahood might be realized. This devaluation, I would say, is what Nietzsche rails against.

The Buddha taught not only the reality of *duhkha*, but also the way for making the present life supremely meaningful. Recognizing life's tragic dimension is necessary, because without that recognition we will never seek the way. There are two sides to awakening—the death of the old self and the birth of a new self. The old self sees impermanence as its enemy, but for an awakened person, impermanence becomes a source of creativity. Rather than the refutation of life, the path of the Buddha leads to the complete fulfillment of human life. Here I see no contradiction with Nietzsche's vision of the awakened person, whom he calls the *Übermensch*.

> The awakened one is the meaning of the earth. Let your will say: The awakened one *shall be* the meaning of the earth!
> I entreat you, my brothers, *remain true to the earth*, and do not believe those who speak to you of otherworldly hopes! Poison-mixers are they, whether they know it or not. Despisers of life are they, decaying ones and poisoned ones themselves, of whom the earth is weary: so away with them!
> Once blasphemy against God was the greatest blasphemy; but God died, and therewith also those sinners. To blaspheme the earth is now the most dreadful sin, and to rate the entrails of the unknowable higher than the meaning of the earth.[479]

At one point, Nietzsche's vision seems to echo Shan-tao's parable of the two rivers and the white path:

> Man is a rope stretched between the animal and the *Übermensch*—a rope over an abyss. A dangerous crossing, a dangerous wayfaring, a dangerous looking-back, a dangerous trembling and halting. What is great in man is that he is a bridge and not a goal.[480]

WHAT SHINRAN TEACHES

Gotama Buddha was not a preacher of death who taught that human life is refuted. Neither was Shinran, but judging by what some of his interpreters have said, you might question my assertion. Certainly, Shinran urges us to confront the reality of our greed, anger, and delusion:

> But with a foolish being full of blind passions, in this fleeting world—this burning house—all matters without exception are empty and false, totally without truth and sincerity.[481]

If this aspect of Shinran's teaching is taken in isolation, it can make him sound like a preacher of death, one who says that the present life is refuted, and hence we must wait for a future existence, call it "birth in the Pure Land," where conditions will be more favorable. However, this interpretation does not accord with Shinran's larger message.

He taught and lived the life of shinjin, or awakening in the present moment "without severing blind passions (*fudan bonnō*)." It is to see what we truly are—foolish beings caught in samsara, "ever sinking and ever wandering in transmigration from innumerable kalpas in the past, with never a condition that would lead to emancipation."[482] Awakening means, *at the same time*, "allowing yourself to be carried by the power of the Vow without any doubt or apprehension," to receive the benefit of a life of humility and creativity here and now, and to realize supreme nirvana as this life draws to an end.

> Beholding the power of the Tathāgata's [*Hongan*], I see that people who entrust themselves to it do not meaninglessly remain in samsaric life here.[483]

> Because sentient beings of the nembutsu have perfectly realized the diamond-like mind of crosswise transcendence, they transcend and realize great, complete nirvana on the eve of the moment of death.[484]

By way of this paradoxical teaching, Shinran guides us to the fulfillment of human life, culminating in perfect completion in the same sense that Gotama experienced it.

The voice of the Dharma summons *all* beings to be liberated, but at times there are *none* with the ears to hear it. Thus, Nietzsche's phrase "a book for all and none"[485] might well be applied to the *Kyōgyōshinshō*. Shinran undertook a radical revaluation of Buddhist values during an era when the light of the Dharma was "concealed in dormancy." Through deep listening and self-reflection, he rediscovered the true heart and mind of the Buddha. The teaching spread widely in the centuries after Shinran's passing—all the while becoming blended with various ideas that served the needs of institutional religion and secular government, thereby obscuring what Shinran had brought forth.[486] Eventually, when Japan was thrown open to Western ideas, there arose a renewed interest in Shinran's teaching, some six hundred years after his death.[487] He might therefore be regarded as a "posthumous man." Could his intent in writing the *Kyōgyōshinshō* be expressed by these haunting words?

> This book belongs to the very few. Maybe not one of them is alive yet.... How *can* I confound myself with those who today already find a hearing? Only the day after tomorrow belongs to me. Some are born posthumously.[488]

True Settlement

Shinjin is an expression of the realization that your life, which is limited and finite, has a place within the infinite. As I strive to express what shinjin is, I have tried to make it my own, which is a most difficult thing.[489]

—Hideo Yonezawa

One of the most ambitious goals that we can aim for is to understand Shinran. He lived eight centuries ago in a culture vastly different from 21st century America. As a Tendai monk, he engaged in austere practices that most of us could never endure. Then, he abandoned monasticism and devoted his life to reflecting on the teaching he had received from Hōnen. Owing to Shinran's personal history, it takes effort on our part to appreciate the context out of which his writings flow.

We have a further challenge. Shinran, like Gotama before him, upended the religious values of his day (and of ours, as well). We have trouble accepting his ideas, because they conflict with our own views and prejudices.

Perhaps the most puzzling aspect of studying Shinran is that each interpreter is influenced by his or her life experience and by the teachers he or she has known. So, if we listen to many talks and read various books about Shin Buddhism, we are bound to find contradictory statements. I don't regard this as a bad thing, because encountering contradictions helps us to think critically. We must engage personally with Shinran's writings, and, with a sense of humility, decide for ourselves what the evidence shows. In this book I have tried to convey what the evidence is telling me.

Here I will focus on an idea that is central to Shinran's teaching—the idea of *true settlement*. The stage of the truly settled (*shōjōju*) is a transformation of one's mind that occurs on the Buddhist path. It is an aspect of *shinjin*, a word that has no precise equivalent in English, but means, roughly, self-awareness or a life of awakening.

During Gotama's lifetime, many disciples attained awakening by listening to his words, but, with the passing of the historical Buddha, this Way of the Hearers (*śrāvakayāna*) became inaccessible. As a remedy, Pure Land teachers taught that at the time of death Amida Buddha welcomes followers to an ideal environment for Dharma listening. Through a long period of practicing in Amida's land, they can realize true settlement, which guarantees the eventual attainment of Buddhahood. Prior to Shinran, the focus was on being born in the after-death Pure Land, which was the critical milestone on the long path to becoming a Buddha. If rebirth in the world of suffering continues, there will be no true settlement and no Buddhahood.

> In the Pure Land tradition prior to Shinran, ["truly settled ones"] referred to beings born in the Pure Land, who attain enlightenment without fail because of the ideal environment there conducive to religious life. Shinran, however, uses "the truly settled" to refer to persons of shinjin, awakened here and now, for they will necessarily attain enlightenment by virtue of the [*Hongan*].[490]

It was an astounding revision. The idea that true settlement could be realized in the present life was not emphasized in the ten centuries of Pure Land Buddhism prior to Shinran. It had, however, been taught by Nāgārjuna in India, as in the following passages:[491]

> If bodhisattvas wish to attain the stage of non-retrogression while in their present existence and realize the supreme, perfect enlightenment, they should think on the Buddhas in the ten quarters and call their names.[492]
>
> The Primal Vow of Amida is, "If one takes refuge in me, while being mindful of me and saying my name, one immediately enters the stage of the definitely settled, and will attain the highest, perfect enlightenment."[493]

Shinran's understanding of true settlement relies on the *Larger Sutra*, particularly the fulfillment statements of Vows 18 and 11, which he reinterprets in surprising fashion:

> [18] *All sentient beings, as they hear the Name, realize even one thought-moment of shinjin and joy, which is directed to them from Amida's sincere mind, and aspiring to be born in that land, they then attain birth and dwell in the stage of non-retrogression....*
>
> *They then attain birth*: *then* (*soku*) means immediately, without any time elapsing, without a day passing....
>
> When we are grasped by Amida, immediately—without a moment or a day elapsing—we ascend to and become established in the stage of the truly settled; this is the meaning of *attain birth*.[494]
>
> [11] *The sentient beings born in that land all dwell among the truly settled, for in that Buddha-land there is not one who is falsely settled or not settled.*
>
> In these words... we find stated the significance of *they then attain birth*; that is, to become established in the stage of the truly settled thus is itself to *dwell in the stage of non-retrogression*. When a person becomes established in this stage, he or she becomes one who will necessarily attain the supreme, great nirvana; hence, it is taught that one realizes the equal of perfect enlightenment.... It is also said that one "immediately enters the stage of the definitely settled."[495]

The meaning that Shinran attaches to the phrase, *they then attain birth*, is to enter the stage of the truly settled and necessarily attain great, complete nirvana (*daihatsu nehan* or parinirvana)—in striking contrast with ideas about the Pure Land that were then prevalent.

> The Pure Land path as seen by Shinran not only leads to non-retrogression in this life, but to the realization of supreme enlightenment at the very moment of death. This view was unheard of in the history of Buddhism.[496]

For a person of shinjin, life concludes in parinirvana—the same as Gotama Buddha. To further describe it is beyond any of our words and concepts. Simply, it means the perfect fulfillment of one's life.

Yet, there seems to be ambiguity regarding Pure Land birth, if conceived of as reappearance in an after-death realm. What could Shinran mean by attaining birth "without a moment or a day elapsing?" Is he a deceiver? Does one "attain birth" only in an indirect sense? As I see it, for a person who awakens to *Hongan* and receives shinjin, Pure Land birth (in the sense of actualizing its symbolic content) is *immediate*. And in the fulfillment statement of Vow 11 presented above ("The sentient beings born in that land all dwell among the truly settled"), I detect no ambiguity in the matter of timing: Pure Land birth cannot be imagined as deferred to a time *subsequent* to true settlement.

> ... allowing oneself to be carried by the power of the Buddha's Vow, quickly [one] attains birth in the land of purity. Supported by the Buddha's power, one immediately enters the group of the truly settled of the Mahāyāna.[497]

> Hearing of the purity and happiness of that land with wholeheartedness, the person who realizes shinjin and aspires to be born there, and the person who has already attained birth, immediately enter the stage of the truly settled.[498]

A commentary suggests that the latter passage "refers to two kinds of people," and suggests that "there is no distinction" between these people.[499] As I see it, the one "who realizes shinjin and aspires to be born" and the one "who has already attained birth" are *the same person*. It is therefore necessary to explain how Amida's Pure Land can extend into our everyday world of greed, anger, and ignorance, which I've tried to do elsewhere in this book.[500]

Many Buddhists think of the Pure Land as an afterworld, and some of Shinran's writings might be interpreted in that way if one insists on equating parinirvana with birth in Amida's land. However, the idea of being reborn in a realm of bliss and beauty—which the sutras describe in lavish detail—seems far removed from the "full extinguishment" that was the culmination of Gotama's bodhisattva career.[501] Nor is it reasonable to equate his parinirvana with boarding a two-way transport system connecting the after-death Pure Land with the present world of suffering.[502] To distinguish from those ideas, let me state plainly that Shinran's path *is* Buddhism; it exhibits a fundamental correspondence with the life and teachings of Gotama. Thus, it is natural that Shinran finds in true settlement the idea of "being the same as Maitreya," the envisioned future Buddha who will be Gotama's successor:[503]

> On realizing true and real shinjin, a person immediately enters the stage of the truly settled. Being the same as Maitreya—of the rank of succession to Buddhahood after one lifetime—this person will attain great, complete nirvana.[504]

It is said that Maitreya, after many kalpas of practicing, now waits in Tuṣita heaven. When he next appears in our world it will be his last birth, wherein he will awaken countless beings and will attain parinirvana "after one lifetime"—the same culmination as reached by his predecessor Gotama. A person of shinjin who is like Maitreya (so it would appear) will have nothing to accomplish by being reborn in an after-death realm.

> Maitreya Bodhisattva will wait 5.67 billion years, but for a person of true shinjin, *satori* opens this time around.[505]

Maitreya's attainment of the perfect enlightenment will be long in coming, but we shall reach nirvana quickly. He awaits the dawn 5.67 billion years hence, but we are as though separated by only a film of bamboo.[506]

It might be objected that my remarks do not conform with Vow 22 of the *Larger Sutra*, which for Shinran is actualized (i.e., becomes "true-and-real") along with Vow 11.[507] The objection would be valid if one regards Amida's land as strictly an after-death realm. However, by "attaining birth" in the present life, the "exceptional" bodhisattvas of Vow 22 perform practices "to guide others freely to enlightenment," and like Maitreya they attain great, complete nirvana when this one lifetime ends.[508]

To enter the stage of the truly settled means that parinirvana is inevitable, as Shinran explains:

> Ordinary people are filled with blind passions; the multitudes subject to birth-and-death are defiled by their misdeeds. However, through [Amida's] directing of virtue in its going aspect they receive the mind and practice. At that moment, they enter and are numbered among the truly settled of the Mahāyāna. Because they dwell in the truly settled stage, they necessarily attain final emancipation (*hisshi metsudo*).[509]

Metsudo (Pāli, *nirodha*) means cessation or extinguishment, and in this context it is synonymous with life's completion. For Shinran, necessarily attaining *metsudo* has eight aspects: perpetual joy, ultimate tranquility, supreme nirvana, unconditioned *dharma-kāya*, true reality, Dharma nature, true suchness, and absolute oneness.[510] Notably absent from the list is Pure Land birth (*ōjō jōdo*).[511]

Another phrase that Shinran uses for life's completion is *daihatsu nehan o satoru*.[512] Because the cycle of birth-and-death has been cut off, it can be said that "*satori* opens this time around," as was the case for Gotama and will be for Maitreya. Shinran employs the word *satori* (verb: *satoru*) only in connection with parinirvana. It is the realization of limitless reality, of which Amida and the Pure Land are symbolic expressions. They are an expedient that we receive as words and images, by means of which the symbolic content becomes true-and-real in the present life. Then, with *satori*—life's completion—the symbols are transcended.

To live a life of awakening or shinjin is to see ourselves just as we are, painful as that may be. We remain foolish beings burdened with greed, anger, and ignorance. As Shinran states, blind passions arise without pause, until the very last moment of life. Out of his deep self-awareness, he confesses,

> I know truly how [sad] it is that I, Gutoku Shinran, am sinking in an immense ocean of desires and attachments and am lost in vast mountains of fame and advantage, so that I rejoice not at all at entering the stage of the truly settled, and feel no happiness at coming nearer to the realization of true enlightenment. How ugly it is! How wretched![513]

These are sobering words for us to reflect on as we try to understand the meaning of true settlement. In another passage, Shinran expresses his deep aspiration and his unavoidable feeling of sadness. Even doubt and slander of the Dharma can be a condition for eventually realizing true settlement:

> Thus, suppressing tears of both sorrow and joy, I record the circumstances that have resulted [in my compilation of this work].... Mindful solely of the profundity of the Buddha's benevolence, I pay no heed to the derision of others. May those who see and hear this work be brought—either through the cause of reverently embracing the teaching or through the condition of doubt and slander of it—to manifest shinjin within the power of the Vow and reveal the incomparable fruit of true enlightenment in the land of peace.[514]

Postscript

Is it necessary to study the Buddhist teachings? Or, can we develop an appreciation by intuition, that is, without the conscious use of reasoning? Both approaches are possible, so we might choose the one that is best for us—study or intuition. We may be able to combine the two; it need not be either/or. But, is it possible to know which approach is more suitable?

Today in America, literacy is prevalent, at least in theory, but that was not the case during much of Japan's history. People struggled to make a living under the threat of famine and natural disasters. Among Shin Buddhist followers, there were some with little or no schooling who arrived at a deep, intuitive understanding of the Dharma, often by enduring personal hardships. Those who were renowned for special insight were called *myōkōnin*, or "wondrously excellent people."[515] Even today we may meet such exemplary followers. The best way for us to become like the *myōkōnin* is to have grown up in the presence of people who themselves had deep, intuitive appreciation. Their self-awareness would have touched our hearts. We might grow to resemble them and to share in their insights.

But, what about the person who did not have such an upbringing, who did not encounter the Dharma until later in life? For that person, the intuitive path to understanding may not be accessible. Nowadays, if he or she is secure in terms of food, clothing, and shelter, then a different way of finding the Shin Buddhist path becomes possible—the way of hearing and reflecting (*monshi*)—which I've attempted to describe in this book. It includes listening to Dharma talks and lectures, reading contemporary books on Shin Buddhism, studying Shinran's writings and the Pure Land sutras, and (most importantly) continuous self-reflection. In his commentaries, Shinran frequently adds the imperative *Let this be known* or *Reflect on this*, after stating key ideas. The phrase is both a reminder to himself and a way to encourage us to persevere in hearing and reflecting. "*Reflect on this* means that a person must understand this in accordance with the way things truly are."[516]

Many Shin Buddhists have arrived at understanding through intuition, but Shinran did not. He was as far from being a *myōkōnin* as one could get. For him to develop an appreciation of Jōdo Shinshū required a tremendous effort to hear the meaning of the *myōgō*, Namo Amida Butsu. He was led to abandon his intuitive notions, to doubt his capacity for liberation. In the process, he became perhaps the greatest Dharma listener in the history of Pure Land Buddhism. It would be foolish to think that we could emulate Shinran's level of listening, but still I would argue that he (rather than the *myōkōnin*) is the appropriate role model for many of us. We engage in study and reflection, because our intuitive notions about Buddhism may well be wrong.

> The Right Dharma is indeed something wonderful, transcending things of this world! Let us, therefore, feel no hesitancy in listening to it and reflecting on it![517]

Conclusion

People of the countryside do not know the meanings of written characters and are painfully and hopelessly ignorant [of sacred texts]. To help them understand, I have repeatedly written the same things over and over. The educated reader will probably find this writing peculiar and may ridicule it. But paying no heed to such criticism, I write only so that ignorant people may easily grasp the essential meaning.[518]

—Gutoku Shinran

About the Author

James Pollard was trained as a physical chemist (B.A., Pomona College; Ph.D., UC Berkeley) and worked for many years as an aerospace engineer. He and his wife are members of the sangha at Orange County Buddhist Church, where he serves on the temple board as vice-president for the religious program.

Notes

[1] Chapter on Practice, *CWS*, vol. 1, p. 55; *Kyō Gyō Shin Shō*, *RTS*, vol. 5, p. 57; *Shinran's Kyōgyōshinshō*, *DTS*, p. 90.

[2] *Inferno*, Canto I, trans. H.W. Longfellow.

[3] *Majjhima Nikāya* 26 (Pāsarāsi Sutta), trans. Bhikkhu Sujato, https://suttacentral.net/. See Bodhi, *IBW*, pp. 55-56.

[4] Ibid. *Nibbāna* or nirvana is the Buddhist world of awakening.

[5] From a 1942 film. Renault: "And what in heaven's name brought you to Casablanca?" Rick: "My health. I came to Casablanca for the waters." Renault: "What waters? We're in the desert!" Rick: "I was misinformed."

[6] Shunryu Suzuki, *Zen Mind, Beginner's Mind*, 21st printing (Weatherhill, 1986), p. 22.

[7] I am indebted to Dr. Nobuo Haneda for emphasizing this point.

[8] Albert Low, *What More Do You Want? Zen Questions, Zen Answers* (Tuttle, 2013), p. 28.

[9] I have never encountered this usage in the Buddhist Churches of America.

[10] Here I might be accused of oversimplifying. See Bodhi, *IBW*, pp, 145-150. Gotama urged those who are spiritually mature to put an end to rebirth and attain *nibbāna*. To those who lack maturity, he taught the path of ethical actions leading to future rebirth in the human or heavenly realms. By contrast, Shinran's exclusive focus is on putting an end to the cycle of birth-and-death, regardless of one's spiritual or ethical capabilities.

[11] *Samyutta Nikāya* 56.11 (Dhammacakkappavattana Sutta). See Rahula, *WBT*, p. 94.

[12] Chapter on Shinjin, *CWS*, vol. 1, pp. 115-116; Notes on the Inscriptions on Sacred Scrolls, pp. 495-497.

[13] *The Larger Sutra, TPLS*, vol. 2, pp. 16-17.

[14] Lamp for the Latter Ages, *CWS*, vol. 1, p. 528. Awakening in Mahāyāna Buddhism is to see that nirvana and samsara are not a

duality. See Ueda and Hirota, "The Structure of Attainment," *SIT*, pp. 83-89.

[15] Belief systems are customarily given -*ism* labels (e.g., Protestantism, Marxism). The term "Buddhism" is of European origin and has no exact counterpart in Asian languages. It serves as a stand-in for the term *kyōgyōshō* (teaching-practice-realization) found in Shinran's writings. Thankfully, labels such as "Jōdo Shinshūism" and "Shinranism" have never gained popularity.

[16] *Majjhima Nikāya* 63 (Cūlamālunkya Sutta). See Bodhi, *IBW*, pp. 230-233.

[17] Chapter on Shinjin, *CWS*, vol. 1, p. 100; *DTS*, p. 134; Chapter on the Transformed Buddhas and Lands, *CWS*, pp. 235-236 (quoting the *Nirvana Sutra*).

[18] *Dīgha Nikāya* 30 (Lakkhana Sutta); *The Larger Sutra, TPLS*, vol. 2, pp. 4-5.

[19] The Pāli suttas describe the stage of "stream-entry" or "invincible faith," which is analogous to the Mahāyāna stage of true settlement. See Bodhi, *IBW*, pp. 85-87.

[20] *Kyō Gyō Shin Shō, RTS*, vol. 5, p. 94 (quoting Shan-tao); Chapter on Shinjin, *CWS*, vol. 1, p. 90.

[21] Blaise Pascal (1623-1662), *Pensées*, trans. W.F. Trotter.

[22] "As it is, these remain: faith, hope, and charity, the three of them; and the greatest of them is charity." 1 Cor. 13:13.

[23] Gen. 18-19, Deut. 20, Josh. 1-12, 2 Sam. 8, Rev. 17-20.

[24] Albert Camus, *The Myth of Sisyphus and Other Essays*, trans. Justin O'Brien (Vintage International, 1983), p. 210.

[25] Dan Arnold and Alicia Turner, "Why Are We Surprised When Buddhists Are Violent?" *The New York Times*, 5 March 2018.

[26] "...all beings, an ocean of multitudes, have since the beginningless past down to this day, this very moment, been evil and defiled, completely lacking the mind of purity." Chapter on Shinjin, *CWS*, vol. 1, p. 95; Hymns of the Dharma Ages, pp. 402, 429; Notes on 'Essentials of Faith Alone,' p. 466.

[27] *Kokoro* Newsletter (New York Buddhist Church, July-August 2018). According to this source, the author of the Golden Chain was Dorothy

Hunt. She and her husband, Rev. Ernest Hunt, espoused a Buddhism based on the ethical teachings of Gotama in the Pāli Canon. See Michihiro Ama, *Immigrants to the Pure Land* (Univ. of Hawaii Press, 2011), pp. 70-73, pp. 93-94.

[28] Chapter on Practice, *CWS*, vol. 1, p. 29; *DTS*, p. 65 (quoting T'an-luan).

[29] Chapter on the Transformed Buddhas and Lands, *CWS*, vol. 1, pp. 228-229; Hymns of the Dharma Ages, pp. 413-417; *RTS*, vol. 5, p. 192.

[30] *The Larger Sutra, TPLS*, vol. 2, pp. 97-99; Hymns of the Dharma Ages, *CWS*, vol. 1, pp. 413-417.

[31] *Anguttara Nikāya* 8.39 (Abhisanda Sutta). See Bodhi, *IBW*, pp. 172-176.

[32] In a strange twist, Theravāda-style precept-taking appeared at Shin Buddhist temples on the West Coast during the 1930s, where it was central to the initiation and ordination ceremonies for Euro-Americans. See Michihiro Ama, *Immigrants to the Pure Land* (Univ. of Hawaii Press, 2011), pp. 97-100.

[33] Notes on 'Essentials of Faith Alone,' *CWS*, vol. 1, p. 458.

[34] Notes on the Inscriptions on Sacred Scrolls, *CWS*, vol. 1, p. 516.

[35] Takamaro Shigaraki, "Shinjin and Social Praxis in Shinran's Thought," trans. David Matsumoto, *Pacific World*, ser. 3, no. 11 (Fall 2009), p. 199.

[36] James C. Dobbins, *Jōdo Shinshū: Shin Buddhism in Medieval Japan* (Univ. of Hawaii Press, 2002), p. 48.

[37] See "Pure Land Birth" in Part III.

[38] Lamp for the Latter Ages, *CWS*, vol. 1, p. 547.

[39] Lamp for the Latter Ages, *CWS*, vol. 1, p. 553.

[40] A Record in Lament of Divergences, *CWS*, vol. 1, p. 671.

[41] James C. Dobbins, *Jōdo Shinshū: Shin Buddhism in Medieval Japan* (Univ. of Hawaii Press, 2002), pp. 66-68, pp. 141-144; Takamaro Shigaraki, "Shinjin and Social Praxis in Shinran's Thought," trans. David Matsumoto, *Pacific World*, ser. 3, no. 11 (Fall 2009), pp. 197-198.

[42] *Majjhima Nikāya* 72. See Bodhi, *IBW*, p. 367.

[43] One might ask, did *nothing* exist before the Big Bang, 13.8 billion years ago? The question appears reasonable, but from the perspective of physics, it is not properly framed. See Sean Carroll, *The Big Picture* (Dutton, 2016), chap. 25; Stephen Hawking, *A Brief History of Time* (Bantam, 1988), chap. 3.

[44] *Samyutta Nikāya* 35.28 (Āditta Sutta), trans. Bhikkhu Sujato, https://suttacentral.net/. See Bodhi, *IBW*, p. 346; Rahula, *WBT*, p. 96.

[45] Chapter on the Transformed Buddhas and Lands, *CWS*, vol. 1, p. 239 (quoting Shan-tao).

[46] *Dīgha Nikāya* 16 (Mahāparinibbāna Sutta). See Rahula, *WBT*, p. 138; Karen Armstrong, *Buddha* (Penguin Books, 2001), p. 187.

[47] *Theragāthā* 2.32 (Sivaka), trans. Bhikkhu Sujato, https://suttacentral.net/.

[48] *Hamlet*, act 3, sc. 1, lines 55-67.

[49] *Macbeth*, act 5, sc. 5, lines 19-28.

[50] *King Lear*, act 4, sc. 6, lines 182-183.

[51] A Record in Lament of Divergences, *CWS*, vol. 1, p. 679.

[52] Albert Camus, *The Myth of Sisyphus and Other Essays*, trans. Justin O'Brien (Vintage International, 1983), p. 3.

[53] Ibid., pp. 21, 28.

[54] Ibid., p. 53.

[55] *Majjhima Nikāya* 36 (Mahāsaccaka Sutta). See Bodhi, *IBW*, pp. 61-67.

[56] "As for me, Shinran, I have never said the nembutsu even once for the repose of my departed father and mother." A Record in Lament of Divergences, *CWS*, vol. 1, p. 664.

[57] James C. Dobbins, *Jōdo Shinshū: Shin Buddhism in Medieval Japan* (Univ. of Hawaii Press, 2002), pp. 82-83, p. 150.

[58] For an interpretation, see "Institutional Buddhism" in Part VI.

[59] James C. Dobbins, "Portraits of Shinran in Medieval Pure Land Buddhism," in *Living Images: Japanese Buddhist Icons in Context*, ed. R.H. Sharf and E.H. Sharf (Stanford Univ. Press, 2001), pp. 31, 33-48.

⁶⁰ *Kyōgyōshinshō* Preface, *CWS*, vol. 1, p. 3; Chapter on Teaching, p. 7.

⁶¹ This discussion draws on Karen Armstrong's superb biography, *Buddha* (Penguin Books, 2004).

⁶² This is my paraphrase of *Anguttara Nikāya* 4.36 (Doṇa Sutta), trans. Bhikkhu Sujato, https://suttacentral.net/.

⁶³ *Samyutta Nikāya* 38.1 (Nibbānapañhā Sutta). See Bodhi, *IBW*, pp. 364-365.

⁶⁴ Hymns of the Dharma-Ages, *CWS*, vol. 1, pp. 402-404.

⁶⁵ Hymns of the Pure Land, *CWS*, vol. 1, p. 354.

⁶⁶ Bodhi, *IBW*, pp. 373-384; Gutoku's Notes, *CWS*, vol. 1, pp. 588-589.

⁶⁷ *Samyutta Nikāya* 48.53 (Sekha Sutta). See Bodhi, *IBW*, pp. 381, 406-407.

⁶⁸ *Gaku* is learning. *Mu* is negation, and hence *mugaku* is non-learning. *Nin* is a person, and hence a *gakunin* is a trainee.

⁶⁹ *Samyutta Nikāya* 56.11 (Dhammacakkappavattana Sutta), trans. Bhikkhu Sujato, https://suttacentral.net. See Rahula, *WBT*, p. 94.

⁷⁰ Toshikazu Arai, *Grasped by the Buddha's Vow: A translation and commentary on Tannishō* (Buddhist Churches of America, Center for Buddhist Education, 2008), p. 132.

⁷¹ Chapter on Shinjin, *CWS*, vol. 1, p. 86 (quoting Shan-tao).

⁷² Nobuo Haneda, lecture given at Orange County Buddhist Church, 31 Mar 2014.

⁷³ My paraphrase of T'an-luan's "Because the cause is pure (*in jō*), the effect is also pure (*ka jō*)." Chapter on Realization, *RTS*, vol. 5, p. 143; *CWS*, vol. 1, pp. 158, 165.

⁷⁴ Takamaro Shigaraki, "The Meaning of Practice in Shin Buddhism," trans. David Matsumoto, *Pacific World*, ser. 3, no. 7 (Fall 2005), p. 3.

⁷⁵ I infer this based on the following points. First, shinjin persons are said to be "of the same stage as Maitreya," a bodhisattva of the highest rank; Notes on 'Essentials of Faith Alone," *CWS*, vol. 1, p. 455. Second, Shinran quotes a passage from the *Nirvana Sutra*: "I have taught that bodhisattvas of the tenth stage see a little of Buddha-

nature," although they "do not see it especially clearly." Chapter on the True Buddha and Land, *CWS*, vol. 1, pp. 189, 202.

[76] See "True Settlement" in Part VIII.

[77] Gyodo Haguri, *The Awareness of Self: A Guide to the Understanding of Shin Buddhism*, trans. William Masuda (Buddhist Education Center, 2015), p. 4.

[78] Takamaro Shigaraki, "The Meaning of Practice in Shin Buddhism," trans. David Matsumoto, *Pacific World*, ser. 3, no. 7 (Fall 2005), p. 3.

[79] See "The Turning Point" in Part I.

[80] In the view of Mahāyānists, sages of the Two Vehicles— *śrāvakas* and *pratyekabuddhas*—mistakenly identify the stage of negation as the culmination of the path.

[81] "Beholding the power of the Tathāgata's [*Hongan*], I see that people who entrust themselves to it do not meaninglessly remain in samsaric life here." Notes on the Inscriptions on Sacred Scrolls, *CWS*, vol. 1, p. 502. See "Is Life Refuted?" in Part VIII.

[82] Ueda and Hirota, "Entrance into Monastic Life," *SIT*, pp. 24-25.

[83] Ueda and Hirota, "Entrance into Monastic Life," *SIT*, pp. 26-27.

[84] See "A Narrow Road to the Interior" in Part VIII.

[85] See "True Teachings and Provisional Teachings" in Part III.

[86] Karen Armstrong, *Buddha* (Penguin Books, 2001), p. xviii.

[87] Robert E. Buswell and Donald S. Lopez, *The Princeton Dictionary of Buddhism* (Princeton Univ. Press, 2014) pp. 513-514.

[88] Ueda and Hirota, "The Mahāyāna Movement," *SIT*, pp. 99-102

[89] Soga Ryōjin, "Shinran's View of Buddhist History," in *Cultivating Spirituality*, ed. M. Blum and R.F. Rhodes (SUNY Press, 2011), pp. 119-138.

[90] The Pāli suttas had Sanskrit counterparts called Āgama sutras, which survive in Chinese translations (*Agongyō*). Shinran knew of these texts but never quoted them. See Chapter on Practice, *CWS*, vol. 1, pp. 28-29.

[91] Chapter on Teaching, *CWS*, vol. 1, pp. 7-10; Passages on the Pure Land, p. 317; Hymns of the Pure Land Masters, p. 379; Lamp for the Latter Ages, pp. 524-525.

[92] Notes on 'Essentials of Faith Alone,' *CWS*, vol. 1, p. 459.

[93] Passages on the Pure Land, *CWS*, vol. 1, p. 295.

[94] Hymns of the Dharma Ages, *CWS*, vol. 1, p. 429.

[95] A Record in Lament of Divergences, *CWS*, vol. 1, p. 679.

[96] In fact, the de-emphasis of Shinran's teaching started much earlier. The first Hongwanji ministers on the West Coast chose general Buddhism as the basis of their outreach activities, as did American-born Nisei ministers prior to World War II. See Michihiro Ama, *Immigrants to the Pure Land* (Univ. of Hawaii Press, 2011), pp. 36-42, pp. 69-70, pp. 93-100.

[97] Chapter on the Transformed Buddhas and Lands, *CWS*, vol. 1, p. 241.

[98] Stephen Batchelor, *After Buddhism: Rethinking the Dharma for a Secular Age* (Yale Univ. Press, 2015), chap. 5.

[99] Chapter on Teaching, *CWS*, vol. 1, pp. 7-10; Passages on the Pure Land, p. 317; Hymns of the Pure Land Masters, p. 379; Lamp for the Latter Ages, pp. 524-525.

[100] *The Amida Sutra, TPLS*, vol. 1, p. 4.

[101] Chapter on Practice, *CWS*, vol. 1, p. 71; Notes on the Inscriptions on Sacred Scrolls, pp. 500-502. Shinran is also prolific in his use of *similes*, as in the Chapter on Practice, pp. 66-67: "The Vow of compassion is like vast space... like an immense cart... like a wonderful lotus blossom... [etc.]"

[102] My italics. *Kyō Gyō Shin Shō, RTS*, vol. 5, p. 17; *Kyōgyōshinshō* Preface, *CWS*, vol. 1, p. 3.

[103] My italics. Chapter on Practice, *CWS*, vol. 1, p. 56.

[104] Beethoven, Piano Sonata in C-sharp minor, op. 27, no. 2.

[105] Leonard Bernstein, "Musical Semantics," Charles Eliot Norton Lecture no. 3, Harvard University, 1973.

[106] *The Amida Sutra, TPLS*, vol. 1, p. 7.

¹⁰⁷ *The Larger Sutra, TPLS*, vol. 2, p. 42.

¹⁰⁸ Ueda and Hirota, "The Unfolding of Wisdom as Compassion," *SIT*, pp. 81-83.

¹⁰⁹ From Joseph Campbell's *The Hero with a Thousand Faces*, Copyright © Joseph Campbell Foundation (jcf.org) 2008. Used with permission. 3rd edition (New World Library), p. 228.

¹¹⁰ As an alternative to the *trikāya*, there is the twofold framework of *dharma-kāya* as suchness and *dharma-kāya* as expedient means. See Notes on 'Essentials of Faith Alone,' *CWS*, vol. 1, p. 461; "Twofold Dharma-Body," *CWS*, vol. 2, p. 104.

¹¹¹ Shūichi Maida, *Heard by Me: Essays on My Buddhist Teacher*, trans. Nobuo Haneda (Frog Press, 1992), pp. 25-32.

¹¹² From Joseph Campbell's *Historical Atlas of World Mythology,* vol. II: *The Way of the Seeded Earth*, Copyright © Joseph Campbell Foundation (jcf.org) 1988. Used with permission. (Harper Perennial), p. 113.

¹¹³ Friedrich Nietzsche, *The Birth of Tragedy*, trans. W.A. Haussmann (1910), sec. 10.

¹¹⁴ Notes on 'Essentials of Faith Alone,' *CWS*, vol. 1, p. 452.

¹¹⁵ Shinran cautions against attaching only personal meaning to the Name: "People make [the *Hongan*'s] auspicious Name their own root of good; hence, they cannot give rise to shinjin and do not apprehend the Buddha's wisdom." Chapter on the Transformed Buddhas and Lands, *CWS*, vol. 1, p. 240.

¹¹⁶ Takamaro Shigaraki, "The Meaning of Practice in Shin Buddhism," trans. David Matsumoto, *Pacific World*, ser. 3, no. 7 (Fall 2005), p. 6.

¹¹⁷ *CWS*, vol. 1, frontispiece, p. xi; "The Name of Amida as Altar Scroll," *CWS*, vol. 2, pp. 140-145; James C. Dobbins, "Portraits of Shinran in Medieval Pure Land Buddhism," in *Living Images: Japanese Buddhist Icons in Context*, ed. R.H. Sharf and E.H. Sharf (Stanford Univ. Press, 2001), pp. 22-24.

¹¹⁸ "*Monmyō* is to hear the Name that embodies the *Hongan*. *Mon* means to hear the *Hongan* and be free of doubt. Further, it indicates shinjin." Chapter on Shinjin, *CWS*, vol. 1, p. 112; Notes on Once-Calling and Many-Calling, p. 474.

[119] Of the *Larger Sutra*'s forty-eight Vows, sixteen of them have to do with hearing the Name. *Larger Sutra, TPLS*, vol. 2, pp. 20-29, 51-52, 57-59.

[120] A Collection of Passages on the Types of Birth in the Three Pure Land Sutras, *CWS*, vol. 1, pp. 639-640.

[121] Refers to Vow 17. *Larger Sutra, TPLS*, vol. 2, pp. 30, 51; Chapter on Practice, *CWS*, vol. 1, pp. 14-17.

[122] Refers to Vow 18. *Larger Sutra, TPLS*, vol. 2, p. 52, fn. 1, p. 57; Chapter on Shinjin, *CWS*, vol. 1, pp. 80-83.

[123] This is my rough translation. See Chapter on Practice, *CWS*, vol. 1, p. 38; *RTS*, vol. 5, p. 48 and footnotes; *DTS*, p. 75.

[124] Notes on the Inscriptions on Sacred Scrolls, *CWS*, vol. 1, pp. 500-502, 504-505.

[125] Lamp for the Latter Ages, *CWS*, vol. 1, pp. 523, 531, 549; A Record in Lament of Divergences, pp. 672-674.

[126] *Kyō Gyō Shin Shō, RTS*, vol. 5, p. 117 and footnotes.

[127] *Kyō Gyō Shin Shō, RTS*, vol. 5, p. 24, fn. 5. The commentator writes, "By hearing alone, one may tend toward a blind faith."

[128] This is my rough translation. Compare Chapter on Practice, *CWS*, vol. 1, p. 54 (quoting Shan-tao); *Kyō Gyō Shin Shō, RTS*, vol. 5, p. 57.

[129] Chapter on the Transformed Buddhas and Lands, *CWS*, vol. 1, p. 235 (quoting the *Nirvana Sutra*). See Chapter on Shinjin, pp. 99-100, 108, 111.

[130] *PLW*, vol. 1, frontispiece, p. vi. The ten characters originated in Vasubandhu's *Pure Land Treatise*. See Notes on the Inscriptions on Sacred Scrolls, *CWS*, vol. 1, pp. 500-502. Shinran also used T'an-luan's Chinese sentence *Namo fukashigikō butsu* as the *myōgō*, meaning "Take refuge in the Buddha of inconceivable light!" See The Virtue of the Name of Amida Tathagata, *CWS*, vol. 1, p. 658.

[131] Lamp for the Latter Ages, *CWS*, vol. 1, pp. 543-545.

[132] My quotation marks. Hymns of the Dharma-Ages, *CWS*, vol. 1, p. 428.

[133] "This Tathāgata is light... [it] is the form of wisdom." Notes on the Inscriptions on Sacred Scrolls, *CWS*, vol. 1, p. 501.

[134] Hōnen Shōnin, *Ichimai-kishōmon* ("One-Sheet Document").

[135] *Shin Buddhist Service Book*, 3rd printing, (Buddhist Education Center, 2016), p. 83.

[136] *Shinran's Kyōgyōshinshō, DTS*, p. 43; *Kyōgyōshinshō* Preface, *CWS*, vol. 1, p. 4.

[137] Passages on the Pure Land, *CWS*, vol. 1, p. 303.

[138] *Dīgha Nikāya* 16 (Mahāparinibbāna Sutta). See Stephen Batchelor, *After Buddhism: Rethinking the Dharma for a Secular Age* (Yale Univ. Press, 2015), p. 281.

[139] From Joseph Campbell's *The Hero with a Thousand Faces*, Copyright © Joseph Campbell Foundation (jcf.org) 2008. Used with permission. 3rd edition (New World Library), p. 275.

[140] Gotama's pedagogy sometimes includes his sharing of parables and myths. These stories-within-the-story are obviously not meant as historical accounts.

[141] From Joseph Campbell's *The Hero with a Thousand Faces*, Copyright © Joseph Campbell Foundation (jcf.org) 2008. Used with permission. 3rd edition (New World Library), p. 221.

[142] Joseph Campbell, *Myths to Live By* (Penguin Compass, 1993), p. 14.

[143] Ibid., pp. 43-60.

[144] Joseph Campbell (with Michael Toms), *An Open Life* (Harper Perennial, 1990), p. 21.

[145] Ibid., p. 22.

[146] Ibid., pp. 21-22.

[147] Chapter on the Transformed Buddhas and Lands, *CWS*, vol. 1, p. 241 (quoting Nāgārjuna).

[148] *The Gospel According to St. John*, chapter 1. A view within Shin Buddhism states that "the Name and its substance are not separate (*myōtai funi*)," suggesting that the Name is a substantial entity, which conveys the same flavor as St. John's Gospel. Prof. Shigaraki has shown that this view does not represent the teaching of Shinran [*Pacific World*, ser. 3, no. 3 (Fall 2001), pp. 34-35].

[149] *The Lotus Sutra*, trans. Gene Reeves (Wisdom, 2008), chap. 2, p. 84; chap. 3, pp. 112-118, p. 123.

^{150} Chapter on the Transformed Buddhas and Lands, *CWS*, vol. 1, pp. 220-222; "Three Types of Religious Existence," *CWS*, vol. 2, pp. 67-69. See "A Narrow Road to the Interior" in Part VIII.

^{151} *Kyō Gyō Shin Shō*, *RTS*, vol. 5, p. 200; Chapter on the Transformed Buddhas and Lands, *CWS*, vol. 1, p. 242.

^{152} Chapter on the Transformed Buddhas and Lands, *CWS*, vol. 1, p. 289.

^{153} Chapter on the True Buddha and Land, *CWS*, vol. 1, p. 203; Chapter on Shinjin, p. 124; Gutoku's Notes, pp. 587-589.

^{154} Chapter on Practice, *CWS*, vol. 1, p. 68; *Kyō Gyō Shin Shō*, *RTS*, vol. 5, p. 79. True-and-real practice corresponds to Vow 17 ("the Vow that all the Buddhas praise the Name"). True-and-real shinjin corresponds to Vow 18 ("the Vow of sincere mind and entrusting"). Shinran gives equal prominence to these two Vows. He is misrepresented if one attempts to reduce his teaching to Vow 18 alone, a view that I sometimes encounter.

^{155} Vows 11, 12, 13, 17, 18, and 22. He calls three of these the "selected Vows" of true-and-real practice (Vow 17), shinjin (Vow 18), and realization (Vow 11). See Passages on the Two Aspects of the Tathāgata's Directing of Virtue, *CWS*, vol. 1, pp. 633-634.

^{156} Vow 19 is "the Vow of meritorious acts" in accord with the *Contemplation Sutra*. Vow 20 is "the Vow of cultivating the root of virtue" in accord with the *Amida Sutra*.

^{157} A Collection of Passages on the Types of Birth in the Three Pure Land Sutras, *CWS*, vol. 1, pp. 639-652.

^{158} *Kyō Gyō Shin Shō*, *RTS*, vol. 5, p. 198. See also, Hymns of the Dharma Ages, *CWS*, vol. 1, pp. 399-403.

^{159} I am indebted to Dr. Nobuo Haneda for a discussion of this point. See the *kanji* in the *Kyōgyōshinshō* chapter titles. *Kyō Gyō Shin Shō*, *RTS*, vol. 5, chap. 1-4, pp. 29, 39, 87, 139.

^{160} *Kyō Gyō Shin Shō*, *RTS*, vol. 5, chap. 5, p. 151.

^{161} "Shinran's Originality," *CWS*, vol. 2, pp. 112-114.

^{162} Chapter on the True Buddha and Land, *CWS*, vol. 1, p. 203; Collection of Passages on the Types of Birth in the Three Pure Land Sutras, pp. 645-652.

[163] This is my rough translation. See Chapter on the Transformed Buddhas and Lands, *CWS*, vol. 1, p. 225; *Kyō Gyō Shin Shō, RTS*, vol. 5, p. 184.

[164] "Shinran's Conception of Means," *CWS*, vol. 2, pp. 69-71. See "A Narrow Road to the Interior" in Part VIII.

[165] Takamaro Shigaraki, "The Problem of True and False in Contemporary Shin Buddhist Studies," trans. David Matsumoto, *Pacific World*, ser. 3, no. 3 (Fall 2001), pp. 27-50.

[166] Notes on "Essentials of Faith Alone," *CWS*, vol. 1, p. 455; Notes on Once-Calling and Many-Calling, pp. 474-475. This is Shinran's commentary on *Soku toku ōjō, Jū fu tai ten*, a key phrase from the *Larger Sutra*. See also, "Shinran's Originality," *CWS*, vol. 2, pp. 112-114.

[167] Notes on Once-Calling and Many-Calling, *CWS*, vol. 1, p. 475.

[168] Gutoku's Notes, *CWS*, vol. 1, pp. 592-593; Passages on the Pure Land, p. 317; Notes on One-Calling and Many-Calling, pp. 484-485.

[169] Chapter on Shinjin, *CWS*, vol. 1, p. 123; Hymns of the Dharma Ages, pp. 404-406; Notes on Once-Calling and Many-Calling, pp. 475-477.

[170] Lamp for the Latter Ages, *CWS*, vol. 1, pp. 523, 531, 549; A Record in Lament of Divergences, pp. 672-674.

[171] Chapter on Shinjin, *CWS*, vol. 1, pp. 79, 93-94, 99; *Kyō Gyō Shin Shō, RTS*, vol. 5, pp. 88,101; Passages on the Pure Land, *CWS*, vol. 1, p. 316; Notes on the Inscriptions on Sacred Scrolls, p. 513.

[172] *Shōshin Ge, RTS*, vol. 1, pp. 21, 35; *Kyō Gyō Shin Shō, RTS*, vol. 5, pp. 50, 119, 175. Compare *CWS*, vol. 1, pp. 38, 69, 72, 112, 221.

[173] Lamp for the Latter Ages, *CWS*, vol. 1, p. 539.

[174] James C. Dobbins, *Letters of the Nun Eshinni: Images of Pure Land Buddhism in Medieval Japan* (Univ. of Hawaii, 2004), pp. 57-73, 107-151.

[175] See "The Teaching for Our Era" in Part VIII.

[176] *Shi soku ze gan ōjō gyō nin, myō yoku jūji, gan riki shōtoku ōjō*. Here is a translation of each *kanji*: "This namely this aspire birth practitioner, life desire final moment, vow power attain birth." See Notes on the Inscriptions on Sacred Scrolls, *CWS*, vol. 1, p. 505.

[177] My rough translation. See Notes on the Inscriptions on Sacred Scrolls, *CWS*, vol. 1, pp. 506-507; Chapter on Practice, *RTS*, vol. 5, p. 45, fn. 3.

[178] Gutoku's Notes, *CWS*, vol. 1, pp. 587-588, 603; A Record in Lament of Divergences, pp. 674-675.

[179] Ueda and Hirota, "Shinran's Reformulation of the Pure Land Path," *SIT*, pp. 138-139.

[180] Ueda and Hirota, "The Significance of Shinjin," *SIT*, pp. 170-173.

[181] Lamp for the Latter Ages, *CWS*, vol. 1, p. 544.

[182] Lamp for the Latter Ages, *CWS*, vol. 1, p. 528; Chapter on Shinjin, p. 116.

[183] Chapter on the Transformed Buddhas and Lands, *CWS*, p. 238 (quoting Shan-tao).

[184] Notes on the Inscriptions on Sacred Scrolls, *CWS*, vol. 1, p. 513.

[185] Hymns of the Pure Land Masters, *CWS*, vol. 1, p. 388-390.

[186] Hymns of the Pure Land Masters, *CWS*, vol. 1, p. 387.

[187] "We foolish beings ever sinking in transmigration—... our self-power failed, and we continued to transmigrate.... We have wandered thus in birth-and-death to this day." Hymns of the Dharma Ages, *CWS*, vol. 1, pp. 402-403.

[188] Chapter on Realization, *CWS*, vol. 1, p. 168 (quoting T'an-luan).

[189] Chapter on Shinjin, *CWS*, vol. 1, p. 103.

[190] Passages on the Pure Land, *CWS*, vol. 1, p. 298.

[191] My rough translation. See Chapter on Teaching, *CWS*, vol. 1, p. 7; *Kyō Gyō Shin Shō*, *RTS*, vol. 5, p. 29; *Shinran's Kyōgyōshinshō*, *DTS*, p. 45.

[192] Chapter on Realization, *CWS*, vol. 1, pp. 153, 158, 174; Passages on the Pure Land, pp. 296-302; Passages on the Two Aspects of the Tathāgata's Directing of Virtue, pp. 633-635; Collection of Passages on the Types of Birth in the Three Pure Land Sutras, pp. 639-652.

[193] Hymns of the Pure Land Masters (T'an-luan), no. 34-36, in my rough translation. Compare *CWS*, vol. 1, p. 370, which contains insertions to suggest that foolish beings are "going forth" and

"returning." See *Kōsō Wasan*, *RTS*, vol. 6, pp. 56-59; Hisao Inagaki, *The Way of Nembutsu Faith: A Commentary on Shinran's Shōshinge* (Horai Assn. 1996), p. 112.

[194] Chapter on Shinjin, *CWS*, vol. 1, p. 112.

[195] Collection of Passages on the Types of Birth in the Three Pure Land Sutras, *CWS*, vol. 1, p. 644.

[196] Notes on Once-Calling and Many-Calling, *CWS*, vol. 1, p. 477 and Shinran's footnote.

[197] *Kyō Gyō Shin Shō*, *RTS*, vol. 5, p. 205.

[198] *Majjhima Nikāya* 22, trans. Bhikkhu Sujato, https://suttacentral.net/.

[199] Albert Camus, *The Myth of Sisyphus and Other Essays*, trans. Justin O'Brien (Vintage International, 1983), p. v, p. 3. See "Dying and Living" in Part II.

[200] Albert Camus, *The Rebel: An Essay on Man in Revolt*, trans. Anthony Bower (Vintage Books, 1956), p. 6.

[201] Albert Camus, *The Myth of Sisyphus and Other Essays*, trans. Justin O'Brien (Vintage International, 1983), p. 123.

[202] For an account of Kent's last days, see Marvin Harada, *Discovering Buddhism in Everyday Life* (Buddhist Education Center, 2011), pp. 78-80.

[203] Kenneth Clark, *Civilisation* (Harper & Row, 1969), p. 241.

[204] Karen Armstrong, *Buddha* (Penguin Books, 2001), pp. 134-135.

[205] Friedrich Nietzsche, *Twilight of the Idols, or How to Philosophize with a Hammer*, trans. A.M. Ludovici (1911), "The Four Great Errors," sec. 8.

[206] See "Looking for the Self" in Part VII.

[207] Rahula, *WBT*, p. 54.

[208] Bodhi, *IBW*, pp. 312-316. See "Cause and Effect" in Part VII.

[209] Shūichi Maida, *Heard by Me: Essays on My Buddhist Teacher*, trans. Nobuo Haneda (Frog Press, 1992), p. 166.

[210] *Majjhima Nikāya* 72 (Aggivacchagotta Sutta), trans. Bhikkhu Sujato, https://suttacentral.net/. See Bodhi, *IBW*, pp. 367, 230-233, 437 n.1.

[211] *Samyutta Nikāya* 44.10 (Ānanda Sutta). See Rahula, *WBT*, pp. 62-65.

[212] From Joseph Campbell's *The Hero with a Thousand Faces*, Copyright © Joseph Campbell Foundation (jcf.org) 2008. Used with permission. 3rd edition (New World Library), p. 221.

[213] Fyodor Dostoevsky, *The Brothers Karamazov*, trans. Constance Garnett, book XII, chap. IX. Dostoevsky describes the condemned man's state of mind in greater detail in the novel, *The Idiot*, part 1, chap. 5.

[214] Ronald Hingly, Introduction to *Memoirs from the House of the Dead* by Fyodor Dostoevsky (Oxford University, 1983), p. ix.

[215] *Anguttara Nikāya* 3.36 (Devadūta Sutta), trans. Bhikkhu Sujato, https://suttacentral.net/. See Bodhi, *IBW*, p. 29.

[216] Hideo Yonezawa, *Awaken to Your True Self: The Shin Buddhist Way of Life* (Buddhist Education Center, 2017), p. 102.

[217] See "The Teaching for Our Era" in Part VIII.

[218] Fyodor Dostoevsky, *Notes from Underground*, trans. Constance Garnett, part I, sec. IX.

[219] The Four Gates story is usually represented as Gotama's biography, but he did not teach it in that way. He taught it as a legend about a buddha called Vipassī who lived in the remote past. See *Dīgha Nikāya* 14 (Mahāpadāna Sutta).

[220] Fyodor Dostoevsky, *Notes from Underground*, trans. Constance Garnett, part II, sec. X.

[221] Notes on Once-Calling and Many-Calling, *CWS*, vol. 1, p. 488.

[222] Fyodor Dostoevsky, *Notes from Underground*, trans. Constance Garnett, part I, sec. XI.

[223] My literary friend, the late Robert Treat Thompson, once remarked, "Jim and I, we're Dostoevsky men!"

[224] *The Larger Sutra, TPLS*, vol. 2, p. 70.

[225] Hailey Branson-Potts and Rosanna Xia, *The Los Angeles Times*, 8 Dec 2011.

[226] *The Larger Sutra, TPLS*, vol. 2, p. 69.

²²⁷ A Record in Lament of Divergences, *CWS*, vol. 1, p. 671; Shūichi Maida, *The Evil Person: Essays on Shin Buddhism*, trans. Nobuo Haneda (Maida Center, 2016), pp. 97-100.

²²⁸ Kurt Streeter, "Killer's Change of Heart Touches Victim's Brother," *The Los Angeles Times*, 22 Dec 2011. Update: Suleika Jaouad, "The Prisoners Who Care for the Dying and Get Another Chance at Life," *The New York Times Magazine*, 16 May 2018.

²²⁹ Edward O. Wilson, *Half-Earth: Our Planet's Fight for Life* (Liveright, 2016). The principal human actions driving global extinction are habitat destruction, transport of invasive species, pollution, human overpopulation, and overhunting/overfishing.

²³⁰ *Tannishō: A Shin Buddhist Classic*, trans. Taitetsu Unno (Buddhist Study Center, 1996), p. 21.

²³¹ Hymns of the Dharma-Ages, *CWS*, vol. 1, p. 422.

²³² In his later commentaries and verses the by-line is simply Gutoku Shinran or Gutoku Zenshin. But after sixteen poems confessing his own insincerity and lamenting the corruption of Buddhist monks, he writes, "Composed by Shaku Shinran," apparently with bitter irony. Hymns of the Dharma-Ages, *CWS*, vol. 1, pp. 421-424.

²³³ I am indebted to Dr. Nobuo Haneda for emphasizing this point.

²³⁴ Chapter on the Transformed Buddhas and Lands, *CWS*, vol. 1, pp. 236-237 (quoting the *Nirvana Sutra*).

²³⁵ *Jōdo no shinshū wa shōdō ima sakari nari.* Kyōgyōshinshō Postscript, *CWS*, vol. 1, p. 289.

²³⁶ *Kyōgyōshinshō* Postscript, *CWS*, vol. 1, p. 289.

²³⁷ Ueda and Hirota, "The Life of Shinran," *SIT*, p. 34.

²³⁸ Hideo Yonezawa, *Awaken to Your True Self: The Shin Buddhist Way of Life* (Buddhist Education Center, 2017), p. 35.

²³⁹ See "True Teachings and Provisional Teachings" in Part III.

²⁴⁰ Ueda and Hirota, "The Significance of Shinjin," *SIT*, p. 171.

²⁴¹ See "A Narrow Road to the Interior" in Part VIII.

²⁴² A Record in Lament of Divergences, *CWS*, vol. 1, p. 663

²⁴³ Lamp for the Latter Ages, *CWS*, vol. 1, p. 555.

[244] A Record in Lament of Divergences, chapter 8. My rephrasing of various translations.

[245] This is my rough translation. See Chapter on Practice, *CWS*, vol. 1, p. 38; *RTS*, vol. 5, p. 48 and footnotes; *DTS*, p. 75; Notes on the Inscriptions on Sacred Scrolls, *CWS*, vol. 1, pp. 500-502. See "Hearing and Reflecting" in Part III.

[246] Chapter on Practice, *CWS*, vol. 1, p. 71; Hymns of the Pure Land, p. 337; Hymns of the Dharma-Ages, p. 406; A Collection of Letters, p. 561; A Record in Lament of Divergences, pp. 672-674.

[247] *Shinjin shōin shōmyō hōon.* "Shinjin is the true cause; reciting the Name is an expression of gratitude." See Mitsuya Dake, "A Contemporary Re-examination of Shin Buddhist Notions of Practice," *Pacific World*, ser. 3, no. 7 (Fall 2005), pp. 107-117.

[248] See "Hearing and Reflecting" in Part III.

[249] Adapted from an explanation that I wrote for the *Shin Buddhist Service Book* (Buddhist Education Center, 2013), p. 28.

[250] Albert Low, *What More Do You Want? Zen Questions, Zen Answers* (Tuttle, 2013), p. 119.

[251] Joseph Campbell, *Myths to Live By* (Penguin Compass, 1993), p. 55.

[252] Joseph Campbell, *Myths to Live By* (Penguin Compass, 1993), p. 130; Karen Armstrong, *Buddha* (Penguin Books, 2001), pp. 88-90.

[253] Joseph Campbell, *Myths to Live By* (Penguin Compass, 1993), p. 57.

[254] See "It's Only a Story" in Part III.

[255] Joseph Campbell, *Myths to Live By* (Penguin Compass, 1993), p. 97.

[256] Edward Gibbon, *History of the Decline and Fall of the Roman Empire*, vol. I, chap. VIII.

[257] See "Beyond Charity" in Part I.

[258] See "Pure Land Birth" in Part III.

[259] Takamaro Shigaraki, "The Problem of True and False in Contemporary Shin Buddhist Studies," trans. David Matsumoto, *Pacific World*, ser. 3, no. 3 (Fall 2001), pp. 27-50.

[260] Lamp for the Latter Ages, *CWS*, vol. 1, pp. 543-545.

[261] A Record in Lament of Divergences, chapter 8. My rephrasing of various translations.

[262] See "Hearing and Reflecting" in Part III.

[263] Notes on 'Essentials of Faith Alone,' *CWS*, vol. 1, p. 459.

[264] Hymns of the Dharma Ages, *CWS*, vol. 1, p. 429.

[265] A Record in Lament of Divergences, *CWS*, vol. 1, p. 663.

[266] "Self-Awareness in Shinjin," *CWS*, vol. 2, pp. 46-47.

[267] At age fifty-eight Shinran abandoned the practice of chanting sutras as being "senseless" and based on self-power faith. He also had an experience at age forty that led him to question the validity of chanting. See James C. Dobbins, *Letters of the Nun Eshinni: Images of Pure Land Buddhism in Medieval Japan* (Univ. of Hawaii, 2004), pp. 30-32.

[268] James C. Dobbins, "Portraits of Shinran in Medieval Pure Land Buddhism," in *Living Images: Japanese Buddhist Icons in Context*, ed. R.H. Sharf and E.H. Sharf (Stanford Univ. Press, 2001), pp. 22-24.

[269] This very popular practice is the BCA's version of continuous walking meditation (*jōgyō zanmai*).

[270] James C. Dobbins, *Jōdo Shinshū: Shin Buddhism in Medieval Japan* (Univ. of Hawaii Press, 2002), p. 23, pp. 26-27.

[271] Those who see a doctrinal objection to our sitting quietly before the altar may have erroneously inferred that we are emulating the meditative practices of Tendai monks. We do not perform austerities, nor is there an attempt to visualize Amida Buddha and the Pure Land. Visualization practice, as taught in the *Contemplation Sutra*, is unknown to most of our participants.

[272] This "routinization of charismatic authority" was identified by sociologist Max Weber (1864-1920). See "Institutional Buddhism" in Part VI.

[273] James C. Dobbins, *Jōdo Shinshū: Shin Buddhism in Medieval Japan* (Univ. of Hawaii Press, 2002), pp. 149-150.

[274] See "A Narrow Road to the Interior" in Part VIII, and "Shinran's Conception of Means," *CWS*, vol. 2, pp. 69-71.

[275] A tragic consequence of the coronavirus pandemic has been the separation of dying patients from their families and friends.

[276] See "Putting Away Samsara" in Part II.

[277] *Tannisho: A Shin Buddhist Classic*, trans. Taitetsu Unno (Buddhist Study Center Press, 1996), p. 5.

[278] Hymns of the Dharma Ages, *CWS*, vol. 1, p. 399. The naga's palace is an inaccessible storehouse at the bottom of the ocean.

[279] This my rough translation. See *Kyō Gyō Shin Shō*, *RTS*, vol. 5, p. 79, p. 40 fn. 1; *Shinran's Kyōgyōshinshō*, *DTS*, p. 103; Chapter on Practice, *CWS*, vol. 1, p. 68.

[280] Chapter on Practice, *CWS*, vol. 1, p. 13; Passages on the Pure Land, p. 296; *Kyō Gyō Shin Shō*, *RTS*, vol. 5, p. 39 fn. 3, p. 40 fn. 1.

[281] *Kyō Gyō Shin Shō*, *RTS*, vol. 5, p. 79; Passages on the Two Aspects of the Tathāgata's Directing of Virtue, *CWS*, vol. 1, p. 633; A Collection of Passages on the Types of Birth in the Three Pure Land Sutras, pp. 639-640.

[282] Hymns of the Pure Land, *CWS*, vol. 1, pp. 342-343.

[283] *Kyō Gyō Shin Shō*, *RTS*, vol. 5, p. 64; Chapter on Practice, *CWS*, vol. 1, p. 57.

[284] Takamaro Shigaraki, *Heart of the Shin Buddhist Path: A Life of Awakening*, trans. David Matsumoto (Wisdom, 2013), p. 53.

[285] *Majjhima Nikāya* 73, trans. Bhikkhu Sujato, https://suttacentral.net/.

[286] I am indebted to Rev. Marvin Harada for this insight.

[287] Hymns of the Pure Land Masters, *CWS*, vol. 1, p. 378.

[288] I am indebted to Dr. Nobuo Haneda for emphasizing this point.

[289] A portion of Rev. Haguri's book, *Shinshin no Kakumei* (1953), was published as *The Awareness of Self*, trans. William Masuda (Buddhist Education Center, 2015).

[290] See "A Narrow Road to the Interior" in Part VIII.

[291] Hymns of the Pure Land Masters, *CWS*, vol. 1, p. 387.

[292] See "'Meditation Is Not Part of Our Tradition'" in Part V.

[293] See "True Teachings and Provisional Teachings" in Part III.

[294] Temple membership and sangha membership are not equivalent. One becomes a member of a BCA temple by paying dues; it is a social and cultural affiliation. One becomes a member of a Shin Buddhist

sangha by gathering with others for the purpose of Dharma listening, without which there can be no sangha.

[295] Michihiro Ama, *Immigrants to the Pure Land* (Univ. of Hawaii Press, 2011), pp. 36-42, pp. 69-70, pp. 97-100.

[296] Duncan Ryūken Williams, *American Sutra: A Story of Faith and Freedom in the Second World War* (Belknap/Harvard, 2019), pp. 62, 144-148.

[297] Ibid., pp. 127-130.

[298] For example, *Buddhist Service Book* (Buddhist Churches of America, 1967, second printing), successor to the *Young Buddhist Companion* (ca. 1952).

[299] Michihiro Ama, *Immigrants to the Pure Land* (Univ. of Hawaii Press, 2011), pp. 24-30.

[300] *Kyōgyōshinshō* Postscript, *CWS*, vol. 1, p. 289; Hymns of the Dharma-Ages, pp. 421-424.

[301] Hideo Yonezawa, *Awaken to Your True Self: The Shin Buddhist Way of Life* (Buddhist Education Center, 2017), pp. 121-122.

[302] Takamaro Shigaraki, *Heart of the Shin Buddhist Path: A Life of Awakening*, trans. David Matsumoto (Wisdom, 2013), pp. 76-80.

[303] Michihiro Ama, *Immigrants to the Pure Land* (Univ. of Hawaii Press, 2011), pp. 20-24.

[304] Mark L. Blum, "Shin Buddhism in the Meiji Period," in *Cultivating Spirituality*, ed. M. Blum and R.F. Rhodes (SUNY Press, 2011), pp. 12-14.

[305] Takamaro Shigaraki, "The Problem of True and False in Contemporary Shin Buddhist Studies," trans. David Matsumoto, *Pacific World*, ser. 3, no. 3 (Fall 2001), pp. 45-47.

[306] Takamaro Shigaraki, "Shinjin and Social Praxis in Shinran's Thought," trans. David Matsumoto, *Pacific World*, ser. 3, no. 11 (Fall 2009), pp. 197-199.

[307] James C. Dobbins, *Letters of the Nun Eshinni: Images of Pure Land Buddhism in Medieval Japan* (Univ. of Hawaii, 2004), pp. 112-113; Mark L. Blum, "Kiyozawa Manshi: Life and Thought," in *Cultivating Spirituality*, ed. M. Blum and R.F. Rhodes (SUNY Press, 2011), pp. 55-65.

[308] For a commentary that considers Shinran's outlook to be medieval rather than universal, see James C. Dobbins, *Letters of the Nun Eshinni: Images of Pure Land Buddhism in Medieval Japan* (Univ. of Hawaii, 2004), pp. 107-151.

[309] Soon after Shinran's death, a blending with Shintō occurred under the leadership of Kakunyo and Zonkaku and was later extended by Rennyo. See Takamaro Shigaraki, "The Problem of True and False in Contemporary Shin Buddhist Studies," trans. David Matsumoto, *Pacific World*, ser. 3, no. 3 (Fall 2001), pp. 29, 45-47.

[310] Duncan Ryūken Williams, *American Sutra: A Story of Faith and Freedom in the Second World War* (Belknap/Harvard, 2019), pp. 241-242.

[311] *Kyō Gyō Shin Shō*, RTS, vol. 5, p. 212; Chapter on the Transformed Buddhas and Lands, *CWS*, vol. 1, p. 291.

[312] Max Weber, *Sociology of Religion* (1920). The pattern is called the "routinization of charismatic authority."

[313] Chapter on the Transformed Buddhas and Lands, *CWS*, vol. 1, pp. 240-253.

[314] "Institutional Buddhism," the title of this essay, is an oxymoron.

[315] James C. Dobbins, *Jōdo Shinshū: Shin Buddhism in Medieval Japan* (Univ. of Hawaii Press, 2002), p. 64.

[316] *Kyōgyōshinshō* Postscript, *CWS*, vol. 1, p. 289.

[317] A Record in Lament of Divergences, *CWS*, vol. 1, p. 662, p. 664.

[318] James C. Dobbins, *Jōdo Shinshū: Shin Buddhism in Medieval Japan* (Univ. of Hawaii Press, 2002), pp. 85-86.

[319] See "Your Island" in Part VI.

[320] Ueda and Hirota, "Shinran: Life and Works," *SIT*, p. 41.

[321] Hymns of the Dharma-Ages, *CWS*, vol. 1, p. 399.

[322] After Shinran's death, Japanese Pure Land Buddhism promptly resumed its medieval slumbers, from which it would not awaken for the next six hundred years. See "Remembering Our Predecessors" in Part VI.

[323] Nobuo Haneda, Maida Center retreat, 2014; "Shinran's Originality," *CWS*, vol. 2, pp. 112-114.

[324] Lamp for the Latter Ages, *CWS*, vol. 1, pp. 524-525.

[325] Shinran considered the Path of Sages to include the "other Mahāyāna teachings" as well as the "Hīnayāna teachings" of the Two Vehicles for *śrāvakas* and *pratyekabuddhas*. Chapter on the Transformed Buddhas and Lands, *CWS*, vol. 1, pp. 222-223; Gutoku's Notes, pp. 587-589.

[326] Notes on the Inscriptions on Sacred Scrolls, *CWS*, vol. 1, pp. 514-515; Lamp for the Latter Ages, pp. 524-525; Gutoku's Notes, pp. 587-589.

[327] They must "nurture their wholesome qualities with the radiant energy of the Dhamma before their mind-streams become mature enough to attain direct realization. This process ordinarily requires many lives, and thus such people have to take a long-term approach to their spiritual development." Bodhi, *IBW*, pp. 145-154.

[328] This is known as the karmic recompense of good and evil. For Shinran's view, see "Beyond Charity" in Part I.

[329] Hymns of the Dharma-Ages, *CWS*, vol. 1, p. 412.

[330] Lamp for the Latter Ages, *CWS*, vol. 1, p. 525.

[331] Notes on Once-Calling and Many-Calling, *CWS*, vol. 1, p. 484.

[332] Chapter on the Transformed Buddhas and Lands, *CWS*, vol. 1, p. 222 (quoting Shan-tao); Notes on Once Calling and Many Calling, pp. 485-486.

[333] Olga Khazan, "Why So Many Americans Are Turning to Buddhism," *The Atlantic* (Mar 7, 2019); Robert Wright, *Why Buddhism Is True* (Simon & Schuster, 2017).

[334] Hymns of the Two Gateways of Entrance and Emergence, *CWS*, vol. 1, p. 628.

[335] Chapter on the Transformed Buddhas and Lands, *CWS*, vol. 1, pp. 207, 240, 289.

[336] Chapter on Shinjin, *CWS*, vol. 1, pp. 115-116; Notes on the Inscriptions on Sacred Scrolls, pp. 495-497.

[337] *Dīgha Nikāya* 16 (Mahāparinibbāna Sutta). See Rahula, *WBT*, p. 61.

[338] "Samsara… is usually compared to an ocean, and what is required in the ocean for safety is an island, a solid land, and not a lamp." Rahula, *WBT*, p. 60, fn. 3. Stephen Batchelor, *After Buddhism: Rethinking the Dharma for a Secular Age* (Yale Univ. Press, 2015), pp. 57-58, 274-275.

[339] *Dīgha Nikāya* 16 (Mahāparinibbāna Sutta). See Stephen Batchelor, *After Buddhism: Rethinking the Dharma for a Secular Age* (Yale Univ. Press, 2015), p. 274.

[340] *Majjhima Nikāya* 73 (Mahāvaccha Sutta). See Stephen Batchelor, *After Buddhism: Rethinking the Dharma for a Secular Age* (Yale Univ. Press, 2015), p. 42; Bodhi, *IBW*, p. 388.

[341] See "True Settlement" in Part VIII.

[342] *Majjhima Nikāya* 26 (Pāsarāsi Sutta). See Bodhi, *IBW*, p. 74.

[343] Ueda and Hirota, "The Life of Shinran," *SIT*, p. 32

[344] Ueda and Hirota, "The Life of Shinran," *SIT*, p. 33.

[345] Ueda and Hirota, "The Life of Shinran," *SIT*, p. 36.

[346] Ueda and Hirota, "The Life of Shinran," *SIT*, p. 19.

[347] Shūichi Maida, *Heard by Me: Essays on My Buddhist Teacher*, trans. Nobuo Haneda (Frog Press, 1992), pp. 189-194; Michihiro Ama, *Immigrants to the Pure Land* (Univ. of Hawaii Press, 2011), pp. 161-163.

[348] I learned this from Rev. Patti Nakai. Shūichi Maida puts it this way: "The independent person lives a life that is severed from both the future and the past. He is not attached to the past; neither does he count on the future."

[349] *Suttanipāta* 3.12 (Dvayatānupassanā Sutta), trans. Bhikkhu Sujato, https://suttacentral.net/.

[350] Charles Darwin, *On the Origin of Species by Means of Natural Selection*, 6th ed., chap. XV.

[351] Microorganisms include bacteria and all unicellular animals, plants, and fungi. Viruses are excluded, as they are generally considered to be non-living.

[352] Michael Specter, "Germs Are Us: Bacteria make us sick. Do they also keep us alive?" *The New Yorker* (22 October 2012).

353 Nobuo Haneda, Lecture at Orange County Buddhist Church, 20 Mar 2012.

354 *Dīgha Nikāya* 16 (Mahāparinibbāna Sutta).

355 Taitetsu Unno, *River of Fire, River of Water: An Introduction to the Pure Land Tradition of Shin Buddhism* (Doubleday, 1998), Prologue and Epilogue.

356 Charles Darwin, *On the Origin of Species by Means of Natural Selection*, 6th ed., chap. IV.

357 Robert L. Dorit, "Rereading Darwin," *American Scientist*, Jan-Feb 2012, p. 21.

358 Charles Darwin, *On the Origin of Species by Means of Natural Selection*, 6th ed., chap. III.

359 Joseph Campbell, *Myths to Live By* (Penguin Compass, 1993), p. 88.

360 Charles Darwin, *On the Origin of Species by Means of Natural Selection*, 6th ed., chap. III.

361 Biological knowledge today incorporates evolutionary pathways that Darwin could not have foreseen in the 1850s. Yet, the principle of natural selection stands as one of evolution's most important driving forces. See Sean Carroll, *The Big Picture* (Dutton, 2016), chap. 33.

362 A rare instance of an origin myth is found in *Dīgha Nikāya* 27 (Aggañña Sutta). Gotama tells this story to explain the arising of India's caste system. He concludes that the caste into which one is born does not determine one's conduct—good or bad—nor is it decisive as far as one's ability to live the holy life.

363 *Samyutta Nikāya* 15.1 (Tinakaṭṭha Sutta). See Bodhi, *IBW*, pp. 37-40.

364 The earliest fossils of algae (*Grypania spiralis*) composed of eukaryotic cells are dated at 2.1 billion years ago. Single-celled prokaryotic organisms must have existed much earlier, but the fossil record is disputed. The oldest fossils of complex, multicellular organisms are 500-600 million years old.

365 Charles Darwin, *On the Origin of Species by Means of Natural Selection*, 6th ed., chap. XIV. Genealogically speaking, Shinran was on the right track in saying, "For all sentient beings, without exception, have been our parents and brothers and sisters in the course of countless

lives in many states of existence." A Record in Lament of Divergences, *CWS*, vol. 1, p. 664

[366] Ibid., chap. XV. Cambrian sediments reveal the rapid diversification of fossilized life forms beginning 550 million years ago.

[367] Katie L. Burke, "Oldest *Homo sapiens* Fossils," *American Scientist*, Sept-Oct 2017, p. 267.

[368] Sandra J. Ackerman, "Prehistoric Arts and Crafts," *American Scientist*, Jan-Feb 2018, p. 8; Richard Potts, et al., "Environmental dynamics during the onset of the Middle Stone Age in eastern Africa," *Science*, 15 Mar 2018; Ian Sample, "World's 'oldest figurative painting' discovered in Borneo cave," *The Guardian* (7 Nov 2018); Gary Tomlinson, *A Million Years of Music: The Emergence of Human Modernity* (Zone Books, 2015).

[369] It appears that our close evolutionary cousins, the Neanderthals, were making cave paintings as early as 65,000 years ago. Deborah Netburn, *Los Angeles Times* (23 Feb 2018).

[370] Transmutation of species had been proposed prior to Darwin. His contribution was to demonstrate that evolution by natural selection could account for the diversity and distribution of life forms that were known in his day. As refined and expanded by Darwin's successors, species evolution is the foundation of modern biology.

[371] Charles Darwin, *On the Origin of Species by Means of Natural Selection*, 6th ed., Introduction and chap. XV.

[372] In this regard, Darwin's investigation was aided and inspired by the pioneering work of German naturalist, Alexander von Humboldt (1769-1859).

[373] "It is almost as if the human brain were specifically designed to misunderstand Darwinism, and to find it hard to believe…. It requires effort of the imagination to escape from the prison of familiar timescales." Richard Dawkins, *The Blind Watchmaker* (Norton, 1987), pp. xi-xii.

[374] Charles Darwin, *On the Origin of Species by Means of Natural Selection*, 6th ed., chap. XV.

[375] Ibid., chap. IV.

[376] Ibid., chap. XV.

[377] Richard Dawkins, *The Greatest Show on Earth: The Evidence for Evolution* (Free Press, 2009), pp. 429-437.

[378] Richard J. Meislin, "U.S. Asserts Key to Curbing Births is a Free Economy," *The New York Times*, 9Aug 1984.

[379] Charles Darwin, *On the Origin of Species by Means of Natural Selection*, 6th ed., chap. III.

[380] Charles A.S. Hall and John W. Day, Jr., "Revisiting the Limits to Growth After Peak Oil," *American Scientist*, May-June 2009, p. 230.

[381] Notes on Once-Calling and Many-Calling, *CWS*, vol. 1, p. 488.

[382] A.A. Michelson and E.W. Morley attempted with great care to measure the motion of matter through the "luminiferous aether." Such motion was found not to exist, implying that the aether itself does not exist.

[383] In 1905 Einstein gave an account of the photoelectric effect and introduced the special theory of relativity, through which he was able to explain the propagation of light without reference to a luminiferous aether. This understanding is reflected in numerous aspects of modern technology.

[384] Friedrich Nietzsche, *The Gay Science*, trans. Thomas Common (1910), book 4, sec. 319.

[385] Nevertheless, anti-scientific and anti-medical extremism flourishes as unscrupulous people use lies to stoke resentment for political advantage.

[386] For a hypothesis to reckoned as scientific, there must, in principle, be a method by which the idea can be shown to be false by observations. This contrasts with revealed religion and speculative philosophy, in which truth-claims are not open to falsification through experiments.

[387] Richard P. Feynman, *The Feynman Lectures on Physics* (Addison-Wesley, 1963), p. 1-1.

[388] *Majjhima Nikāya* 22 (Alagaddūpama Sutta), trans. Bhikkhu Sujato, https://suttacentral.net/.

[389] *Samyutta Nikāya* 22.59 (Anattalakkhana Sutta). See Bodhi, *IBW*, pp. 341-342.

[390] In the suttas, human experience is described (1) by the *five aggregates of attachment*, (2) by the *eighteen sensory elements*, and (3) by *name-form and consciousness*. These are loosely overlapping lists of categories encompassing the various aspects of experience. See Bodhi, *IBW*, pp. 305-312; Stephen Batchelor, *After Buddhism: Rethinking the Dharma for a Secular Age* (Yale Univ. Press, 2015), pp. 178-205.

[391] *Samyutta Nikāya* 22.56 (Upādānaparipavatta Sutta). See Bodhi, *IBW*, pp. 335-337.

[392] In response to a demand for speculative answers, Gotama related the famous parable of the poisoned arrow. *Majjhima Nikāya* 63 (Cūlamālunkya Sutta). See Bodhi, *IBW*, pp. 230-233.

[393] Stephen Batchelor, *After Buddhism: Rethinking the Dharma for a Secular Age* (Yale Univ. Press, 2015), p. 201.

[394] Albert Einstein, quoted in Walter Isaacson, *Einstein: His Life and Universe* (Simon & Schuster, 2007), p. 548. The statement is applicable as well to two of my other heroes, Charles Darwin and Joseph Campbell.

[395] See "Beginner's Mind" in Part I.

[396] Tony Rothman, "The Secret History of Gravitational Waves," *American Scientist*, Mar-Apr 2018, p. 96.

[397] Amina Khan, "Einstein was right: we can hear the universe," *The Los Angeles Times*, 12 Feb 2016. Three of the project leaders shared the 2017 Nobel Prize in physics.

[398] Joey Shapiro Key and Tyson Littenberg, "Gravitational Wave Astronomy," *American Scientist*, Sept-Oct 2018, p. 276.

[399] Alexander Pope (1688-1744).

[400] This is my paraphrase of a statement written by Einstein in 1917; quoted in Abraham Pais, *Subtle is the Lord: The Science and Life of Albert Einstein* (Oxford Press, 1982), p. 325.

[401] Einstein disagreed with the probabilistic interpretation of quantum mechanics. This might be seen as a loss of his beginner's spirit regarding the scientific revolution that he helped to initiate. On the other hand, his disagreement might be looked on as coming from the beginner's spirit that aims for an ever-deepening understanding.

[402] Albert Einstein, quoted in Walter Isaacson, *Einstein: His Life and Universe* (Simon & Schuster, 2007), p. 388.

[403] Abraham Pais, *Subtle is the Lord: The Science and Life of Albert Einstein* (Oxford Press, 1982), p. vii.

[404] *Sanbutsuge*, trans. Nobuo Haneda, *Dharma Breeze: Essays on Shin Buddhism* (Maida Center, 2007), p. 35.

[405] *Suttanipāta* 3.9 (Vāsettha Sutta). See *The Suttanipāta*, trans. Bhikkhu Bodhi (Wisdom, 2017), p. 268.

[406] A modern-day despot, similarly aggrieved, would tweet, "Bad climate! Baaaad!"

[407] *The Odyssey*, trans. E.V. Rieu (Penguin, 1986), p. 26.

[408] Carl Sagan, *The Demon-Haunted World: Science as a Candle in the Dark* (Ballantine, 1996), chap. 18; Armand Marie Leroi, *The Lagoon: How Aristotle Invented Science* (Viking, 2014).

[409] Charles Darwin, *On the Origin of Species by Means of Natural Selection*, 6th ed., chap. IV.

[410] Carl Sagan, *The Demon-Haunted World: Science as a Candle in the Dark* (Ballantine, 1996), chap. 1.

[411] Richard Dawkins, *The Greatest Show on Earth: The Evidence for Evolution* (Free Press, 2009), pp. 429-437.

[412] "Sharp Partisan Divisions in Views of National Institutions," Pew Research Center (10 July 2017).

[413] Friedrich Nietzsche, *The Anti-Christ*, trans. A.M. Ludovici (1911), sec. 49.

[414] Here, I refer to actions and results in the macroscopic world, as perceived by human sense faculties; that is the domain of applicability. I do not refer to the elementary constituents of matter and the physical laws that govern them. See Sean Carroll, *The Big Picture* (Dutton, 2016), chap. 3, chap. 7.

[415] Thorstein Veblen, *The Theory of the Leisure Class* (Dover, 1994), p. 171.

[416] Alexander Jones, *A Portable Cosmos: Revealing the Antikythera Mechanism* (Oxford Univ. Press, 2017), pp. 190-191.

[417] *Majjhima Nikāya* 26 (Pāsarāsi Sutta). See Bodhi, *IBW*, pp. 47, 69-70, 312-316, 430. See Stephen Batchelor, *After Buddhism: Rethinking the Dharma for a Secular Age* (Yale Univ. Press, 2015), pp. 55-59.

[418] *Samyutta Nikāya* 12.37 (Natumha Sutta), trans. Bhikkhu Sujato, https://suttacentral.net/.

[419] *Kyō Gyō Shin Shō*, *RTS*, vol. 5, p. 9; Chapter on the Transformed Buddhas and Lands, *CWS*, vol. 1, p. 274.

[420] Notes on 'Essentials of Faith Alone,' *CWS*, vol. 1, p. 459.

[421] Hymns of the Dharma-Ages, *CWS*, vol. 1, p. 400.

[422] For Shinran, all of the eighty-four thousand gateways are provisional Buddhism. They are expedient means that can guide us to the teaching of *Hongan*, which he calls the One Vehicle. See Chapter on the Transformed Buddhas and Lands, *CWS*, vol. 1, p. 222; Notes on Once-Calling and Many-Calling, pp. 485-486.

[423] Passages on the Pure Land, *CWS*, vol. 1, p. 295.

[424] *Matsudai* or "latter age" is a contraction of *mappō no jidai*, the age when the Dharma is coming to an end. See *Kyō Gyō Shin Shō*, *RTS*, vol. 5, p. 84; Chapter on the Transformed Buddhas and Lands, *CWS*, vol. 1, pp. 240-253.

[425] *The Tale of the Heike*, trans. A.L. Sadler (Asiatic Society, 1918), vol. 1, chap. 1.

[426] *The Tale of the Heike*, trans. Royall Tyler (Viking, 2012), p. 191.

[427] *The Tale of the Heike*, trans. Royall Tyler (Viking, 2012), p. 327.

[428] Kamo no Chōmei, *Hōjōki*, trans. Meredith McKinney (Penguin 2013). This is an eyewitness account of the catastrophic events of 1177-1185.

[429] *The Tale of the Heike*, trans. Royall Tyler (Viking, 2012), pp. 533-537.

[430] Ibid., pp. xxix, 12, 93.

[431] Hymns of the Dharma Ages, *CWS*, vol. 1, pp. 422-423.

[432] Notes on Once-Calling and Many-Calling, *CWS*, vol. 1, p. 484.

[433] Chapter on the Transformed Buddhas and Lands, *CWS*, vol. 1, p. 274 (quoting the *Sutra of the Vows of Medicine Master Buddha*).

[434] Lamp for the Latter Ages, *CWS*, vol. 1, pp. 523, 531, 549; A Record in Lament of Divergences, pp. 672-674.

[435] See "Cause and Effect" in Part VII.

[436] Taira no Kiyomori is a model for the persona of Donald Trump, a white tribalist cult leader, autocrat, and poison-mixer who has promoted and exploited all of the aforementioned tendencies. His incitement of an armed mob to attack the U.S. Capitol forms a striking parallel to Kiyomori's order to attack the Nara temples.

[437] Notes on Once-Calling and Many-Calling, *CWS*, vol. 1, pp. 485-486.

[438] Albert Camus, *The Myth of Sisyphus and Other Essays*, trans. Justin O'Brien (Vintage International, 1983), p. 84.

[439] *Kyōgyōshinshō* Postscript, *CWS*, vol. 1, p. 289; *Kyō Gyō Shin Shō*, *RTS*, vol. 5, p. 205.

[440] Passages on the Pure Land, *CWS*, vol. 1, p. 304.

[441] Takamaro Shigaraki, "Shinjin and Social Praxis in Shinran's Thought," trans. David Matsumoto, *Pacific World*, ser. 3, no. 11 (Fall 2009), pp. 197-199.

[442] See "Remembering Our Predecessors" in Part VI.

[443] Ueda and Hirota, "The Life of Shinran," *SIT*, pp. 35-38; James C. Dobbins, *Jōdo Shinshū: Shin Buddhism in Medieval Japan* (Univ. of Hawaii Press, 2002), p. 66.

[444] Ueda and Hirota, "The Life of Shinran," *SIT*, pp. 38-39.

[445] *Shin Buddhist Service Book*, 3rd printing, (Buddhist Education Center, 2016), p. 83.

[446] Resources are available: *Shōshin Ge*, *RTS*, vol. 1; Hisao Inagaki, *The Way of Nembutsu Faith: A Commentary on Shinran's Shōshinge* (Horai Assn. 1996).

[447] Study and reflection being the aim, it's doubtful that Shinran would encourage chanting of the *Shōshinge* with no understanding of the words. However, that is the manner in which it generally takes place today.

[448] Passages on the Pure Land, *CWS*, vol. 1, pp. 304-309. *CWS* has a printer's error on page 306: lines 15 through 18 should be deleted.

449 Hymns of the Two Gateways of Entrance and Emergence, *CWS*, vol. 1, pp. 621-629; vol. 2, p. 166.

450 In these lines, Shinran has versified a passage by Hōnen's disciple Seikaku (1166-1235), who had drawn on a passage by Shan-tao. *Shin Buddhist Service Book*, p. 144; Hymns of the Dharma-Ages, *CWS*, vol. 1, p. 412; Notes on the Inscriptions on Sacred Scrolls, pp. 514-517.

451 *Shōshin Ge, RTS*, vol. 1, p. 38; Chapter on the Transformed Buddhas and Lands, *CWS*, vol. 1, pp. 240-253; *CWS*, vol. 2, pp. 75-76, 99-100.

452 *Kyō Gyō Shin Shō, RTS*, vol. 5, p. 198; Chapter on the Transformed Buddhas and Lands, *CWS*, vol. 1, p. 240.

453 Hymns of the Dharma-Ages, *CWS*, vol. 1, p. 397.

454 Hymns of the Dharma-Ages, *CWS*, vol. 1, p. 399.

455 Hymns of the Dharma-Ages, *CWS*, vol. 1, p. 400.

456 Hymns of the Dharma-Ages, *CWS*, vol. 1, p. 403.

457 *Kyōgyōshinshō* Postscript, *CWS*, vol. 1, p. 292 (quoting the *Garland Sutra*).

458 "Calculation," *CWS*, vol. 2, p. 174.

459 Lamp for the Latter Ages, *CWS*, vol. 1, pp. 525-526.

460 A Record in Lament of Divergences, *CWS*, vol. 1, pp. 663.

461 *Kyō Gyō Shin Shō*, RTS, vol. 5, p. 64; Chapter on Practice, *CWS*, vol. 1, p. 57.

462 A Record in Lament of Divergences, *CWS*, vol. 1, pp. 663.

463 Concerning "beings who are difficult to cure," Shinran quotes a Mahāyāna version of the story in which Śākyamuni guides Ajātaśatru to liberation from suffering [Chapter on Shinjin, *CWS*, vol. 1, pp. 125-140]. Compare that with a Pāli version of the story where Gotama responds to Ajātasattu's questions with a discourse on moral discipline and announces that Ajātasattu will *not* find liberation [*Dīgha Nikāya* 2 (Sāmaññaphala Sutta)].

464 Introduction, *TPLS*, vol. 1, p. xx.

465 *Kyōgyōshinshō* Preface, *CWS*, vol. 1, p. 3; Passages on the Pure Land, p. 302; Hymns of the Pure Land, p. 346.

466 Friedrich Nietzsche, *Thus Spoke Zarathustra: A Book for All and None*, trans. Thomas Common (1909), "The Way of the Creator."

467 *Oku no hoso michi* is the title of a celebrated travel diary by the *haiku* poet, Matsuo Bashō (1644-1694). I learned from Rev. Gyoko Saito's writings that Bashō's title aptly describes the Shin Buddhist path.

468 Shinran identifies the three stages with Vows 19, 20, and 18 in the *Larger Sutra*. Chapter on the Transformed Buddhas and Lands, *CWS*, vol. 1, p. 240; *RTS*, vol. 5, p. 197; Hymns of the Pure Land no. 24, *CWS*, vol. 1, p. 330. See the commentaries in *CWS*, vol. 2, pp. 64-71.

469 I am indebted to Dr. Nobuo Haneda for his instruction on this topic.

470 Chapter on the Transformed Buddhas and Lands, *CWS*, vol. 1, p. 240; *RTS*, vol. 5, p. 196, fn. 3; Gutoku's Notes, *CWS*, vol. 1, pp. 587-589. Dharmākara vows to be the "hidden treasure-store," i.e., latent shinjin that is the "cause of supreme enlightenment." Chapter on Practice, *CWS*, vol. 1, pp. 14-15.

471 *Kyōgyōshinshō* Postscript, *CWS*, vol. 1, pp. 290-291.

472 Lamp for the Latter Ages, *CWS*, vol. 1, pp. 525-527.

473 This is my rough translation. See Chapter on Practice, *CWS*, vol. 1, p. 62; *Kyō Gyō Shin Shō*, *RTS*, vol. 5, p. 69; *Shinran's Kyōgyōshinshō*, *DTS*, p. 98.

474 Notes on 'Essentials of Faith Alone,' *CWS*, vol. 1, p. 459.

475 Kiyozawa Manshi, "Negotiating Religious Morality and Common Morality," in *Cultivating Spirituality*, ed. M. Blum and R.F. Rhodes (SUNY Press, 2011), pp. 82-84.

476 Takamaro Shigaraki, "The Pure Land," essay published in Japan, ca. 1980; trans. Marvin Harada (2013).

477 Friedrich Nietzsche, *Thus Spoke Zarathustra: A Book for All and None*, trans. Thomas Common (1909), "The Preachers of Death."

478 "Buddhism is a hundred times more realistic than Christianity—it is part of its constitutional heritage to be able to face problems objectively and coolly, it is the outcome of centuries of lasting philosophical activity. The concept 'God' was already exploded when it appeared. Buddhism is the only really *positive* religion to be found in history, even in its epistemology (which is strict phenomenalism)—it no longer

speaks of the 'struggle with *sin*' but fully recognizing the true nature of reality it speaks of the 'struggle with *pain.*' It already has—and this distinguishes it fundamentally from Christianity—the self-deception of moral concepts beneath it—to use my own phraseology, it stands *Beyond Good and Evil.*" Friedrich Nietzsche, *The Anti-Christ*, trans. A.M. Ludovici (1911), secs. 20-23.

[479] Friedrich Nietzsche, *Thus Spoke Zarathustra: A Book for All and None*, trans. Thomas Common (1909), Prologue 3.

[480] Ibid., Prologue 4.

[481] A Record in Lament of Divergences, *CWS*, vol. 1, p. 679.

[482] Chapter on Shinjin, *CWS*, vol. 1, p. 85 (quoting Shan-tao).

[483] Notes on the Inscriptions on Sacred Scrolls, *CWS*, vol. 1, p. 502.

[484] Chapter on Shinjin, *CWS*, vol. 1, p. 123.

[485] "Ein Buch für Alle und Keinen" is the subtitle of *Thus Spoke Zarathustra.*

[486] Takamaro Shigaraki, "Shinjin and Social Praxis in Shinran's Thought," trans. David Matsumoto, *Pacific World*, ser. 3, no. 11 (Fall 2009), pp. 197-199.

[487] See "Remembering Our Predecessors" in Part VI.

[488] Friedrich Nietzsche, *The Anti-Christ*, trans. A.M. Ludovici (1911), Preface.

[489] Hideo Yonezawa, *Awaken to Your True Self: The Shin Buddhist Way of Life* (Buddhist Education Center, 2017), p. xi. The epigraph evokes the "two aspects of deep mind." See Chapter on Shinjin, *CWS*, vol. 1, p. 85; *Kyō Gyō Shin Shō*, *RTS*, vol. 5, p. 91.

[490] "Truly Settled Ones," in Glossary of Shin Buddhist Terms, *CWS*, vol. 2, pp. 214-215.

[491] Shinran cites Nāgārjuna's teaching in Chapter on Practice, *CWS*, vol. 1, pp. 22-23, 38, 54.

[492] Nāgārjuna's *Chapter on Easy Practice*, *PLW*, vol. 1, p. 7.

[493] Nāgārjuna's *Chapter on Easy Practice*, *PLW*, vol. 1, p. 19.

[494] *The Larger Sutra*, *TPLS*, vol. 2, pp. 51-52; Notes on Once-Calling and Many-Calling, *CWS*, vol. 1, pp. 474-476.

⁴⁹⁵ *The Larger Sutra, TPLS*, vol. 2, pp. 51-52; Notes on Once-Calling and Many-Calling, *CWS*, vol. 1, pp. 474-476.

⁴⁹⁶ "Birth in the Pure Land," *CWS*, vol. 2, p. 110.

⁴⁹⁷ Chapter on Practice, *CWS*, vol. 1, p. 26 (quoting T'an-luan).

⁴⁹⁸ Notes on Once-Calling and Many-Calling, *CWS*, vol. 1, p. 477, fn. 12.

⁴⁹⁹ "Realization as Supreme Nirvana," *CWS*, vol. 2, pp. 51-52.

⁵⁰⁰ See "Pure Land Birth" in Part III.

⁵⁰¹ *Samyutta Nikāya* 6.15 (Parinibbāna Sutta); *Dīgha Nikāya* 16 (Mahāparinibbāna Sutta).

⁵⁰² See "'He Returned to the Pure Land'" in Part III.

⁵⁰³ *The Larger Sutra, TPLS*, vol. 2, pp. 76, 112; "Maitreya," *CWS*, vol. 2, p. 194 and "Succession to Buddhahood After One Lifetime," p. 208.

⁵⁰⁴ My rephrasing of Hymns of the Dharma-Ages, *CWS*, vol. 1, p. 406. See also, Chapter on Shinjin, pp. 122-123; Notes on 'Essentials of Faith Alone.' p. 455; Notes on Once-Calling and Many-Calling, pp. 476-478; Lamp for the Latter Ages, p. 528.

⁵⁰⁵ My rough translation. See Hymns of the Dharma-Ages, *CWS*, vol. 1, p. 405.

⁵⁰⁶ Lamp for the Latter Ages, *CWS*, vol. 1, p. 544.

⁵⁰⁷ Vow 22 is "the Vow of directing virtue in the returning aspect." *The Larger Sutra, TPLS*, vol. 2, pp. 23-24, 59-60; Chapter on Realization, *CWS*, vol. 1, pp. 153-174.

⁵⁰⁸ See "'He Returned to the Pure Land'" in Part III.

⁵⁰⁹ My rough translation. See *Kyō Gyō Shin Shō*, *RTS*, vol. 5, p. 140; *Shinran's Kyōgyōshinshō*, *DTS*, p. 191; Chapter on Realization, *CWS*, vol. 1, p. 153.

⁵¹⁰ *Kyō Gyō Shin Shō*, *RTS*, vol. 5, p. 140; *Shinran's Kyōgyōshinshō*, *DTS*, p. 191; Chapter on Realization, *CWS*, vol. 1, p. 153.

⁵¹¹ In the Chapter on Realization of the *Kyōgyōshinshō*, Shinran's own statements never mention Pure Land birth.

⁵¹² Hymns of the Dharma Ages, nos. 21, 27, *CWS*, vol. 1, pp. 404-405.

⁵¹³ Chapter on Shinjin, *CWS*, vol. 1, p. 125.

[514] *Kyōgyōshinshō* Postscript, *CWS*, vol. 1, p. 291.

[515] Taitetsu Unno, *River of Fire, River of Water: An Introduction to the Pure Land Tradition of Shin Buddhism* (Doubleday, 1998), pp. 104-107; D.T. Suzuki, *Buddha of Infinite Light* (Shambala, 1998), pp. 69-84.

[516] Notes on 'Essentials of Faith Alone," *CWS*, vol. 1, p. 466.

[517] *Shinran's Kyōgyōshinshō*, *DTS*, p. 43; *Kyōgyōshinshō* Preface, *CWS*, vol. 1, p. 4.

[518] My rephrasing of Notes on Once-Calling and Many-Calling, *CWS*, vol. 1, p. 490.

Made in the USA
Las Vegas, NV
17 January 2025